Enforcing Intellectual Property Rights

Enforcing Intellectual Property Rights

A Concise Guide for Businesses, Innovative and Creative Individuals

JANE LAMBERT

Routledge
Taylor & Francis Group

LONDON AND NEW YORK

First published in paperback 2024

First published 2009 by Gower Publishing

Published 2016 by Routledge
4 Park Square, Milton Park, Abingdon, Oxon OX14 4RN

and by Routledge
605 Third Avenue, New York, NY 10158

Routledge is an imprint of the Taylor & Francis Group, an informa business

Publisher's Note
The publisher has gone to great lengths to ensure the quality of this reprint but points out that some imperfections in the original copies may be apparent.

British Library Cataloguing in Publication Data
Lambert, Jane
  Enforcing intellectual property rights : a concise guide
  for businesses, innovative and creative individuals
  1. Intellectual property – Great Britain
  I. Title
  346.4'1048

Library of Congress Control Number: 2007943377

ISBN : 978-0-566-08714-1 (hbk)
ISBN : 978-1-03-283783-3 (pbk)
ISBN : 978-1-315-57960-3 (ebk)

DOI: 10.4324/9781315579603

Contents

List of Figures

List of Tables

Glossary of Intellectual Property Terms

Berne Convention	Berne Convention for the Protection of Literary and Artistic Works: international agreement establishing Berne Union and providing for copyright protection of artistic and literary works of contracting parties' nationals on a reciprocal basis.
Brand	The sign by which a product or service is recognized in the market.
Chancery County Court	The Central London County Court or a county court that is attached to a chancery district registry (e.g. Birmingham, Bristol, Caernarfon, Cardiff, Leeds, Liverpool, Manchester, Mold, Newcastle upon Tyne and Preston County Courts).
Community Design ('CD')	A design that is protected under the Community Design Regulation. It may be registered Community design or an unregistered Community design.
Community Design Regulation	Council Regulation (EC) No 6/2002 of 12 December 2001 on Community designs (OJ EC No L 3 of 5.1.2002, p. 1). The legislation that provides for Community designs.
Community Trade Mark ('CTM')	A trade mark that is registered with OHIM under the provisions of the Community Trade Mark Regulation.
Community Trade Mark Regulation	Council Regulation (EC) No 40/94 of 20 December 1993 on the Community trade mark. The legislation that establishes OHIM and provides for the registration of trade marks as Community trade marks.
Confidence	A duty not to disclose or use secret technical, commercial or otherwise sensitive information that is entrusted to another ('the confidante') expressly in confidence (i.e. when the confidante signs a confidentiality or non-disclosure agreement) or in circumstances giving rise to an obligation of confidence (i.e. discussing an invention with a patent agent).
Convention	Treaty or other international agreement between sovereign governments. Includes Berne, Paris and Rome Conventions, Washington Treaty, European Patent Convention, Patent Co-operation Treaty, Madrid Protocol and Hague Agreement.
Copyright	Exclusive right to copy, issue copies to the public, lend, rent, perform, communicate to the public or adapt original artistic, dramatic, literary or musical works, broadcasts, films, sound recordings or typographical arrangements of published works. These are 'economic rights'. Some authors also have moral rights in respect of their works.
Creative Work	Work of art or literature. Works of art include plastic arts such as collages, drawings, etchings, engravings, graphics, images on a computer, paintings, sculptures, media such as animations, films, sound recordings and videos, musical works such as a score and performing arts such as ballet, drama, singing and other musical performances. Works of literature include not just novels and poems but also compilations of data, mathematical tables, street directories, traders' catalogues and computer software.

Design	The shape or configuration of an article or part of an article. The topic really breaks into functional designs and ornamental designs.
Design Right	The right conferred by an unregistered design right. Not to be confused with unregistered Community designs or registered designs.
Designs Directive	Directive 98/71/EC of the European Parliament and of the Council of 13 October 1998 on the legal protection of designs OJ L 289, 28.10.1998, p. 28–35: Council directive harmonizing national registered design law. Implemented in the UK by The Registered Designs Regulations 2001 which amended the Registered Designs Act 1949 of the member states.
Economic Rights	Rights relating to the exploitation of copyright or right in performance as opposed to a moral right. They include reproduction, publication, renting, lending, performing, communicating the public and adapting.
European Patent Convention ('EPC')	Agreement between over 30 European countries establishing the European Patent Office and providing for the grant of European patents that stand alongside national patents in each of the contracting states,
European patent	Patent granted by the European Patent Office for one or more countries that are party to the European Patent Convention on behalf of the contracting government(s).
European Patent Office ('EPO')	Intergovernmental agency established by the European Patent Convention to grant European patents on behalf of the governments(s) of one or more of the contracting parties to that Convention to take effect alongside national patents.
Functional Design	The design of a mechanism, electrical circuit or other functional object.
Hague Agreement	The Hague Agreement Concerning the International Deposit of Industrial Designs: international agreement to facilitate registered design protection by facilitating applications to multiple design registrations forma single filing. The EU is party to this agreement but the UK is not as yet.
Infringement	Violation of an intellectual property right as in infringement of a patent, copyright or trade mark. It is, however, permissible to refer to a 'breach of confidence'.
Intellectual Asset	Investment in brands, design, technology or creative work.
Intellectual Property ('IP')	Collective name for the bundle of rights that protect intellectual assets at law. They include patents, trade marks, copyrights, and rights in performances, registered and unregistered designs.
Intellectual Property Right ('IPR')	Legal protection of an intellectual asset: i.e. patent, trade mark, copyright, registered design, right to bring an action for passing of breach of confidence.
Madrid Protocol	Protocol Relating to the Madrid Agreement Concerning the International Registration of Marks: international agreement to facilitate trade mark registration permitting applications to trade mark registries in several contracting countries form a single filing.
Moral Right	Right to preserve the dignity and integrity if a copyright work or performance and the reputation of the author or performer such as the right to be identified, the right not to have work treated derogatively and right not to have other work attributed to the author.
OHIM (Office for Harmonization in the Internal Market)	European Community trade mark and designs registry established by the Community Trade Mark Regulation and the Community Design Regulation.

Ornamental Design	The appearance of the whole or a part of a product resulting from the features of, in particular, the lines, contours, colours, shape, texture and/or materials of the product itself and/or its ornamentation.
Paris Convention	Paris Convention for the Protection of Industrial Property: international agreement establishing the Paris Union and providing for the legal protection of the inventions, trade marks and designs of contracting parties on a reciprocal basis and the suppression of unfair competition.
Passing Off	Common law action (occasionally called 'palming off' in USA) and closely related to unfair competition whereby a trader who uses a name, mark or get-up that is similar to that of an established trader can be liable for any damage that he or she causes by the use of that sign.
Patent	A monopoly granted by a state of the manufacture, distribution, importation use of a new product, the use of a new product or the distribution, importation or use of products made form such process.
Patent Agent	In the UK and most other countries, an interchangeable and less misleading term for patent attorney. In the USA, a professional who is not a lawyer who applies for patents, other registered rights, advises on intellectual property and does most of the work of a patent attorney.
Patent Attorney	In the USA, a lawyer specializing in patent and other intellectual property work. In the UK and some other countries a professional with some specialist legal knowledge who applies for patents and other registered IP rights, advises on the law, represents clients in the UK-IPO, EPO and OHIM and sometimes appears in the Patents and Patent County Courts, Chancery Division and Chancery County Courts. Patent agents have recently started to use the term 'patent attorney' because they feared that they were perceived as somehow inferior to US patent lawyers.
Patent Co-operation Treaty ('PCT')	International agreement to facilitate patent applications permitting applications to patent offices in several contracting countries from a single filing.
Patents County Court	A county court designated by the Lord Chancellor for patents and designs litigation. The Central London County Court s the only county court that is so designated.
Patents Court	Judges of the Chancery Division specializing in patents, registered and registered Community design and semiconductor topography litigation.
Performance	A performance by an actor, dancer, singer, musician or other performing artiste.
Publication Right	Right of a publisher of a previously unpublished work that is out of copyright at the time of publication to prevent copying, further publication, renting, lending or adapting the work.
Registered Community Design	A new design having individual character which is registered with OHIM under the Community Design Regulation.
Registered Design	A new design having individual character which is registered with the UK Intellectual Property Office under the Registered Designs Act 1949 as amended. Designs registered with OHIM under the Community Design Regulation are known as registered Community Designs.
Right in a Performance	The right of an actor, dancer, musician, singer or other artiste not to have his or her performance broadcast, filmed or taped without his or her consent. Also, the right of a broadcaster, film or recording studio who has contracted with the performer to broadcast film or tape the performance to object to anyone else's broadcasting, filming or taping the performance. These are economic rights. Performers now also have moral rights in relation to their performances.

Rome Convention	Rome Convention for the Protection of Performers, Producers of Phonograms and Broadcasting Organizations: international agreement providing for protection of broadcasts, live performances and films and tapes of such performances of nationals and residents of contracting states on a mutual basis.
Semiconductor Topography	The design of the layout of a semiconductor chip which is protected in the UK as unregistered design rights by The Design Right (Semiconductor Topographies) Regulations 1989. See also The Washington Treaty.
Trade Mark	A sign capable of being represented graphically, consisting of words, including personal names, designs, letters, numerals, the shape of goods or of their packaging, that is capable of distinguishing the goods or services of one supplier from those of others. NB. 'Trade mark' is spelt as two words in the UK and as one in the USA.
Trade Mark Agent	In the UK and most other countries, an interchangeable and less misleading term for trade mark attorney. In the USA, a professional who is not a lawyer who applies for trade marks advises on intellectual property and does most of the work of a trade mark attorney.
Trade Mark Attorney	In the USA, a lawyer specializing in trade mark work. In the UK and some other countries a professional with some specialist legal knowledge who applies for trade marks and designs, advises on the law, represents clients in the UK-IPO and OHIM and sometimes appears in the Chancery Division and Chancery County Courts. Trade mark agents have recently started to use the term 'patent attorney' because they feared that they were perceived as somehow inferior to US trade mark lawyers.
Trade Marks Directive	First Council Directive 89/104/EEC of 21 December 1988 to approximate the laws of the Member States relating to trade marks: Council directive harmonizing the trade mark laws of the member states. Implemented in the UK by the Trade Marks Act 1949.
TRIPs (Agreement on Trade-Related Aspects of Intellectual Property Rights)	Annex 1C to the WTO Agreement. An agreement for WTO member states to provide minimum legal protection for intellectual assets, to comply with the Berne, Paris and Rome Conventions and the Washington Treaty and to provide civil remedies and criminal penalties for infringement.
UDRP (Uniform Domain Name Dispute Resolution Policy)	Form of alternative dispute resolution for disputes over generic top level domain names (those ending in .com, .org, .net, .info et cetera) incorporated by reference into every contract for the registration of such a domain name.
UK Intellectual Property Office ('UK-IPO')	New name for the Patent Office. Executive agency established to examine and grant patents, trade marks and registered designs for the UK under the Patents Act 1977, Trade Marks Act 1994 and the Registered Designs Act 1949.
Unregistered Community design	Automatic 3-year EU wide protection from copying of a design that could have been registered as a registered Community design or as a registered design in the UK.
Utility Models	Short term protection for new inventions similar to a patent but usually granted on less rigorous examination available in most of Europe including Ireland where they are called 'short term patents' but not yet in the UK. Also known as 'innovation patents' in Australia. The UK protects many inventions that would qualify for utility model protection by design rights.
Washington Treaty	Washington Treaty on Intellectual Property in Respect of Integrated Circuits: treaty providing for mutual protection of semiconductor circuit designs of residents and nationals of contracting parties. Not yet in force but implemented by several governments including HMG.

WIPO	World Intellectual Property Organization: UN specialist agency for intellectual property, custodian of most of the IP Conventions and important domain name dispute resolution service provider. NB The initials are pronounced separately 'W', 'I', 'P', 'O' – never as 'wipe-oh' as though it were a brand of window cleaner.
The World Trade Organization ('the WTO')	A multilateral international organization consisting of most of the world's developed and developing nations regulating trade and development.
WTO Agreement	Marrakesh Agreement establishing the World Trade Organization ('the WTO') and regulating trade between WTO members.

Glossary of Terms used in Litigation

Affidavit	A written statement verified on oath. Making an untrue statement under oath is perjury.
Affirmation	A written statement verified by a solemn declaration. Making an untrue statement under affirmation is perjury.
Anton Piller	The term formerly used for a search order before 23 April 1999 after the decision in *Anton Piller KG v Manufacturing Products Ltd.* [1976] Ch 55.
Applicant	Party seeking an interim injunction or other relief. Usually a claimant but can be a defendant in a security for costs application.
Application	An application to the court for an interim injunction or other relief. Replaced 'motions' (applications to a judge in open court) and 'summonses' (applications to a judge or master in chambers).
Application by order	Time set aside by the court for hearing of an application that is unlikely to be determined in less than 2 hours.
Application Day	A day in which an applications judge hears applications for interim injunctions and other relief. Called a 'motions day' before 23 April 1999.
Applications Judge	A judge who hears applications for interim injunctions and other relief.
Central London County Court	The county court for central London enjoying patent and chancery jurisdiction.
Chancery	A body of law and practice developed by the Court of Chancery before 1873 and followed after that date by the Chancery Division of the High Court of Justice, the Central London County Court and certain chancery county courts.
Chancery County Courts	A county court which shares judges, staff and offices with a Chancery District registry and can therefore hear chancery claims. They include the Birmingham, Bristol, Caernarfon, Cardiff, Leeds, Liverpool, Manchester, Mold, Newcastle and Preston County Courts. The Central London County Court can also hear chancery cases.
Chancery District Registry	A branch of the High Court with district judges and administrative staff capable of managing Chancery cases.
Chancery Division	One of the Divisions of the High Court of Justice established by the Supreme Court Act 1981. S.61 and para. 1 of Sched. 1 to the Act assigns a number of causes of action to the Chancery Division including patents, trade marks, registered designs and copyright.

Civil Procedure Rules ('CPR')	The code of procedure of the Senior Courts and the county courts of England and Wales. The CPR consist of the rules divided into a number of parts supplemented by Practice Directions. These rules replaced separate rules for the County Courts ('the County Court Rules') and the Supreme Court ('the Rules of the Supreme Court') on 26 April 1999.
Claim	Court proceedings in which a claimant seeks an injunction, damages or other relief from a defendant.
Claimant	The party who brings a claim or action. Called a 'pursuer' in Scotland and a 'plaintiff' elsewhere.
Committal	Order sending a contemnor to prison until her or she corrects or purges his or her contempt of court.
Contemnor	Person guilty of contempt of court
Contempt of Court	Obstruction of the administration of justice (e.g. disobeying an injunction or breach of an undertaking.)
County Courts	The lower tier of civil courts of England and Wales established by the County Courts Act 1984.
Cross Undertaking	An undertaking given by an applicant in exchange for an undertaking given by, or an injunction restraining, the other side.
Cross Undertaking as to Damages	A cross undertaking to compensate the respondent in damages should the respondent suffer any by reason of the order that the court finds that the applicant should pay.
Defendant	The party against whom a claim is made.
Final Injunction	An order made after the determination of the issues in dispute. Sometimes called a 'perpetual injunction'.
Freezing Injunction	Order requiring a respondent not to remove from the jurisdiction of the court, hide or otherwise dissipate any assets against which a judgement could be executed.
High Court	The trial level of the Senior Courts of England and Wales for civil claims. Established by the Supreme Court Act 1981, the High Court was formed from the merger of common law and chancery courts in 1873 and continues to sit in three separate divisions, namely the Chancery, Queen's (or King's) Bench and Family Division.
Injunction	An order of the court order prohibiting a person from doing something or requiring him or her to do something. In Scotland and a number of other countries such an order is called an 'interdict'.
Interim injunction	An order to refrain from doing something (or occasionally to do something) by a specified date and time or stage of the proceedings such as judgment in the action.
Judgment	Final decision in a case or part of a case.
Mareva Injunction	The name used for a Freezing Injunction before 23 April 1999 after The Mareva, *Mareva Compahia Naviera SA v International Bulk Carriers SA* [1979] 2 Lloyds LR 508.
Minute of Order	Instrument signed by the judge and sealed by the court recording his or her order.

Patents County Court	A county court that has been designated by to hear patent and design claims. The Central London County Court is the only Patents County Court.
Patents Court	Specialist court within the Chancery Division that hears patent, registered design, registered Community design and semiconductor topography claims.
Perpetual Injunction	See Final Injunction
Respondent	Party against whom an application is made. Usually but not always a defendant.
Search Order	Order requiring the person in charge of a building or vehicle to admit a supervising solicitor and members of the applicant's solicitors to enter the premises and carry out a search for documents and other evidence which may otherwise have been lost or hidden and to make copies of those documents or copies of such evidence. Formerly known as an Anton Piller order.
Security for Costs	An order that a company or occasionally individual claimant shjold deposit funds or give some other security for the defendant's costs.
Senior Courts	The superior courts of England and Wales consisting of the Court of Appeal, the High Court and the Crown Court. Formerly called the Supreme Court even though it was inferior to the House of Lords.
Supervising Solicitor	A solicitor independent of the parties who serves and executes a search order and certain other relief.
Supreme Court	The old name of the Senior Courts.
Undertaking	Promise to the court to do something or refrain from doing something. A breach of an undertaking is contempt of court which may be punished by a fine, prison or other penalty.
Vice-Chancellor	Full title is the 'Vice Chancellor of the County Palatine of Lancaster'. A High Court judge who presides over the Chancery Division in the North of England. The head of the Chancery Division, who is now known as the Chancellor, used to be called the Vice-Chancellor.
Witness statement	Written evidence verified by a statement of truth. An untrue statement is a contempt of court.

Foreword: What This Book is About and Why You May Want to Read it

Purpose of the book

The title should say it all. This is not a law book though lawyers should find it useful. Much less is it a students' book though it does no harm for students to see how the law works in practice. The purpose of this book is to guide businessmen and women through the maze of IP law so that they avoid mistakes that have threatened the livelihoods and, occasionally, ruined the lives of many of their number.

Why you need to worry about Intellectual Property

It is very tempting to resolve never to have any truck with the law or lawyers, but that is not always possible. You may have to seek a court order against a former employee who sets up in competition with you, having first removed your customer list and other confidential documents. Similarly, action may be unavoidable if complaints roll in from customers who have bought products that look a bit like yours and may even bear a similar label but turn out to have been made in East Asia out of inferior materials with very poor workmanship without your knowledge or consent. Alternatively, you may be accused of infringing someone else's intellectual property. You may be about to launch a new product having spent a small fortune on advertising and promotion. Just before the launch you receive a solicitors' letter complaining that your product infringes their client's trade mark or registered design and warning of imminent litigation unless you give grovelling undertakings. In each of those circumstances you will be faced with a hard choice. Do you give in and accept serious, possibly catastrophic, damage to your business or do you risk thousands of pounds on legal fees without any guarantee of success?

Litigation is carrying on business by other means

Each of those situations could have been mitigated or even avoided by forward planning and good management. The German thinker von Clausewitz observed that 'war is politics by other means'.* It may perhaps be helpful to think of litigation and other forms of dispute resolution as 'doing business by other means'. Disputes are emergencies just like fires, floods, labour disputes, computer crashes and other hazards of doing business. Business people invariably

---

*   Carl von Clausewitz: 'Der Krieg ist eine bloße Fortsetzung der Politik mit anderen Mitteln.' (para 24 Chapter 1 'Vom Krieg' at http://www.clausewitz.com/CWZHOME/VomKriege/Book1Ch01VK.htm

plan for those other emergencies and take steps to manage them by, for example, installing fire doors, second sourcing and, above all, taking out the appropriate insurance. In the same way, you can give yourself the best possible chance of protecting your intellectual assets (that is to say the brands, product designs, technology and creativity that give your company an edge over the competition) by say obtaining optimum trade mark, patent, registered design or other intellectual property protection, training your staff in handling and securing trade secrets and other confidential information and taking out appropriate intellectual property insurance.

Handling emergencies

Planning for any emergency requires identifying and prioritizing risks, devising effective counter-measures and putting as many as possible into effect within the constraints of your budget. Applying that approach to the law, an obvious risk of putting a new product on the market is that you may infringe someone else's patent, registered design or other intellectual property right. Patents and literature searches should reduce that risk and insurance is available against claims by third parties. Another risk is that your product may be copied. Patents, design and trade mark registration in your principal markets and any place where lookalikes are likely to be made can deal with that. Of course, taking precautions against a risk is never enough in itself. When an emergency threatens, a swift response by management is also required. Just as production may have to be shifted quickly to temporary accommodation if your factory is damaged by fire, so an interim injunction may be needed if someone else's goods are passed off as yours, your customers are canvassed by your former sales manager or your patent, trade mark or design is infringed.

Structure of the book

This book sets out to give you, the proprietor or manager of a business, the knowledge that you need to take crucial decisions on protecting your intellectual assets before it is too late. It is intended to be kept close at hand for use in emergencies just like a first aid manual. It is not comprehensive but then it does not have to be any more than a first aid manual has to be a medical text book. Its purpose is to alert you to problems so that you can take the right steps to manage them in consultation with your professional advisors before they develop into crises.

Because different readers are likely to have different needs and different levels of knowledge about intellectual property law this book is organized as follows:

* **Chapter 1: Setting the Scene:** The chapter begins with a dialogue of a typical conference in chambers between a specialist IP counsel and his clients, a businessman and counsel's instructing solicitors. The dialogue illustrates the sort of issues that arise. I have tried by this technique to communicate in everyday speech concepts and information that most business people find arid – just as DEFRA communicates tedious farming information though 'The Archers' or Plato philosophical concepts through the lips of Socrates. You could skip this chapter but I hope you will not because I have tried to make it funny. †

---

†   Whether or not it is funny is for you, the readers, to judge. I have been told that it is by my long suffering spouse, my honorary niece and the head honcho of the Huddersfield Business Generator. All three have acquired Yorkshire bluntness through residence, education or birth in this great county and they would have no qualms about telling me to cut it out if it bored them.

- **Chapter 2: Introduction to Intellectual Property:** This explains what intellectual property is and what it does. It offers an overview of the IP system starting with the implied bargains that the state makes with inventors, entrepreneurs and creative individuals. It explains the policy issues behind the creation of intellectual property law.
- **Chapter 3: How the Law Protects Different Intellectual Assets:** This chapter outlines the intellectual property system, the WTO agreement, TRIPS, the cornerstone treaties and their implementation into European and national law. It explores the specific means of protecting brands, designs, technology and creative works. It suggests further reading on the internet and in print. Readers will probably need to dip into this chapter from other parts of the book from time to time but they do not need to read all of it unless they want to do so.
- **Chapter 4: Dispute Resolution Options:** This starts with the machinery for enforcing rights. It introduces the common and civil law families of legal systems. It outlines the legal systems of the United Kingdom. It highlights the international obligations upon all WTO member states to provide effective means of enforcing intellectual property rights. It discusses the legal systems of the countries in which UK businesses are most likely to seek intellectual property protection; the UK's main trading partners. Finally, it introduces alternatives to litigation such as arbitration, mediation, expert determination and other forms of ADR (alternative dispute resolution). Again, it will be necessary to consult this chapter from other parts of the book from time to time. It also provides some basic information that is often assumed in law books.
- **Chapter 5: Woolf Rules OK:** Lord Woolf (who served as the most senior judge in England and Wales) will always be remembered for two masterly reports on the English and Welsh civil justice system which proposed far reaching reforms. Sadly, his vision of a change of landscape has never been achieved but he did persuade the government of the day to modernize the rules of civil procedure with a comprehensive code that now applies to all civil courts. This code, known as the Civil Procedure Rules (CPR), governs court proceedings in England and Wales and influences all other forms of dispute resolution. For instance, TPN 1/2000 which modernized the practice and procedure of the UK Intellectual Property Office tribunals was strongly influenced by the CPR. This chapter is an introduction and guide to the rules. If you read nothing else in this book, read this chapter.
- **Chapter 6: So You Want to Sue Somebody:** Basically this chapter tries to persuade you to think long and hard before you do anything so silly as go to law – especially in England. A famous 19th century judge said a patent suit was the next worst thing to your whole family catching bird flu. However, if you must, and sometimes litigation can't be avoided, it tells you how to set about it to mitigate the grief. And there are plenty of pitfalls from Belgian torpedoes (does Belgium actually have a navy) to threats actions (for once, I am not talking about typical weekend banter on Deansgate, the Pier Head, Sauchiehall Street or any other town centre after the pubs close). Good luck. You will need it.
- **Chapter 7: What Happens If Neither Side Gives in:** Now we are getting to the heavy stuff. There are only two ways to settle a dispute: consensual methods such as negotiation and mediation and adjudicatory methods such as litigation, arbitration or expert determination. This chapter discusses both of them. It introduces principled and positional negotiation and provides an overview of court and tribunal procedure in England and Wales and elsewhere.
- **Chapter 8: How to Prepare Your Case:** This is where most of the money goes in litigation. This chapter tells you how to prepare your case. You should start preparing

before you get a problem. If you have a choice, you should think long and hard about where you want to sue. Belgium and Italy are favourite if you want a declaration of non-infringement; Germany or the Netherlands if you want a good, fast cost effective judgment by judges who know what they are doing; England if you are Mr Moneybags and you think your opponent is likely to be short of brass. The chapter explains the importance of getting your pleadings and witness statements right, preparing a good bundle and lodging your skelly (skeleton argument) in time.

- **Chapter 9: What Happens on the Big Day:** This chapter discusses different types of dispute resolution including domain name dispute resolution procedures, getting a search order and what to do if you are searched and mediation. It also mentions procedures that most people have seen on television if not in real life such as trials. Less detail is given to trials because everyone knows all about that having watched *Rumpole* and *Ally McBeal*.
- **Chapter 10: Where to Get Help:** This chapter introduces you to the professionals you are likely to need such as barristers, patent agents and solicitors. It introduces the Legal Services Act 2007 which should make a big difference to the availability, cost and quality of legal services in the UK. It also gives you some useful sources of information if you are mad enough to (or so poor that you must) draft your own patent claims or litigate in the High Court.
- **Chapter 11: Threats Actions:** If you are a solicitor in general commercial practice this is for you because you are most likely to be caught in a non-specialist-solicitor-trap. It is a bit like a heffalump trap only worse because you have a conflict of interest with your client but still have to defend a law suit. However, it is also something that business people and other non-lawyers should read because they can get caught too. The chapter covers what is a threats action, what is a threat, who can be sued, some possible defences and some practical consequences. *Moral* – Don't go to 'Sue, Grabbit & Run LLP' in the High Street for IP work however good they are at commercial leases and estate planning and however glossy their brochure. Go to a firm that belongs to the *Intellectual Property Lawyers Association* or has some other credible intellectual property credentials.
- **Chapter 12: A Few Last Tips:** Twelve last tips for Chapter 12. Basically a distillation of the advice that I have been giving throughout the book. I shall not repeat them here. They are all listed in the first paragraph of the chapter.

At the end of the book there are samples of the documents referred to in the book.

How this book may be used

Someone setting up a new business can probably make best use of this book. That is because he or she can plan an enforcement strategy at leisure, seek the optimum patent or registered trade mark or design protection and secure the appropriate insurance to make sure that a fund is available to enforce those patents, trade marks or other protection as and when necessary. He or she will start with the dialogue and then perhaps move to Chapter 4 to begin planning. There may be concepts that he or she does not fully understand or terms and expressions that he or she has never met before. Such a reader will turn to the relevant parts of Chapters 3 and 4 for an explanation. Possibly a more typical reader will be someone in trouble. He or she will have to make fast decisions in very little time. Maybe the Supervising Solicitor is even in his or her office armed with a search order. He or she is likely to start with the section on what to do on the Big Day and carry on from there. Whatever the starting point, I have tried to cross reference the text and make each chapter a standalone guide.

Feedback and further information

Despite the pain in writing this book which I mention at the start of the book, I hope fervently that this will not be the last edition of this little guide and I hope that the next one will be very much better. To make sure that it is better I really do need to know what works for you and what does not. More importantly, your feedback will help me improve my service and that of my colleagues in chambers, in the rest of the bar and in other professions. Throughout the last 10 years I have tried through my website,‡ blog,§ newsletters, seminars and clinics to offer high quality specialist advice and representation to the small and medium businesses in Lancashire and Yorkshire who need it most and can often afford it least. So please send your comments favourable or otherwise directly to our chambers manager, Toni Wilson, at toni.wilson@ nipclaw.com. Every serious comment and suggestion will be considered and where appropriate acted upon immediately. If you want advice and can get to Huddersfield or Bradford I hold regular free advice sessions at the Huddersfield Media Centre between 11:00 and 13:00 on the last Friday of every month and run patent clinics with Ged Doonan and Stef Stephenson of Leeds Central Library Patents Information Unit and local patent and trade mark attorneys and business advisors in Huddersfield and Bradford on the third Thursday of alternate months. Details will always be displayed on Upcoming.¶ Just search under Huddersfield and Bradford. Good luck!

Dedication

Finally, a dedication. First, to my favourite little girl, Dunni, my honorary niece, without whom this book would never have been written. 'Come on, Uncle**, I know you can do it', she used to urge when I was on the point of writing a cheque to return my publisher's advance. Secondly, to my dear, long suffering spouse, Iyamide, who warned me sagely not to touch this project with tongs for the miserly consideration that Gower were offering. She always had better things for me to do on the rare occasions that inspiration dawned, such as driving her to Waitrose or wheeling out the green bins on the even rarer occasions that Kirklees Borough Council collects recyclable waste. You will judge which one of them was right.

Jane Lambert
nipc®
The Media Centre
7 Northumberland Street
Huddersfield
United Kingdom
HD1 1RL
Tel: +44 (0)870 990 5081
E-mail: Jane.lambert@nipclaw.com
http://nipclaw.blogspot.com

---

‡ www.ipit-update.com.
§ www.nipclaw.blogspot.com.
¶ http://upcoming.yahoo.com.
** I should explain that I am transsexual and that I was still living as a male when I delivered the manuscript.

1 *Setting the Scene*

How this book came to be written

This book has been a real pain to write. It should have been easy enough. I earn my living from advising on IP (intellectual property) law and have done for more than 20 years. It is something I do almost every day whether as counsel,[1] mediator, domain name panellist, patent clinic advisor, inventors' club organizer, blogger or otherwise. Yet although I know something about the topic, I have started and abandoned this chapter no less than 17 times and trashed hundreds of pages in the process. More than once I thought of returning the publisher's advance. If this was a book that was easy or even possible to write - I have said to myself – someone else would have written it.

There is no shortage of well written books on patents, designs, trade marks, copyrights, passing off and other intellectual property rights. Most of them have at least a chapter on enforcement. Why another? Yet almost every day, whenever I have a conference like the one that I am about to describe, I am reminded why a book like this has to be written. Sometimes I am consulted after thousands of pounds have been wasted on actions that should never have started. Other times I am approached after years of investment in research and development have been lost through inadequate legal protection or, more frequently, through bungled attempts to enforce such protection as did exist.

The reason that I have started and abandoned this book so many times is that it has been very difficult to pitch it at the right level. My early drafts were written in the style that I write opinions. Fine for lawyers but terribly dull for everyone else. Later drafts went to the other extreme so that they read like school civics. Throughout these struggles with writers' block my spouse has been powering ahead with a riveting tale about a gender dysphoric barristers' clerk. 'If only this were a novel,' I thought. And then it dawned on me: 'why not write it like a novel?' It is, after all, the fascinating detail of reported cases that enables lawyers to discern legal principle. Indeed, it is such detail that makes the study of law bearable. Detail such as the incredulity of anyone, even in the late 19th century, who would seriously believe that sniffing fumes from a hollow rubber ball containing a powder treated with carbolic acid would actually ward off a particularly virulent strain of influenza. Or, indeed, that its supplier was serious in offering to pay £100 to anyone who caught flu after such sniffing.[2] So let's see what can be learned from a typical conference in chambers.

---

1 In the UK,'counsel' means a higher court advocate, usually but nowadays not exclusively a barrister.
2 See Stephanie Pain 'Mrs Carlill lays down the law' from issue 2534 of *New Scientist* magazine, 14 January 2006, p. 50.

A typical client

Mr. Aardvark – or rather his company – imports to the UK a range of external wall mounted ornaments that he markets as 'distelfinks' which are made in China to his order. 'Fink' means 'finch' in Old Dutch so each of those plaques bears a stylized image of a finch – chaffinch, greenfinch, bullfinch and so on. Distelfinks are new to Britain but they are very common in parts of Pennsylvania where they have appeared on the walls of Dutch settlers' houses for centuries. Mr. Aardvark's distelfinks have been something of a craze. Featured in the style pages of the qualities, they have sold like hot cakes in retail establishments throughout the land and over the internet. So popular had they become – particularly in the North of England – that rural parts of the county of Lancaster began to resemble faintly parts of Lancaster County.[3]

A typical problem

It was to be expected that anything as popular and profitable as Mr. Aardvark's distelfinks would spawn plenty of cheap and nasty imitations and so there were. The finches on some of them looked nothing like Mr. Aardvark's or, indeed, any finch that has ever flown into my garden. Others were made of inferior materials so that the colours began to run whenever it rained - which happens occasionally in Manchester. But what stung Mr. Aardvark particularly was a range of distelfinks that seemed to resemble his in every detail even down to their four layers of packaging and the wording of the mounting instructions.

Enquiries made by his agent in China revealed that they had actually come from a sub-contractor to one of Mr Aardvark's manufacturers. Harsh words had apparently been said but the sub-contractor stood his ground. He replied, not unreasonably, that the foreigner's design did not appear to be protected in China. Nobody had ever told him that there was anything special about the design or that there was any reason to query the subsequent order. He was just a small factory owner trying to earn an honest living to educate his children so that they could enjoy better opportunities in life than he had had. So what was all the fuss? The agent said he could stop placing orders with the offending contractor, but did Mr. Aardvark really want him to do that. That particular contractor was very good and it would be difficult to find anyone else whose quality came close. And there was nothing that he could do to prevent the sub-contractor selling distelfinks to other customers. Indeed, he was doing a roaring trade right now because a craze for distelfinks had begun to take hold in some of the smarter suburbs of Chongqing.

A typical conference

So my clerk, Fred, had booked in Mr. Aardvark in for a 9 am conference in my chambers in Central Manchester, together with his solicitor, Samuel Pepys, knowing that I would have to traipse across the Pennines on a frosty morning and that I am not the world's best timekeeper. Bundling into the lift of our office block at about 9:07 am our fees clerk, Susie, called me on my mobile to tell me that 'Mr Peppies' (sic) and 'Mr Hard Work' (sic) had been pacing the clerks' room since 8:25 that morning and what could she tell them. Nobody ignores Susie because

---

3   The part of Pennsylvania where the Dutch settled.

she has a particularly whiney voice which comes in very useful for chasing fees. Susie even managed to collect from Mary Burke, a lady solicitor in one of the better firms in Liverpool, full of her sense of self-importance, who was always far too busy to attend to the trivial matter of paying counsel 'who were already grossly overpaid as it was'.[4] *She achieved that by calling Mrs Burke on her direct line at the start of every day as soon as the fee note was due with her usual greeting: 'Mrs Burke, it's Su-u-u-u-sie from Mr. A's' or Ms. B's chambers in Manchester.' Mary was pretty good at standing up to most people but not to Susie, and not at 9:30 am every morning. She tried diverting her phone to Emma, her secretary, but that was fatal because Emma could put up with the whine for just three consecutive calls. She intervened with her boss: 'Look couldn't you just pay this fee and go to other chambers in future.' 'I'm on my way Susie,' I replied, 'I'm in the lift as we speak.' 'Which lift, Mr Lammburrt?' asked Susie before the signal was lost. She really ought to have been a cross-examiner.*

Mr. Aardvark, whose DNA would have been coded with almost religious respect for punctuality inherited from 200 years of the factory system, and Mr Pepys who was given to panic, must have been fuming like the smoke ball while waiting for me to arrive. They had nothing to read save one of Fred's discarded motoring magazines, an out of date chambers brochure and a well-thumbed, 2 year old edition of Cheshire Life, and nothing to consume save Justin the junior's very weak tea in a plastic cup with a stained spoon complete with tea bag served with two unappetizing digestive biscuits. But whatever their frustration they greeted me cordially enough.

'Very nice to see you, Mr. Lambert', fawned Mr. Pepys, 'so good of you to make the time. I've told Mr Aardvark how busy you are.'

'Not from your work, Samuel', I felt like saying, but instead what came out with something vaguely like a smile was: 'Oh that's alright, Mr. Pepys. I understand how important this is to your client. Have you had tea or coffee? Have you tried one of Susie's home-baked pastries?[5] *No, well, never mind, that's a pleasure to come. Shall we make a start?'*

Typical instructions

Once in my room in chambers (out of which Justin had ejected Sally, a family practitioner, who was much more accustomed to kicking me out for her conferences) I opened the conference after making sure that everyone was seated and that Justin had taken everyone's coats, no doubt to be draped over a towel rail in the gents.

'Now, Mr Pepys', I began, 'I have read your instructions.'

That was not strictly true as Mr Pepys's instructions tended to be over 20 pages long of which no more than 5 lines were ever relevant. As usual they comprised an ample description of every letter, fax, email and other document in his file, whether enclosed with his instructions or not, together with a regurgitation of his notes on the law of copyright gleaned from a one-day

---

4   Mary may have had a point there. One young criminal practitioner of my acquaintance is said to have earned £85,000 in his first year and blown it all on a Lotus.
5   Susie was reported once to have managed to shove a ready meal into a microwave when her mum was ill. This was my revenge for the dialogue in the lift though I am not sure that Susie appreciates irony.

seminar on intellectual property that he had attended to get his points many years ago. But I had at least spotted quite quickly and read those relevant 5 lines.

Some typical misconceptions

'I see you want me to get an "Anton Piller Order" to close down the importers of the product that has been sourced from one of Mr Aardvark's manufacturers?'

'Yes, that's quite right, Mr Lambert.' replied Mr. Pepys. 'My client also wants you to get additional and conversion damages for breach of copyright and costs on the indemnity basis too. And I have already prepared letters to go off to all the retailers warning them that we will go after them too unless they give us undertakings and offer us damages.'

'Well steady on, Mr Pepys,' I said, 'you haven't sent any of those out, I hope.'

'Not yet.' he replied, the colour beginning to drain from his face. 'Is there a problem?'

'Not if you haven't posted them', I reassured him. 'Have you ever heard of a threats action?' It was clear from his face that he hadn't.

Taking the last volume of the latest edition of Laddie Prescott & Vitoria[6] from my bookcase, I read the following words of S.253 (1) of the Copyright, Designs and Patents Act 1988:

'Where a person threatens another person with proceedings for infringement of design right, a person aggrieved by the threats may bring an action against him claiming—

    (a) a declaration to the effect that the threats are unjustifiable;
    (b) an injunction against the continuance of the threats;
    (c) damages in respect of any loss which he has sustained by the threats.'[7]

'We should be all right, shouldn't we?' said Mr Pepys. 'After all, we are complaining of breach of contract.'

'Copyright may subsist in the artwork for the finches', I agreed, 'but, if I understand Mr Aardvark's concern correctly, you also complain about the whole assembly.'

'That's right,' beamed Mr. Pepys, 'didn't you see the design drawings at Tabs 2 and 3 of your instructions?'

'I did indeed see the design documents', I said, 'but if I can refer you to S.51 (1) of the same Act, it is no longer an infringement of copyright in a design document for anything other than an artistic work to make an article to the design or to copy an article made to the design.[8] "Design", so that we are all clear, is defined as:

---

6   *The Modern Law of Copyright*, 3rd edition, Butterworths.

7   http://www.opsi.gov.uk/acts/acts1988/Ukpga_19880048_en_17.htm.

8   'It is not an infringement of any copyright in a design document or model recording or embodying a design for anything other than an artistic work or a typeface to make an article to the design or to copy an article made to the design.'

"the design of any aspect of the shape or configuration (whether internal or external) of the whole or part of an article, other than surface decoration."[9]

"Design document" means:

"any record of a design, whether in the form of a drawing, a written description, a photograph, data stored in a computer or otherwise."[10]

In other words, copyright no longer protects 3-dimensional industrial designs. The law has changed.'

'Goodness! When did that happen?' asked Mr. Pepys.

'The commencement order came into force on 1 August 1989.'[11] I said.

'So does that mean that any bugger can rip off my distelfinks?' asked Mr Aardvark, looking accusingly at his solicitor.

'No, copyright protection for industrial designs has been replaced by a new intellectual property right called "unregistered design right"', I reassured him, trying to put them at their ease. 'It works very like copyright, but there are some differences. The term is much shorter.'

'Oh, how long?' asked Mr. Aardvark.

'In most cases, 10 years from the end of the calendar year in which articles from the design were first put on the market[12], I replied, 'though in the last 5 years anyone in the world including an infringer can apply for permission to do anything that would otherwise be an infringement of design right.'[13]

'I suppose that's long enough', reflected Mr Aardvark. 'I should have something else on the market long before then.'

'And then there are threats actions', I continued. 'A threats action is a statutory right of action that also exists under the Patents Act 1977,[14] Trade Marks Act 1994[15] and Registered Designs Act 1949.[16] The intention is to discourage intellectual property owners from abusing their

---

9   S.51 (3) http://www.opsi.gov.uk/acts/acts1988/Ukpga_19880048_en_4.htm#mdiv51.
10   Ibid.
11   Art 2 of The Copyright, Designs and Patents Act 1988 (Commencement No. 1) Order 1989, SI 1989 No. 816 (http://www.opsi.gov.uk/si/si1989/Uksi_19890816_en_1.htm).
12   S.216 (1) provides:
        Design right expires—
        (a) fifteen years from the end of the calendar year in which the design was first recorded in a design document or an article was first made to the design, whichever first occurred, or
        (b) if articles made to the design are made available for sale or hire within five years from the end of that calendar year, ten years from the end of the calendar year in which that first occurred.
13   S.237 (1) of the Act provides:
        Any person is entitled as of right to a licence to do in the last five years of the design right term anything which would otherwise infringe the design right.
(http://www.ipo.gov.uk/acts/acts1988/Ukpga_19880048_en_15.htm#mdiv237.)
14   S.70 Patents Act 1977 as amended (http://www.ipo.gov.uk/patentsact1977.pdf).
15   S.21 Trade Marks Act 1994 (http://www.patent.gov.uk/tmact94.pdf).
16   S.26 Registered Designs Act 1949 as amended (http://www.ipo.gov.uk/regdesignact.pdf).

monopolies or other exclusive rights. In the late 19th century, patentees used to queer the pitches of their competitors by threatening to sue distributors who stocked or sold anything but the patented product. That was quite a potent threat because intellectual property litigation has always been prohibitively expensive ...'

'Aye, happen.' interjected Mr Aardvark.

'... and hence wholesalers and retailers would often ditch perfectly legitimate products rather than risk being drawn into a patent infringement claim.'

'But, as I said, we are threatening copyright infringement not design right', protested Mr. Pepys.

'Doesn't matter', I replied. 'The threat doesn't have to be spelt out. It's what a person standing in the shoes of the distributor might think.[17] If you tell someone to stop stocking or selling distelfinks or else, that person is entitled to think that you are asserting a design right.'

'Oh I see', said Mr Pepys.

'And another thing,' I added. 'It isn't just the party who issues the threat who is liable for a groundless threat under S.253. A claim can also be made against the solicitor who writes the offending letter. Indeed, one of the reasons for bringing a threats action is to drive a wedge between the solicitor and his client.'

Mr Pepys began to look decidedly uncomfortable and muttered something about making a telephone call.

'Do you want to use my phone?' I asked.

Interim injunctions

After Mr Pepys had told his secretary to retrieve the letters to the distributors from the post room I raised another point.

'At the start of this conference you said that you wanted an "Anton Piller Order"[18] to close down the importers who had imported the offending distelfinks.'

'Yes. That's right.'

'Why?'

---

17   As Mr Justice Lightman put it in L'Oreal (UK) Ltd and another v. Johnson & Johnson and another [2000] EWHC Ch 129 (7th March, 2000): 'The test is whether the communication would be understood by the ordinary recipient in the position of the claimant as constituting a threat of proceedings for infringement.' (http://www.bailii.org/ew/cases/EWHC/Ch/2000/129.html.)

18   *Anton Piller KG v Manufacturing Process Ltd.* [1976] Ch 55, [1976] 1 All ER 779.

'Because it would force them to let me and members of my staff into their offices and search their computers and filing cabinets. Possibly even their homes and cars. It holes them up in their offices for hours preventing them from talking to anybody else, except perhaps their solicitor so long as they are quick about it. Since solicitors with experience of these orders tend to be few and far between it will cost them a pretty penny to take legal advice. So we can knock the stuffing out of them before they have even started.'

'It would be even better if we could combine it with a "Mareva order"[19], mused Mr Pepys, 'because that prevents them from transferring cash or assets outside the jurisdiction or even spending their money beyond legal advice and normal business or household expenditure. And again because lawyers cost money ...'

'Well, for a start, Anton Piller orders are now called search orders and Mareva orders are freezing injunctions and have been since 26 April 1999', I interrupted.

'I suppose that's part of those Woolf reforms', observed Mr Pepys.

'Quite so,' I replied. 'There was a whole change of terminology. Marevas are now freezing injunctions, interlocutory injunctions are now called interim injunctions, motions are applications', motions day is the Chancery interim applications day and the motions judge is now the Chancery interim applications judge. It's all supposed to simplify the law and make it more user friendly. However, the main point is that search orders and freezing injunctions are not and never have been intended to cripple defendants before they could get their cases off the ground, though that was, and is, regrettably, all too often the effect. And it is not just respondents who go to the wall as a result of these orders. They are expensive to get. Like all interim injunctions they are granted only on undertakings to compensate the other side for any loss it may have sustained as a result of the order if the court concludes at the end of the day that the order should not have been granted. If you close down a company's headquarters for a day while your assistant solicitors and experts are scavenging their records, those losses can be enormous. And so, of course, can the compensation that the applicant be ordered to pay.'

'Bloody hell', said Mr Aardvark, glaring at his solicitor who was no doubt wondering why he had not gone to that nice young Mr Smith from Palatinate Chambers who has just been adopted as a New Labour prospective Parliamentary candidate or the very lovely Ms Jones from Market Street, who is also doing well with Mr Cameron's Conservatives. They may not be intellectual property specialists but they do a lot of other commercial work such as insolvency and landlord and tenant. And most of all they do not raise awkward questions in conference. They just do what they are told though they are a bit pricey.

'The purpose of a search order is to recover and preserve documents or other relevant evidence that would otherwise be destroyed, removed or hidden', I explained, 'just as a freezing injunction is designed to keep within the jurisdiction of the court assets against which a judgment can be executed. These orders are right at the edge of the court's jurisdiction and their purpose is to ensure that justice is not defeated by the machinations of an unscrupulous defendant. They are made in the absence of the intended defendant and stretch almost to breaking point several rights guaranteed by the Human Rights Act 1998 and common law.

---

19   'The Mareva', *Mareva Compania Naviera SA v International Bulk Carriers SA* [1975] 2 Lloyds Reps. 509, [1980] 1 All ER 213.

The courts know that it can be very frightening and confusing to be on the receiving end of a search order. Accordingly they developed rules for the execution of these orders long before the Civil Procedure Rules[20] came into force. Most importantly the search team must now be supervised by an experienced solicitor in independent, private practice called 'a supervising solicitor' who represents the court in the premises to be searched. He or she is there to see fair play. The supervising solicitor serves the order and explains its effect and the respective rights of the parties in everyday language. He or she decides how the search is to proceed. At the end of the search the supervising solicitor has to submit a report as to what happened to the court that made the order.'

'That sounds like it could be expensive', observed Mr Aardvark.

'Indeed, it can', I agreed, 'particularly since there are only a small number of solicitors with the right experience and they tend to be with firms like Addleshaws, Eversheds or DLA Piper.'

'Oh!'

'I do have a supervising solicitor panel on my website,' I suggested.

'No, I think we are all right, lad', said Mr Aardvark. 'I don't think the other side would try to hide or destroy evidence. The lass who's importing those distelfinks used to work for me. That's how she knows where to go for them.'

'She wasn't working for you when you were sourcing your distelfinks?' I asked hopefully, probing the possibility of a breach of confidence claim.

'No,' he replied, 'that were years ago when young Elsie worked for us. No I got the idea for distelfinks long after Elsie set up on her own.'

'So the only reason you were thinking of getting a search order was to inflict suddenly a massive financial burden on Elsie's company?'

'No, lad! It was to bring her to the negotiating table', responded Mr Aardvark, 'just to see if we can't do some kind of deal.'

'Well why don't you do that anyway?' I asked.

Before he could answer Mr Pepys exclaimed: 'But surely we need an interim injunction to stop these distelfinks flooding the market at the very least?'

'How long have you known about Elsie's distelfinks?' I asked.

'Oh weeks, maybe months', he replied.

'And what did you do about it?'

---

20   The rules that govern civil procedure in England and Wales which can be viewed on the Ministry of Justice website at http://www.justice.gov.uk/civil/procrules_fin/index.htm.

'I had a word with Mr Pepys.'

I turned to the solicitor.

'Well, it was during the summer. I was on holiday and then my secretary, Tracy, was off. Then we had our big reception in October to launch our new offices in the town centre. You remember. You were there. And then it was half term and Tracy took more time off to be with her children. And then there was Christmas. And I went off skiing. You know how it is.'

'Indeed, I do', I replied, 'I am not criticizing anybody. But the court may well conclude that if Mr Aardvark can put up with these imports since the summer he can put up with them for a little bit longer, say until trial. I am sure I don't need to tell you that an injunction is an equitable remedy, Mr Pepys, and that delay defeats equity. There are exceptions such as Cavendish House[21] where interim injunctions have been available despite the lapse of time but I can't think of any reasons why the court should make an exception in this case. Besides; applying for an interim injunction can double the cost of litigation and delays its resolution for months.'

'Oh well. We don't want that', responded Mr Aardvark.

'Quite so!' said Mr Pepys, imagining himself in conference with Ms Jones and vowing silently to send all his IP work to her in future, should he be unlucky enough ever to get any more.

Design protection

'The other things you have asked for are additional and conversion damages', I said, turning to Mr. Pepys.

'Yes', said Mr Pepys, 'I understand that every copy of a copyright work made without the copyright owner's permission is deemed to belong to the copyright owner who can therefore demand their delivery up and damages for conversion for any of those copies that have been sold on. Quite a little bill for young Elsie in this case, I shouldn't wonder', he said with a smile.

'Well; infringing copies and infringing articles can still be delivered up'[22] I said, 'and it is still possible to recover additional damages where the justice of the case so requires,[23] but I am afraid that S.10 (1) of the Copyright Act 1956 which treated the copyright owner as the owner of the infringing copies and the plates or means for making them has not been re-enacted in the 1988 Act.'

'He's too clever for his own good', thought Mr Pepys, 'and he is undermining my credibility with my client. I don't think Sarah or Nigel would have done this to me,' as he contemplated the charming Ms Jones and the sleek and elegant Mr Smith.

---

21   *Cavendish House (Cheltenham) Ltd. v Cavendish-Woodhouse Ltd.* [1970] RPC 234.
22   Ss.96 (2), 99 (1) and 114 (1) (a) of the Copyright Designs and Patents Act 1988 (http://www.ipo.gov.uk/cdpact1988.pdf) in respect of copyright and ss. 229 (2) and 230 (1) of that Act in respect of unregistered design right (http://www.opsi.gov.uk/acts/acts1988/Ukpga_19880048_en_14.htm#mdiv229).
23   S.97 (2) and S.226 (3) ibid.

'Besides', I added,'the only thing that may be protected by copyright is the artwork for the finches.'

'May I look at one of those samples, Mr Aardvark?' I asked. One was produced and handed to me. It was packaged very tastefully in a cardboard box with scenes of what I assume to be the Pennsylvania countryside. Before I could open it, the following words caught my attention:

"Authentic Reproduction of an Eighteenth Century Pennsylvania, Dutch Design"

'Oh dear', I exclaimed, 'Those words don't help do they?'

'Waddya mean?' chorused Mr Aardvark and his solicitor.

'Well, copyright lasts for 70 years plus the life of the author. Unless these finches were drawn by Methuselah...'

Mr Pepys's face sank in his hands.

'Cheer up!' I said, 'My little joke. I assume that you employed artists and craftspeople to adapt the traditional designs and prepare them for mass production, Mr Aardvark?'

'Oh aye.'

'And would you say that substantial skill and labour was expended by your team?'

'They cost me enough in wages.'

'Well, in that case you probably still have one or more original artistic works in which copyright subsists. Copyright accrues to value added. Suppose you take a picture of Mr. Pepys coming out of Kendals.[24] That is an original artistic work the copyright of which belongs to you. Suppose that I take a copy of the negative with your permission and add Mickey Mouse ears to Mr. Pepys' head. I create a new artistic work the copyright in which belongs to me.'

'What about my copyright?' Mr Aardvark asked.

'That continues to subsist', I explained, 'but I get a new copyright because I added value to the photo.'

Mr Aardvark turned to his solicitor and could not resist a snigger.

'Now suppose someone copies my work without our consent, both of us have a complaint.'

'I see', said Mr Aardvark doubtfully.

---

24   Kendals or Kendal Milne is a large department store on Deansgate which used to be as grand as Harrods.

'If they only copy the picture of Mr Pepys without the ears then they have not infringed my copyright even though they have reproduced part of my work, because the part that they have reproduced is not the value that I added.'

'You mean the Mickey Mouse ears?' asked Mr Pepys.

'Yes', I replied, 'but they would have infringed Mr Aardvark's copyright because they copied the bit that he made.'

'Ah', said my clients in unison, the penny having obviously dropped.

'If Elsie has gone to the same source in Pennsylvania and employed her own commercial artists to make her own artwork without reference to your distelfinks then you can't really say that she has copied your value added.'

'But she has not done that', said Mr Pepys, 'she has gone to our supplier in China and bought a stock of distelfinks just like ours.'

'Well, you are probably right', I agreed. 'Although the manufacturer may have done nothing wrong in China, the manufacture of distelfinks in the UK without Mr Aardvark's licence might well have infringed some copyright or design right.'

'And remember', I added, 'it is only surface decoration that could be protected by copyright. Designs of three-dimensional articles are protected by unregistered design right.'

Patent and Trade Mark attorneys

'I have been looking through my instructions to see whether you have registered your design under the Registered Designs Act 1949 or as a registered Community design', I observed, 'but I can't find a certificate of registration. Have you applied to register your design, Mr Aardvark?'

'Have I what?' answered Mr Aardvark. 'Mr Pepys, you never told me anything about design registration.'

'Mr Pepys wouldn't', I said coming to his rescue. 'The person who might would have been a patent or trade mark attorney.'

'A what?'

'Patent or Trade Mark attorney', I explained, 'they used to be known as patent or trade mark agents but they now call themselves patent attorneys. I suppose it is because the public associate agents with estate agents and attorneys with LA Law. Anyway their job is to help people protect their investment in brands, design, research and development, publishing and entertainment.'

'How do they do that?' asked Mr Aardvark.

'Well, think of them as a bit like conveyancers', I replied. 'Just as you would instruct a solicitor or licensed conveyancer to buy or sell a house or plot of land, so you would instruct a patent attorney to apply for a patent, trade mark or registered design.'

'And a trade mark attorney?'

'A trade mark attorney advises and assists with applications to register trade marks and designs. Most patent attorneys are also trade mark attorneys although by no means all trade mark attorneys are patent attorneys.'

'Oh?'

'Patent attorneys have science, engineering or technology degrees', I explained, 'and quite a few have doctorates.'

'Clever halfpenny worths.'[25]

'Well they spend a lot of time at university', I agreed, 'so they would probably be otherwise unemployable. But they can sometimes be very useful to inventors, designers and business people.'

'Oh! What do they do?'

'Well. For a start, they can carry out an audit of all the new products, production processes and other technologies in your business to see what is potentially patentable, what could be registered as a design and so on. That's called an "intellectual property audit".'

'Oh aye.'

'They check to see whether you own that intellectual property and if not what you can do about it.'

'What's this intell-ec-tummel (sic) property when it's at home?'

'Intellectual property is the collective name we give to the bundle of laws that protect the kind of investment in brands, design, technology and the arts that I mentioned just now.'

'You mean like pay-tents?' asked Mr. Aardvark.

'Well, yes, except it's pronounced with a short "a" like "grass". "pat-tent".[26] *I said.*

'Oh!'

---

25   Literally,'half-penny worth'. A half-penny in pre-decimal coinage days was pronounced 'hape penny' and a half-penny's worth as 'ape-uth'.

26   This will not be understood in the South of England or even parts of Wilmslow and Harrogate.

'Well, patents are a type of intellectual property. They can confer a monopoly of the manufacture, sale, importation or use of a new product in the United Kingdom for up to 20 years. It is one of the ways of protecting investment in research and development.'

'Can I get one of them patents for my distelfink?' asked Mr Aardvark.

'No', I replied, 'for many reasons. But you might have been entitled, and indeed may still be entitled, to a registered design or registered Community design and we shall discuss that in a minute.'

'Right you are, lad.'

'We were talking about IP audits. The great advantage of that exercise is that it identifies not only potential assets for your company but also flags up possible risks such as possible claims by third parties.'

'What sort of claims?' asked Mr Aardvark with a frown.

'Let's just suppose that someone registered a design for a distelfink either in England under the Registered Designs Act 1949 or at the Community trade marks and designs registry which rejoices under the wonderfully apt name of "Office for Harmonization for the Internal Market" or "OHIM" in Alicante. He or she may not have made or marketed any distelfinks. You may never have heard of his or her registration unless you check the register. But that person would have the exclusive right to make and market distelfinks in the UK or EC depending on whether it is a national or Community registration. And if you make any without his or her licence – that is to say permission – he or she could go after you for injunctions, damages, delivery up et cetera, even though you may have acted in good faith.'

'Oh heck.'

'Patent and trade mark attorneys check the registers and sometimes other sources such as published literature to see whether your invention or design really is "new."'

'I see.'

'They also keep – or more usually employ someone else to keep – a lookout to see whether anyone has applied for a patent, trade mark or registered design anywhere in the world where you carry on business which could affect your trade.'

'Oh.'

'And if they find anything, they tell you about it and advise you about what you can do. If, for example, you want to warn someone that you have a patent, trade mark or registered design, a patent attorney can bring it to that person's notice taking care not to get you or themselves into a threats action. If that does not work, they may make representations to the Intellectual Property Office, European Patent Office, OHIM, or wherever. And if that still doesn't work they may file proceedings in the appropriate intellectual property office.'

'What sort of proceedings?'

'Well, the IP Office has a number of tribunals to determine disputes between people who claim the same intellectual property and disputes between applicants and examiners as to whether an application for a patent or trade mark should be granted. I was referring to proceedings before those tribunals.'

'Have you heard of them tribunals, Sam?' Mr Aardvark asked.

Before Mr Pepys could answer, I interjected: 'Solicitors don't usually do much of that work. They tend to leave it to patent and trade mark attorneys. They can and usually do address those tribunals but if there is a particularly difficult point they may instruct a barrister specializing in intellectual property like me.'

'Should I have gone to one of them patent attorneys rather than young Samuel here?' asked Mr. Pepys.

'Well, some of them do have the right to conduct litigation in the courts, especially the Patents Court and Patents County Court; and they also advise on licensing and draft agreements as solicitors and barristers do. But patent attorneys are very specialized and intellectual property cases do not usually come neatly packaged as they do in law school exams. For instance, some people acquire IP rights from administrators so there are often insolvency issues or there may be tax considerations. The advantage of a good solicitor like Mr Pepys from a first class firm like Deweys[27] is that they can supply all your legal needs.'

'Yes that's right', said Mr Pepys, preening himself and forgetting for a moment Ms Jones's pheromones.

'We do try to look after our corporate clients very well.'

'I'm sure you do', I said. Using a backhand that would raise a cheer at Wimbledon,[28] I added: 'Horses for courses. Were you ever unfortunate enough to find yourself in the Stockport County Court, who better to represent your interests than Mr Pepys? After all, you sit as a deputy district judge in the county court these days don't you?'

'How do I get one of them pay- I mean pat-tent attorneys?' asked Mr Aardvark, pronouncing 'attorney' with a liquid, rolling Lancastrian 'R'.

'If you have a word with the clerks on the way out, they'll give you a list of the ones that come to me.'

'You'll have a long wait', replied Mr Pepys sensing an opportunity for revenge, 'Fred's never there. Susie's always filing her nails except when she is harassing me or my secretary for counsels' fees. And as for young Justin, I would check the calendar if he told me that it was Tuesday today.'

---

27   'Deweys' is a re-brand. It was formerly known as 'Dewey, Screwem & Howe.'
28   So long as it was wielded by a British player.

'Very wise, Mr. Pepys, seeing as it happens to be Wednesday', I responded. 'Well, another thing you can do is have a look at the "CIPA" website at www.cipa.org.uk. CIPA stands for the Chartered Institute of Patent Attorneys which is the professional body for patent attorneys in the UK. They have a database of patent attorneys' firms that is searchable by geography. Or if you want a trade mark attorney you can look at the ITMA[29] site at www.itma.org.uk which has something similar. I think you will find quite a few in the North including several in Manchester. Of course, you can instruct one from anywhere. If you anticipate a hearing in London you may prefer to instruct one near Bouverie Street who could stroll down from say Staple Inn between lunch and tea rather than someone round here who would have to charge you his return train fare from the North and possibly overnight accommodation in London even though I am sure he would do his best to keep the costs down, especially if the hearing happened to coincide with something else like a test match or Harrods's sale. And since many of the intellectual property rights that you may require are Community trade marks or designs or applications for patents or other intellectual property protection in more than one country you are not even restricted to patent attorneys in the UK. The European Patent Office website keeps a searchable database of European patent attorneys from all contracting states. My advice to you is to make thorough enquiries and shop around.'

Registered designs

'Anyway', I observed, 'we seem to have been diverted from the topic of registered designs. Had you registered the design of your distelfink as a registered Community design you would have enjoyed throughout the EC the exclusive right to use it and to prevent any third party not having your consent from using it.[30] Such use would have covered making, offering, putting on the market, importing, exporting or using of a product in which the design was incorporated or to which it was applied, or stocking such a product for those purposes.'[31]

'Can you be a bit more precise as to what is meant by design?' asked Mr Aardvark.

'Well', I said, 'design is defined as … and you will have to excuse me for a moment while I look it up:

> "the appearance of the whole or a part of a product resulting from the features of, in particular, the lines, contours, colours, shape, texture and/or materials of the product itself and/or its ornamentation".'[32]

'Is a distelfink a product?' asked Mr Aardvark.

'Can be', I said. 'The regulation defines product as:

> "any industrial or handicraft item, including inter alia parts intended to be assembled into a complex product, packaging, get-up, graphic symbols and typographic typefaces, but excluding computer programs".'

---

29   Institute of Trade Mark Attorneys.
30   Art 19 (1) Community Design Regulation (Council Regulation (EC) No 6/2002 of 12 December 2001 on Community designs, http://oami.europa.eu/en/design/pdf/reg2002_6.pdf).
31   Ibid.
32   Art 3 (a) ibid.

'Handicrafts, eh!' queried Mr Pepys. 'I remember Mr Smith – who's very good as you know, telling me that there had to be a minimum production run.'

'I know Mr Smith has an excellent reputation for landlord and tenant', I agreed. 'I think you are thinking of the old law.'

'The Registered Designs Act 1949 has not been repealed, Mr Lambert. I know that much', insisted Mr Pepys, smirking.

'Quite right, Mr. Pepys. But it has been amended many times. On two occasions quite out of recognition. First, by the Copyright Designs and Patents Act 1988[33] and more recently by The Registered Designs Regulations 2001.[34] If you want to follow the Act easily I recommend your downloading the unofficial consolidation of the Act[35] from the IPO website.'

'Thank you', said Mr Pepys, scribbling down a note.

'Anyway, getting back to the point. Had you registered the design the scope of your protection would have included not just identical designs but any design that did not produce a different overall impression on the informed user.'[36]

'I think you mentioned a while back that I might still be entitled to register a design or registered Community design?' asked Mr Aardvark hopefully.

'And so you might.' I replied. 'When did you first make your design available to the public?'

'What do you mean by making available to the public?' enquired Mr Aardvark.

'Publishing, exhibiting, use in the trade or otherwise', I suggested.

'Well the first ones went on sale in this country the Easter before last.'

'Pity', I said.

'Why?'

'Well, a design can be registered to the extent that it is new and has individual character.[37] A design is considered to be "new" for the purposes of registration if no identical design has been made available to the public before the date of filing.[38] And it is considered to have "individual character" if the overall impression it produces on the informed user differs from the overall impression produced on such a user by any design which has previously been made available to the public.[39] However art. 7(2) provides that disclosures by the designer during the 12 month

---

33   See schedule 4 of the Copyright Designs and Patents Act 1988 at http://www.opsi.gov.uk/acts/acts1988/Ukpga_ 19880048_en_25.htm#sdiv4.
34   SI 2001 No. 3949 (http://www.opsi.gov.uk/si/si2001/20013949.htm).
35   http://www.ipot.gov.uk/regdesignact.pdf.
36   Art 10 (1) Community design regulation.
37   Art 4 (1) ibid.
38   Art 5 (2) (b) ibid.
39   Art 6 (1) (b) ibid.

period preceding the date of filing of an application are not to be taken into consideration. The Act as amended has a similar provision though it is expressed in a rather more long winded fashion.[40] *I am sorry to say that you are well outside that 12 months grace period.'*

'Oh!' groaned Mr. Aardvark.

'Registration would probably have taken a lot of time and cost you a lot of money', said Mr Pepys, anticipating another accusing glare from his client.

'No it wouldn't have', I said. 'There is almost no formal examination and it is very easy. A lot of people do it themselves without instructing a patent or trade mark attorney. The IPO has produced some very simple, very useful guidance on its website. Anyone can do it.'[41]

'Does he have to tell him this?' mused Mr Pepys. 'Before long he will be telling them how to litigate.'

'You said earlier that someone might have registered a distelfink on the register. How do we find that out?' asked Mr Aardvark.

'We could do a simple search over the internet here and now', I suggested, 'there are a number of classes under which it could be registered.'

'Oh dear!' I exclaimed.

'What's the matter?' asked my clients.

'Well, there is an image here that looks very like your distelfink,' I said. 'In fact, it is called a "distelfink". It was registered not all that long ago by Or Else Novelties Ltd.'

'That's Elsie's company', said Mr Aardvark. 'The cow! She's nicked my design and registered it as her own. She can't do that.'

'Well, I explained that there was no real examination and that it was very easy.'

'Does that mean that she can stop Mr Aardvark selling his distelfinks?' asked Mr Pepys.

'No; for two reasons. The first is that the registration is probably invalid and we could challenge it if we wish.'

'We bloody do', said Mr Aardvark.

'Just as well that I told you about patent attorneys', I said, 'And also, registration does not affect bona fide *prior use.'*

'That's something, I suppose.'

---

40   S.1B (6) Registered Designs Act 1949 as amended.
41   'Designs application procedure' at http://www.ipo.gov.uk/design/d-applying/d-apply.htm.

'And there's something else. It may be too late to apply for a registered or registered Community design but you may still be entitled to an unregistered Community design for up to 3 years from the date upon which your design was first made available to the public. You are still well within that period.'

'What do I have to do to get that?'

'Nothing. It comes into being automatically so long as your design is "new" and has "individual character", which we talked about before.'

'But hasn't Elsie's registration overridden that?' asked Mr Pepys.

'No. One intellectual property right doesn't override another though it may affect its exercise. And as I said Elsie's registration may well be invalid.'

'An unregistered Community design applies throughout the whole EC', I added, cheering up my clients.

'The protection is the same. The only differences, and they are big ones, are that you have to prove copying in the case of an unregistered Community design but not for a registered design and the term is much shorter.'

'So I still have a few shots in my locker?' asked Mr Aardvark hopefully.

'Indeed, you have, Mr Aardvark. In addition to your unregistered Community design you still have your national unregistered design right and your artistic copyrights in the drawings of the finches.'

'Well that's good enough for us, isn't it Mr Lambert?' exclaimed Mr Pepys.

'Maybe', I said, 'but a design registration would have been better. Subject only to a validity challenge, subsistence of the intellectual property right and title are givens. You don't even have to prove copying. Just similarity. With copyright, design right or unregistered Community design you have to prove that the right subsists in the first place. That is not always straightforward. Take design right, for instance: not only must your design be original in the sense that it is not copied from a design that already exists. It may not be commonplace in the design field at the time of creation.[42] The bar for unregistered Community design is set even higher in that you have to prove both novelty and individual character. Then there is title. For copyright and unregistered design right you have to satisfy a qualification test. That's easily achieved for copyright because citizenship or residence of a country that is party to the Berne or Universal Copyright Conventions is enough and all industrial countries are party to one or other of those Conventions. But for design right there are very few countries outside Europe whose citizens qualify. Americans, Chinese, Indians, Japanese and Koreans are excluded except for semiconductor chip topographies.'

'Semiconductor topographies!' said Mr Aardvark. 'What are they when they are at home?'

---

42   S.213 (4) Copyright Designs and Patents Act 1988 (http://www.opsi.gov.uk/acts/acts1988/Ukpga_19880048_en_13.htm#mdiv213).

'Layouts of integrated circuits,' I replied. 'You know, for your PC or mobile phone. I don't think you need to worry about them just yet.'

'That's something, I suppose.'

'But the real nightmare with all these rights is proving copying. The problem is that it is very rare to catch somebody at it. So the law provides the following process. First, you have to prove that the alleged original and the putative copy are similar. Then you have to show that the copyist had an opportunity to copy the original. If you can do that, the other side has to explain the reason for the similarity. There may be all sorts of perfectly good, innocent explanations. There may be only one way of making the product in question. Or it may even be coincidence. If the other side can give a credible explanation the claim will fail.

That's why it takes a lot longer and costs a lot more money to prove infringement of an unregistered right like copyright or design right than it does to prove infringement of an unregistered design.

Also, it's probably fairer to the public. If a design is registered everybody is given fair warning of the existence of the right.'

Pre-action conduct

'Well by the sound of things you are not telling me that I don't have a case?' asked Mr Aardvark.

'No, the likelihood is that you do have a case. But perhaps it is not quite as overwhelming as you had hoped. I think you can see how risky it would have been to apply for a search order. Since you would have made the application in Elsie's absence you would have had to disclose to the court anything that the court would need to consider when deciding whether or not to grant your case. And clearly they would have needed to know about Elsie's design registration.'

'I suppose so.'

'Also, I have not seen anything yet to suggest that Elsie has acted flagrantly or that any benefits have accrued to her to justify additional damages under S.97 (2) or S.229 (3) of the Copyright Designs and Patents Act 1988.'

'No.'

'And as indemnity costs are a sanction for improper or unreasonable conduct of litigation I think it is too early to be thinking about them since we have yet to hear from Elsie.'

'That's true.'

'When I asked you why you wanted a search order just now, you said that you wanted to force Elsie to the negotiating table, but how do you know that she won't come willingly when she learns about your complaint?'

'Well, she might.'

'Precisely. Put yourself in Elsie's shoes. Would you be more likely to respond positively to a fully documented letter of claim or a bunch of strangers forcing their way into your office with a court order and rummaging through your files all day?'

'Oh I'd play pop, me if someone barged into my office like that', said Mr. Aardvark, his face reddening, 'but it would be different if they wrote to me nicely.'

'And does Elsie allow folk to push her around?'

'No way', he replied, 'she's got spirit has that lass.'

'Well then', I said.

Mr Aardvark nodded and Mr Pepys glowered.

'Mr Pepys has probably told you that the court expects parties to litigation to act reasonably in exchanging information and documents relevant to the claim and generally in trying to avoid the necessity for the start of proceedings.'[43]

'Yes, that's quite right', interrupted Mr Pepys nodded like a donkey.

'Did you?' asked Mr Aardvark looking confused.

'Parties to a potential dispute should follow a reasonable procedure, suitable to their particular circumstances, to avoid litigation', I continued. 'That usually involves the claimant writing to give details of the claim, the defendant acknowledging the claim letter promptly, to be followed up within a reasonable time by a detailed written response and the parties conducting genuine and reasonable negotiations with a view to settling the claim economically and without court proceedings.'[44]

'I see', said Mr Aardvark.

'You should set out the details of your claim in a document called a "letter of claim" ', I said. Opening my white book[45] I read:

> 'The claimant's letter should—
> (a) give sufficient concise details to enable the recipient to understand and investigate the claim without extensive further information;
> (b) enclose copies of the essential documents which the claimant relies on;
> (c) ask for a prompt acknowledgement of the letter, followed by a full written response within a reasonable stated period;

---

43   Para 4.1 PD-Protocols (http://www.justice.gov.uk/civil/procrules_fin/contents/practice_directions/pd_protocol.htm#IDAROMSC).
44   Para 4.2 Ibid.
45   *Civil Procedure* (published every year by Sweet & Maxwell).

(For many claims, a normal reasonable period for a full response may be one month.)

(d) state whether court proceedings will be issued if the full response is not received within the stated period;

(e) identify and ask for copies of any essential documents, not in his possession, which the claimant wishes to see;

(f) state (if this is so) that the claimant wishes to enter into mediation or another alternative method of dispute resolution; and

(g) draw attention to the court's powers to impose sanctions for failure to comply with this practice direction and, if the recipient is likely to be unrepresented, enclose a copy of this practice direction.'

'That seems an awful lot of work, Mr Lambert; are you sure that it is really necessary?' asked Mr Pepys.

'Well, it's in the white book', I said, 'ignore it at your peril.'

'What if we do ignore it?' asked Mr Aardvark.

'If you do, the court has a whole armoury of sanctions,' I replied. 'It could disallow some or all of your costs should litigation be inevitable. It could even make you pay some of Elsie's. If you wanted more time to meet a deadline, the court could refuse to give it to you. But the real point is that you can have meaningful negotiations with someone only if he or she understands your case. Presumably you want to settle this amicably if you can?'

'It depends whether she meets our demands', said Mr Pepys.

'You do know how much High Court litigation could cost you, don't you Mr. Aardvark?'

'No, go on, tell me: £20,000, £25,000 ....more than that?'

'Potentially much more', I replied. 'IPAC, which stands for Intellectual Property Advisory Committee, the government's high level advisory committee on intellectual property, published a report in 2003 entitled "The Enforcement of Patent Rights."[46] At the back of the report is a table comparing the costs and other aspects of patent litigation in England and Wales with those in France, Germany, the Netherlands and the USA.[47] The figure for the High Court was £1 million and between £150,000 and £250,000 even for the Patents County Court.'

'Hell's bells!' exclaimed Mr Aardvark, practically falling off his chair.

'The figure for the USA is even higher – between US$2 and 4 million but remember that the losing party in the States does not usually have to pay the winner's lawyers' fees and many counsel are prepared to represent clients on a contingency fee.'

'What about the rest of Europe?' asked Mr Aardvark. 'You can be charged an arm and a leg for a coffee in the Champs Elysées.'

46   http://mandyhaberman.com/media/IPAC-18-11.pdf.

47   Page 50.

'Lawyers come a bit cheaper there, Mr Aardvark', I replied, 'the figures range between €10,000 for summary proceedings in the Netherlands to €50,000 in France and Germany.'

'That's patent litigation though, isn't it, Mr Lambert?'

'Is it the same for designs and copyright?' asked Mr Pepys.

'If anything a good deal more', I replied. 'Most people instruct the same lawyers and, of course, trials over unregistered rights like unregistered design rights and copyrights require a lot more evidence and take a great deal longer than fights over registered rights like patents and designs.'

'Oh Mother', winced Mr Aardvark. 'I'm surprised that anybody can afford to go to law in this country. Is there anything that you can suggest?'

'Well, you could consider intellectual property insurance,' I replied. 'It is a lot cheaper insuring before a dispute arises than it is after litigation starts. There are about 4 or 5 insurers who will quote you before-the-event cover for £4,000 to £5,000. If you wait until a dispute arises the underwriter will quote you one third of your costs and then only on a favourable opinion from counsel which will cost you because the barrister will want to be very thorough before expressing a view. At least I would.'

'The other thing to remember is that there are now some alternatives to litigation', I continued. 'The IPO provides staff mediators for the resolution of intellectual property disputes or they can put litigants in touch with some of the others including me.'[48]

'What's mediation?' asked Mr Aardvark.

'Think of it as chaired negotiation', I replied. 'The reason it works is that the mediator is entrusted with information about the dispute from each of the parties that neither wants to disclose to the other but which enables the mediator to see a solution that could not have occurred to the parties.'

'And there is yet another thing', I added. 'PD-Protocols, which I mentioned above, are supplemented by a code of practice for pre-action conduct in intellectual property disputes which you can download from the CIPA website.[49] That code was produced by a committee of experienced lawyers, patent attorneys and a former Patents Court judge. The chair was Michael Skrein who was a partner of the well-known London solicitors, Richards Butler. It was intended to be a pre-action protocol for intellectual property litigation but was put on ice when the Department for Constitutional Affairs decided to investigate the possibility of a general pre-action protocol for all disputes. That idea was dropped and for some reason or other the idea of an IP Pre-Action Protocol was never revived. But the code is very sensible and I always consult it. It amplifies paragraph 4.3 of PD-Protocols as to the contents of a letter of claim which we discussed above. If I were you, Mr Pepys, I would refer to both paragraph 4.3 of PD-Protocols

---

48   See the UK Intellectual Property Office's list of mediation providers at http://www.ipo.gov.uk/mediationproviders.
pdf.
49   http://www.cipa.org.uk/download_files/code_of_practice.pdf.

and paragraph 3 and Appendix B of the code. Do you want me to review your letter of claim to Elsie before you post it?'

'That would be very kind', said Mr. Pepys.

'Not at all', I replied.

'Just one thing, Mr Lambert', said Mr Aardvark. 'What do you think Elsie will do when she gets Mr Pepys's letter?'

'Difficult to say', I replied, 'but if she is properly advised, and I think she is, she will point to her design registration which we shall say is invalid. One thing you should bear in mind is that paragraph 6 of the code suggests four alternatives to litigation:

- further dialogue;

- mediation;

- expert determination; and

- arbitration.

I urge you to consider all those possibilities, particularly mediation and expert determination.'

'Do mediation and expert determination work for IP disputes?' asked Mr Pepys.

'Spectacularly', I replied. 'Nearly all generic and many country code top level domain name disputes are resolved by expert determination. Indeed, I have resolved a few myself.'

'It seems to me that you really have to plan ahead when it comes to this sort of malarkey', said Mr Aardvark.

'If you remember nothing else you must never forget that', I replied.

'Well, thank you very much', said Mr Pepys.

'Don't mention it', I answered. 'You'll be getting my fee note soon. And if that's not dealt with promptly, you'll be hearing from Susie – literally.'

'I don't think I will, Mr Lambert', Mr Pepys replied. 'I'm going on holiday a month from now.'

'What! You've only just come back from skiing', I exclaimed.

'It's the work-life balance', said Mr. Lambert. 'I've got three young children. It'll be half term again for the two girls. They need quality time with their dad.'

'You know what they say, Mr Pepys. Familiarity breeds contempt. Oh well, have a nice time away.'

'Thank you, Mr Lambert', said Mr Aardvark. 'I can't pretend that I liked everything that you had to say. But I have learned a lot today. I am sure you have saved me a lot of time and money.'

'I'm sure I have, Mr. Aardvark. Good luck with your business.'

Alternative dispute resolution

A few days later Mr Pepys sent me his idea of a letter of claim which came nowhere close to the specifications of paragraph 4.3 of the PD-Protocols or paragraph 3 of the code. I rewrote it completely and sent it off to him. I heard nothing more from him.

A few months later I met him in the Chancery interim applications court in Liverpool. His counsel, Mr Nigel Smith, was being buffeted from pillar to post by one of my colleagues from London. I spoke to him outside court while we were waiting for our respective cases to be called on.

'What happened to the distelfink case?' I enquired.

'Well, it sort of resolved itself', replied Mr Pepys. 'Elsie's solicitors, Fowl & Fowl of London, sent a very detailed letter of response. We decided to meet at their premises in accordance with paragraph 6 of the Code of Practice as you kindly suggested. Arthur asked to have a word with Elsie in private. She agreed. After a very long interview they emerged holding hands and said everything was settled. I was never told the exact terms but the last I heard was that Elsie is now Mrs. Arthur Aardvark.'

Future work for Sally, perhaps, I mused.

'Well I am delighted to hear that', I replied. 'I assume that you are now in funds.'

'Oh yes, Mr Lambert.'

'Good! I'll tell Susie. You'll be hearing from her in the morning.'

The next morning a smiling Susie greeted me.

'You know that con you had with that Mr Hard Work and Mr Peppies, Mr Lambert?'

'Yes, Susie', I replied.

'Well here's his cheque', she beamed, handing me the fee.

'Oh just one thing, Sir', said Fred handing me a chit. 'Err... clerk's fees, Mr Lambert.'

So what did we learn?

Mr Aardvark put his finger on the point when he remarked that you really have to plan ahead when it comes to intellectual property. The time to think about dealing with infringement is not when it occurs nor even when the intellectual property right is granted but before it is sought. Consideration should be given to the appropriate protection for intellectual assets at the earliest possible stage.

As was the case with Mr Aardvark's designs, there may be several ways of protecting investment in brands, designs, technology, publications and other intellectual assets. Some arise automatically such as copyrights, unregistered design rights and unregistered Community designs. Others, such as registered designs and registered Community designs, require registration with the UK-IPO, OHIM or some other agency. Registered rights generally afford greater certainty and better protection than unregistered rights in that they are cheaper and easier to enforce.

The starting point should be an intellectual property audit. Such an audit will identify potential assets as well as possible risks. A patent or trade mark attorney will often assist with such an audit. They will of course help with applications for patents, trade marks and designs but they can also advise on licensing and enforcement. The Chartered Institute of Patent Attorneys and the Institute of Trade Mark Attorneys maintain searchable databases of members on their respective websites.

Enforcement of intellectual property rights is expensive, particularly in England and Wales. It is often many times more expensive than in the rest of Europe. There are a number of initiatives to bring down the cost in England such as mediation and expert determination. Also, insurance cover may be available. Although a number of emergency remedies are available to preserve evidence or assets that might be lost or removed from the jurisdiction, they have to be exercised with very great care. Litigants are required to act reasonably to avoid the need for litigation particularly when exchanging information and documents.

Lastly, and very importantly, intellectual property owners and indeed their lawyers should be aware that threatening proceedings for patent, design or trade mark infringement can be actionable. They should seek specialist advice before issuing such proceedings. It is tragic when clients with legitimate complaints find themselves on the receiving end of a threats action simply because they or their solicitors have gone about raising the complaint the wrong way. Not only is the original complaint often forgotten but the rights owner may end up paying money to the infringer. The reaction of many inventors and professional advisors when I warn them of this risk is that the law is an ass. But the law is the law. There is a very good reason for it. It is one of the realities with which business people have to live.

2 Introduction to Intellectual Property

Context

There was a limit to what I could do for Mr. Aardvark because he did not have the optimum legal protection for his product. He would have been in a much better position if he had registered the designs of his *distelfinks* as UK registered designs or registered Community designs but he had never heard of design registration before he came to see me. Indeed, he had not even heard of intellectual property before then. Mr. Aardvark was not the first businessperson to be in that position and he is unlikely to be the last. Maybe the best way to help folk like him is to explain some basic concepts.

What is meant by the term Intellectual Property'?

In response to Mr. Aardvark's question, 'What's this intell-ec-tummel property when it's at home?' I replied that intellectual property is 'the collective name we give to the bundle of laws that protect the kind of investment in brands, design, technology and the arts.' Brands, design, technology and creative works are known collectively as 'intellectual assets'. These are the investments that give one business an advantage over another. Governments try to encourage those investments because they benefit the public at large. Brands help consumers identify the products and services they really want but they also serve businesses by providing a focus for advertising. Design makes things look better and sometimes helps them to work better. Technology provides the public with all sorts of new products and services as well as new ways of making them. The arts – music, drama, literature, television, literature – entertain us and help us understand the world and ourselves.

Why the law protects Intellectual Property

There are basically two ways in which the governments can encourage such investment. One way is for the state to pay for them. That is what happens in command economies like the former Soviet Union. Ballet dancers, rocket scientists, athletes and others the government wanted to encourage were rewarded with better accommodation, higher status and privileges such as the right to travel abroad. The other way and the way that we tend to use in the United Kingdom is to allow the market to reward innovation and creativity. Ballet dancers, athletes and entertainers, for example, get rich because fans pay to see them perform and buy their merchandise. Rocket scientists and indeed all other folk who develop new technologies get rich because people buy their rockets, medicines, electronic equipment and other things.

However, market mechanisms will not work unaided. If, for example, DVDs of the latest *Harry Potter* film sell like hot cakes it is very tempting to buy one, copy it and offer those copies to consumers. Obviously the author, the makers of the film and original DVDs and their distributors have to able to stop such copying and sales. Otherwise they will all be out of business. The law assists them by giving authors the exclusive right to reproduce or authorize others to reproduce their manuscripts. That is called 'copyright' and it is an example of 'intellectual property'. The law confers copyrights on all the other businesses that made the DVD possible such as the film studio that made the film and the commercial artists who designed the sleeve. It also confers rights on actors not to have their performances recorded without their consent as well as a similar right on any film studio that has contracted for the right to film such performances. These are known as 'rights in performances' and they are also examples of intellectual property. Yet another example is the name 'Harry Potter' which has been registered as a Community trade mark throughout the European Union for a range of goods and services in classes 9, 16, 20, 21, 25 and 28 under CTM registration number 935593 since 9 September 1998.[1]

Monopolies and non-monopoly rights

You may already have noticed that there are two kinds of intellectual property rights. Some are monopolies such as the exclusive right to make or sell new products having specific features known as 'patents', or the exclusive right to sell goods under a word or sign that is registered with the Trade Marks Registry known as a trade mark. Others are rights-to-prevent-other-people-from-doing-something-without-permission such as running a computer program (copyright), selling goods in packaging that is likely to be mistaken for someone else's (passing off) or making use of secret information that is disclosed in confidence (confidentiality). The difference between monopolies and rights-to-prevent-other-people-from-doing-something-without-permission can be very significant both legally and commercially. For instance, the copyright in a drawing entitles the copyright owner to prevent people from copying the drawing but it does not prevent them from making a similar or even identical drawing so long as the drawing is not copied. Two paintings or photos of the same scene taken at about the same time from the same angle would probably be very similar but neither would be a copy of the other. The registration of a design, however, would entitle the registered proprietor to prevent anyone using a similar design even if the similarity is entirely coincidental. It is usually much easier to prove similarity than copying.

Rights that can be registered and those that arise spontaneously

Monopolies require registration with a patent office such as the UK Intellectual Property Office, the United States Patent and Trademarks Office, the Office for Harmonization in the Internal Market or otherwise. Registration may involve extensive searches and examinations to make sure that the rights sought satisfy the legal requirements for registration. That is the case with patents and to a lesser extent trade marks. Rights-to-prevent-other-people-from-doing-something-without-permission, by contrast, tend to come into being spontaneously whenever certain specified conditions apply. Thus, a copyright comes into being in the UK whenever a citizen or resident of the UK makes an artistic, dramatic, literary or musical work without

---

1   See http://oami.europa.eu/CTMOnline/RequestManager/en_DetailCTM_NoReg.

copying or otherwise referring to an antecedent work[2] and an obligation of confidence arises whenever a confider discloses secret information to a confidante in confidence.[3]

Summary of Intellectual Asset Protection in the UK

The following table summarizes the available legal protection for intellectual assets in the United Kingdom:

Intellectual Asset	Type of Protection	Description
Brands	Registered Trade Mark	Renewable exclusive right to supply goods or services in the UK under a sign that is registered with the Trade Marks Registry of the UK Intellectual Property Office (UK-IPO).
	Community Trade Mark	Renewable exclusive right to supply goods or services in the EU under a sign that is registered with the Office for Harmonization in the Internal Market (OHIM).
	Passing-off	Right to prevent others from supplying goods or services in such a way as consumers are likely to believe that they were supplied by or are connected with the complainant.
	Geographical Indication	EU wide assurance that produce comes from, or has been processed in a particular region renowned for the quality of such goods.
	Domain Name	Mnemonic for the digital address of a computer on the internet.
Design	Registered Design	Exclusive right to use a design that has been registered with the Designs Registry of the UK-IPO for up to 25 years in the UK.
	Registered Community Design	Exclusive right to use a design that has been registered with OHIM for up to 25 years throughout the EU.
	Unregistered Community Design	EU-wide right to prevent others from copying design that could have been registered as a registered Community design for up to 3 years from the date the design is first made available to the public.
	Unregistered Design Right	Exclusive right to make articles in the UK to an original design for up to 10 years subject to a licence of right in the last 5 years.
Technology	Patent	Monopoly for up to 20 years of the manufacture, distribution and use of an inventive and useful new product or of the use of a new process including a monopoly of the distribution and use of products made by such process.
	Semiconductor Chip Topography	Modified 25 year unregistered design right in respect of the design of semiconductor chips.
	Confidentiality	Right of confider to prevent unauthorized use or disclosure of secret technical information acquired in confidence.
	Software copyright	Exclusive right to load, run and copy computer programs for the life of the author plus 70 years.

---

2   S.1 (1) and (3) of the Copyright Designs and Patents Act 1988.
3   Jane Lambert, 'Confidential Information', IPIT Update (http://www.ipit-update.com/conf.htm).

Works of Art and Literature	Copyright	Exclusive right to copy, publish, rent, lend, perform, communicate or adapt an original artistic, dramatic, literary or musical work, broadcast, film or sound recording or published edition of a published work.
	Publication Right	Exclusive right to copy, publish, rent, lend, perform, communicate or adapt the first publication of a previously unpublished work in which copyright has expired.
	Rights in Performances	Exclusive right of actor, dancer, musician, singer or other performer or their broadcaster, film or recording studio to authorize broadcasting, filming or taping of a live performance.

Broadly similar protection is available in most other advanced countries of the world although there are some variations from country to country. For instance, the UK is virtually unique in protecting the functional as well as outward appearance aspects of a product by a spontaneously arising design right. On the other hand, many countries protect such aspects by a type of simplified patent known in most counties as a 'utility model'. You should also note that the list is by no means comprehensive. I have left out a number of important rights from the list such as 'moral rights', 'database rights' and 'plant breeders' rights, some of which I will mention later.

The unspoken bargains

I said above that governments protect intellectual assets in order to encourage investment in branding, design, technology and culture. Essentially they bargain with entrepreneurs, innovators and other enterprising and creative people. In exchange for dedicating the fruits of their labour, ingenuity or creativity to the public, they are allowed to entrench the market advantage that their work confers on them over competitors. This is best illustrated by the bargain that the state makes with inventors. Here is a summary of those terms:

'If you can persuade us that you have invented a new, inventive and useful product or process that does not fall within a number of exceptions, if you teach everyone in the industry how to make or use it, and then pay us a lot of money we shall register a specification of your invention at our intellectual property office. Registration will give you the monopoly of that product or process in our territory known as a "patent" and so long as you keep paying us a lot of money periodically, you can enjoy that monopoly for a up to 20 years. We can't promise that you will make any money from your invention. That's up to you and your customers. If they like it they will buy it and if they don't they won't. However, if the public do buy your product or products made from your process, you have the right to prevent others from making, importing, supplying or using your invention during the term. That should be more than enough time for you to recoup your costs and make a tidy sum on the side if your invention is any good. If anyone tries to make, import, sell or use your invention during that time, you have the right to ask our courts for "injunctions" or orders to stop them, order them to pay "damages" to compensate for any loss or damage that you may suffer or both. Of course, you must have a good case and be prepared to pay your costs of going to court and maybe the other side's if you lose. It will not be a crime to infringe your patent, so you won't be able to complain to the police as you can if someone steals your watch or handbag. You must remember that while your patent is in force there will be restrictions on what you can do with it. You may not, for instance, threaten to sue

shopkeepers just because they stock a product that you think may infringe unless it turns out that it does in fact infringe. After your term is up, anyone in the world can make the product or use the process in this country. Oh, and if at any time we find that we should not have granted a patent in the first place (which we may well do when you try to enforce it in infringement proceedings) we can take away your monopoly just like that. If we do that, you won't be able to rely on any trade secret or other legal protection because the whole point of this bargain from our perspective is that you dedicate your invention to us. If we do take away your monopoly, all your efforts and investment will have come to nought, but, hey, that's life. These are our terms, mate. Take them or leave them.'

The bargain that the European Union and its member states make with product designers is similar. Designers are granted a monopoly of the appearance of a product so long as that appearance is new, has individual character and is registered with the national intellectual property office of a member state or with OHIM,[4] the EC trade marks and designs registry in Alicante. 'Appearance' for this purpose means the lines, contours, colours, shape, texture and materials of a product or its ornamentation. It does not include the workings of a product though they can often be protected by other rights. 'Individual character' means not reminiscent of an earlier design. The monopoly lasts initially for 5 years but may be registered up to 5 times giving protection for up to 25 years. Unlike patents there is no examination of registered design applications. However, as with patents, the validity of the registration can be challenged at any time. There are some fees to pay but nowhere near those needed to apply for and renew a patent. Proprietors of design registrations have to go to court to enforce their rights.

As for brands, those who supply or intend to supply goods or services under a name, logo or other sign that can and does distinguish their goods from everyone else's can then register the sign with OHIM or a national intellectual property office as a trade mark. There are restrictions on what can be registered. Signs incorporating national emblems or that are judged to be obscene, for example, are excepted matter. Registration gives you the exclusive right to supply specified goods or services under that sign. Unlike patents and registered designs, trade mark infringement can be a serious criminal offence in some circumstances. However, it is still necessary to go to the civil courts for an injunction or damages with all that entails. Fees are also payable for trade marks though, again, not on the same scale as for patents. Registration lasts initially for 10 years and can be renewed indefinitely. Trade marks can be declared invalid if, for instance, the courts or intellectual property office finds that the mark should never have been registered and a registered trade mark can also be revoked on a number of grounds such as non-use.

A somewhat different deal is struck with those who create original artistic, dramatic, literary or musical works, broadcasts, films, sound recordings or published editions. There are no fees and no registration. All that is required is that the work meets a geographical qualification test and results from independent skill and labour. Except for broadcasts, a work qualifies for protection if it is created by a citizen or resident of the UK or some other country that protects the work of British citizens or if it is first published in one of those countries. If those conditions are satisfied the work can be copied, published, broadcast, performed or adapted only with the owner's consent. Most copyrights last very much longer than patents and registered designs – up to 70 years plus the life of the author in the case of an original book, drawing, play, musical score or computer program but only 25 years in the case of a published

---

4   Office for Harmonization in the Internal Market (http://oami.europa.eu).

edition. The infringement of a copyright can be a criminal offence in certain circumstances, but is it still necessary to go to court for injunctions and damages .

In the last century broadcasting, film and sound recording technology made it possible for the first time to capture, preserve and disseminate the art of actors, dancers, musicians, singers and others who perform their works either on a stage or in a studio. Broadcasts and recordings of those artists' performances on film or tape are and have been for many years protected by copyright; but not the performance itself. Since the mid 1950s states have offered performing artists the right to object to the broadcasting and recording of their performances. This is known as a 'performer's right' and there is a parallel right for a performer's film or recording studio or broadcaster to prevent illicit recording known as 'recording right'. Performers' and recording rights are called collectively 'rights in performances'. Those rights are very much like copyright and are easily confused with it since there's a lot of overlap. Like copyright there is a geographical qualification test. The right is infringed by broadcasting or recording a performance without the performer's consent. There are criminal sanctions as well as civil remedies for infringement as there are with copyright and trade marks.

There are many innovations that do not justify a 20-year monopoly either from the perspective of the public or of the person responsible for the innovation but are nevertheless worth protecting from plagiarism. Some countries provide for the registration of an innovative product as a 'utility model.' Such registration provides similar protection to a patent but for a much shorter term. In the UK many of the things that are protected elsewhere as utility models are protected from copying by an intellectual property right that is almost unique to the UK known as 'unregistered design right'. This right subsists automatically in aspects of shape or configuration of articles or parts of articles. There is no need for novelty or individual character and the right can subsist in purely functional designs as well as aesthetic ones. The design has to be original and recorded in a design document which can include a CAD file or be embodied in a prototype. Design right protection lasts for 15 years – or 10 if articles were made to the design – and anyone in the world, including an infringer, is entitled to a licence to make articles to the design as of right on terms to be decided by the Intellectual Property Office if not agreed during the last 5 years of the term. There is a geographical qualification test as for copyright and rights in performances but as there is no unregistered designs convention, only nationals or residents of EU and EFTA states and a handful of other colonies or former colonies actually meet it.

International agreements

As well as bargaining with businesses and individuals for the protection of intellectual assets, governments make agreements with each other. Since 1 January 1995, favourable access to the markets of the world's richest countries has been conditional upon providing basic legal protection for brands, designs, technology and creative works. That is because the governments of most of the world's richest countries are party to the Marrakech Agreement Establishing the World Trade Organization (the WTO agreement).[5] That agreement requires contracting states to allow the nationals of other countries that are party to the WTO agreement access to their markets on the most favourable terms. The WTO Agreement has a number of annexes, one of which is TRIPS (Trade-Related Aspects of Intellectual Property Rights).[6] That annexe

---

5   http://www.wto.org/english/docs_e/legal_e/04-wto_e.htm.
6   http://www.wto.org/english/docs_e/legal_e/27-trips_01_e.htm.

obliges WTO members to provide minimum standards of legal protection for brands, design, technology and creative works. The reason for that requirement is that disparity in legal protection could distort markets of goods, services and capital. This international obligation will be discussed in more detail in the next chapter.

Enforcement

Except for bootlegging,[7] counterfeiting[8] and piracy,[9] intellectual property infringement is not regarded everywhere as a crime. Enforcing intellectual property rights is primarily the responsibility of owners. Except where parties agree to resolve their dispute in some other way, IPR are enforced through proceedings in the civil courts. Civil litigation is expensive everywhere, but it is particularly so in countries such as the UK and the USA where the parties rather than the court determine the issues to be tried and the evidence to be considered. Copyright owners and performers are often assisted in enforcing their rights by collecting societies (that is to say, associations of authors, composers, musicians to enforce the copyright or other IPR of their members). There are also professional and trade associations such as ACID (Anti Copying in Design)[10] for designers and FAST (The Federation against Software Theft)[11] for software.

Competition Law

Because intellectual property laws create monopolies and other restrictions on competition and customer choice, there have to be limits to the exercise of intellectual property rights. The Treaty of Rome that establishes the European Community prohibits agreements and other arrangements between businesses which restrict competition[12] and the abuse of market dominance[13] in so far as they affect trade between member states. Similar provisions have been introduced into the laws of several member states including the UK.[14] Exercising intellectual property rights does not usually infringe these laws so as to amount to an abuse but there are circumstances when it might. The prohibitions of anti-competitive transactions in European and national law, for instance, can affect licences, assignments and other agreements relating to intellectual property in that they strike down potentially unfair, unreasonable or discriminatory terms in such agreements. For example, when a national broadcasting authority sought to use its copyrights in radio and television listings to restrict competition from other publishers, the European Competition intervened to prevent it from doing so.[15]

---

7   Wilful Infringement of rights in performances on a commercial scale.
8   Wilful infringement of trade marks on a commercial scale.
9   Wilful copyright infringement on a commercial scale.
10   http://www.acid.uk.com.
11   http://www.fast.org.uk.
12   Art 81 Treaty of Rome (http://eur-lex.europa.eu/LexUriServ/LexUriServ.do?uri=CELEX:12002E081:EN:NOT).
13   Art 82 Ibid. (http://eur-lex.europa.eu/LexUriServ/LexUriServ.do?uri=CELEX:12002E082:EN:NOT.)
14   For instance, S.2 and S.18 of the Competition Act 1998.
15   Joined Cases C-241/91 P and C-242/91 P *Radio Telefis Eireann (RTE) and Independent Television Publications Ltd (ITP) v Commission of the European Communities* [1995] ECR-00743 (http://eur-lex.europa.eu/smartapi/cgi/sga_ doc?smartapi!celexplus! prod!CELEXnumdoc&numdoc=61991J0241&lg=en).

Remember

The tension between IPR and competition law is helpful for understanding how intellectual property is supposed to work. By conferring monopolies and other exclusive rights which give one supplier a competitive advantage over another, states try to provide incentives for the development of new and better products and services through competition. Unless they are regulated, however, those same rights that provide incentives can prevent or diminish competition. Intellectual property laws in conjunction with competition laws therefore strike a balance between the competing public interests of encouraging creativity and innovation and ensuring competition and consumer choice through freedom to trade.

3 *How the Law Protects Different Intellectual Assets*

The last chapter introduced the legal protection that is available for brands, design, technology and creative works. This chapter will explore the sources of that law. It will discuss the international agreements upon which nearly all industrial countries base their intellectual property law as well as European Union and national legislation that implements these agreements.

Importance of international agreements

For many situations such as buying a house, paying taxes or just driving along the highway it is enough to know the local conveyancing, revenue or motoring law. Because of the ubiquity of the internet and the reality that few national markets are large enough to generate an adequate return on the investment required to develop and market a new product, businesses have to concern themselves not just with their own national or local intellectual property laws but also those of the country in which their goods are to be made and of the countries in which they are to be sold.

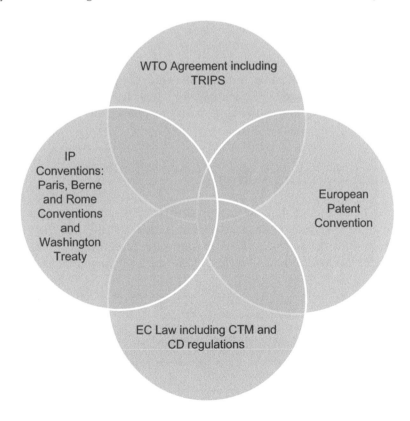

Mr. Aardvark's distelfinks are a case in point. The idea was American. They are a traditional decoration of the Pennsylvania Dutch. But the product was developed and first marketed in Britain. The distelfinks were made in China. The success of the product in the UK and of the lookalikes in China suggests worldwide demand. Governments have recognized that reality ever since the 19th century and have constructed a number of multilateral agreements that are sometimes called 'conventions' or 'treaties' that establish yardsticks for national law. Until 1994 accession to those conventions and treaties was voluntary and the incentive to enter these agreements was essentially the promise of reciprocal protection for their citizens' intellectual assets. As I explained in the previous chapter, favourable access to the markets of the most advanced trading nations is now conditional upon implementing TRIPS[1] which obliges WTO member states to provide at least some legal protection for intellectual assets within their borders.

The cornerstone conventions

TRIPS reinforces the provisions of the following cornerstone conventions:

- **Paris** The *Paris Convention for the Protection of Industrial Property*[2] established a union of countries known as the 'Paris Union' which agree to protect on a reciprocal basis the brands, designs and technology of each other's nationals and residents in their territories through patent, design, trade mark and other intellectual property rights.
- **Berne** The *Berne Convention for the Protection of Literary and Artistic Works*[3] established another Union known as the Berne Union whose members agree to protect works of art and literature of each other's members and nationals through copyright and related rights.
- **Rome** The *Rome Convention for the Protection of Performers, Producers of Phonograms and Broadcasting Organizations*[4] requires contracting countries to protect actors, dancers, musicians, singers and other performing artistes, their broadcasters and recording studios from unauthorized broadcasting, filming and taping of their performances.
- **The Washington Treaty** The *Washington Treaty on Intellectual Property in Respect of Integrated Circuits*[5] requires contracting parties to protect the layout of semiconductor chips.

Other international agreements

There are over 24 international intellectual property treaties and conventions.[6] Most of these complement those four international agreements either globally like the PCT (*Patent Co-operation Treaty*)[7] and the *Madrid Protocol*[8] by providing machinery for processing multiple patent and trade mark applications, or regionally like the EPC (*European Patent Convention*)[9] and

1   http://www.wto.org/english/docs_e/legal_e/27-trips_01_e.htm.
2   http://www.wipo.int/treaties/en/ip/paris/trtdocs_wo020.html.
3   http://www.wipo.int/treaties/en/ip/berne/trtdocs_wo001.html.
4   http://www.wipo.int/treaties/en/ip/rome/trtdocs_wo024.html.
5   http://www.wipo.int/treaties/en/ip/washington/trtdocs_wo011.html.
6   Most of these are listed on the WIPO website at http://www.wipo.int/treaties/en.
7   http://www.wipo.int/pct/en/texts/articles/atoc.htm.
8   http://www.wipo.int/madrid/en/legal_texts/trtdocs_wo016.html.
9   http://www.european-patent-office.org/legal/epc/e/contents.html.

the *Eurasian Patent Convention*[10] which establish patent unions for Europe and the successor states to the former Soviet Union.

WIPO

The Paris[11] and Berne Conventions[12] established international bureaux or secretariats for the Paris and Berne Unions. Those secretariats merged in 1893 to form a 'United International Bureaux for the Protection of Intellectual Property.' The United International Bureau changed its name to the WIPO (World Intellectual Property Organization)[13] in 1974. The WIPO administers most of the intellectual property treaties and conventions. It has also promoted many of the recent supplemental treaties, some of which such as the *WIPO Copyright Treaty*[14] and the *WIPO Performances and Phonograms Treaty*[15] actually incorporate the Organization's name. It promotes intellectual asset protection around the world by drawing up model legislation, training patent office staff from the less developed nations and publications. The WIPO's Arbitration and Mediation Centre[16] is an important forum for the resolution of international intellectual property disputes, particularly domain names. Perhaps most importantly, the WIPO provides the machinery for processing multiple patent and trade mark applications through the PCT and Madrid Protocols.

TRIPS

TRIPS requires WTO members to comply with the substantive provisions of the Paris Convention[17] and to make laws covering:

*   copyright and related rights[18]
*   trade marks[19]
*   geographical indications[20]
*   industrial designs[21]
*   patents[22]
*   topographies of integrated circuits,[23] and
*   protection of undisclosed Information.[24]

WTO member states must also make provision for enforcing such laws including civil remedies,[25] customs controls at air and sea ports and frontiers[26] and criminal sanctions

---

10   http://www.eapo.org/eng/documents/konvenci.html.
11   Art 15 (http://www.wipo.int/treaties/en/ip/paris/trtdocs_wo020.html#P302_47515).
12   Art 24 (http://www.wipo.int/treaties/en/ip/berne/trtdocs_wo001.html#P282_50905).
13   http://www.wipo.int.
14   http://www.wipo.int/treaties/en/ip/wct/trtdocs_wo033.html.
15   http://www.wipo.int/treaties/en/ip/wppt/trtdocs_wo034.html.
16   http://www.wipo.int/amc/en.
17   Art 2 (1).
18   Arts 9–14.
19   Arts 15–21.
20   Arts 22–24.
21   Arts 25–26.
22   Arts 27–34.
23   Arts 35–38.
24   Art 39.
25   Arts 41–49.
26   Arts 51–60.

for copyright piracy and trade mark counterfeiting.[27] The most advanced countries had to implement TRIPS at once.[28] Less developed countries were allowed to phase in its provisions over a number of years.[29]

European law

Since all the countries of the European Union are also party to the WTO, the governments of the EU member states have chosen to implement some of their TRIPS obligations collectively. The instruments by which they have implemented those obligations include:

- **Directives**: instructions from the Council of Ministers (representatives of the governments of the member states) to national governments to make specified laws; and
- **Regulations**: legislation made by the Council of Ministers or its executive known as the European Commission (the Commission) that comes into being automatically in all the member states.

Thus, the Council of Ministers has adopted a number of directives requiring member states to bring their copyright, design, trade marks and even certain aspects of their patent laws into line with TRIPS. Other Council directives introduce new intellectual property rights into English law such as database, publication and artists' resale rights. The Council has also adopted regulations establishing the OHIM (Office for Harmonization in the Internal Market) which registers the '*Community trade marks*' and '*registered Community designs*' that I mentioned in the previous chapter.

Intellectual asset protection in the UK

Brands, designs, technology and creative works are protected in the UK by a mix of legislation and judge-made law. UK legislation consists of *Acts of the United Kingdom Parliament* (known as '*statutes*') and orders and regulations made by ministers or other authorities under powers granted by statute ('*secondary legislation*' or '*statutory instruments*'). Many statutes and statutory instruments are intended to give effect to Directives of the European Council or the UK's obligations under TRIPS and the other international agreements. Judge-made law (or '*common law*' as it is usually called) consists of general principles discerned from the reasoning of judges in a succession of cases.

Cornerstone statutes

The following Acts of Parliament are the cornerstones of intellectual property law in the UK:

- **Patents Act 1977**[30] which authorizes the UK-IPO (*UK Intellectual Property Office*) and the EPO to grant *patents* or *European patents (UK)* for inventions in the UK;

---

27   Art 61.
28   Art 65 (1).
29   Arts 65 (2), (3) and (4) and 66.
30   http://www.ipo.gov.uk/patentsact1977.pdf.

- **Registered Designs Act 1949**[31] which provides for the registration of new designs with the Designs Registry of the UK-IPO as *'registered designs'*;
- **Trade Marks Act 1994**[32] which provides for the registration of signs that distinguish one supplier's goods or services from those of all others with the Trade Marks Registry of the UK-IPO as *'registered trade marks'*;
- **Copyright, Designs and Patents Act 1988**[33] (often abbreviated to 'the CDPA') which confers copyrights, rights in performances and unregistered design rights.

All of those Acts have been amended many times to bring them into line with EU directives, treaties, conventions and other international agreements. The Registered Designs Act 1949, in particular, has been transformed almost out of recognition first by the Copyright Designs and Patents Act 1988 and more recently by The Registered Designs Regulations 2001 in order to implement the European designs directive.

New Intellectual Property rights

There are also rights that are created entirely by secondary legislation such as database right which protects investment in obtaining, verifying or presenting the contents from unauthorized extraction and re-utilization, and publication right which protects publication of previously unpublished material that is no longer protected by copyright.

Common law rights

Over many years, judges of the courts of England and Wales, Scotland and Ireland have developed rules through a series of cases that prevent:

- one supplier from misrepresenting his or her goods, services or business as those of another supplier by using through the same or similar trade name, trade mark, packaging of his or her products or presentation of services known as *'the action for passing off'*; and
- those who have received secret technical or commercial information in confidence from using or disclosing such information known as *'the obligation of confidence'*.

The action for passing off and the obligation of confidence are sometimes referred to as 'common law rights' to distinguish them from the rights created by legislation.

Where to find the law on the internet

TRIPS and the other annexes to the WTO Agreement are to be found at the WTO website at www.wto.org. You will also find plenty of news, commentary and discussion on intellectual property as it affects international trade on that site. Most of the global intellectual property treaties and conventions are found on the WIPO site at www.wipo.int. You will also find a wealth of other useful materials including a comprehensive collection of national intellectual property laws in English and several other languages, presentations, leaflets, newsletters and

---

31   http://www.ipo.gov.uk/regdesignactchanges.pdf.
32   http://www.ipo.gov.uk/tmact94.pdf.
33   http://www.ipo.gov.uk/cdpact1988.pdf.

much, much more. The EPC, the regulations and protocols that implement the Convention, the cases that interpret it and all sorts of other information on patents in general and European patents in particular are to be found on the European Patent Office at www.epo.org. Similar information on Community trade marks and designs is to be found on OHIM's website at oami. europa.eu. Consolidated versions of the cornerstone statutes plus the Rules that implement those statutes, and other important statutory instruments, relevant case law, manuals, practice notes and guides to UK intellectual property law are available on the UK-IPO website at www. ipo.gov.uk. Probably the best source of legislation and case law for the UK and Irish Republic is the *British and Irish Legal Information Institute* (BAILII) at www.bailii.org. BAILII links to the websites of similar legal institutes containing collections of laws from Australia, Canada, Hong Kong, South Africa, USA and most of the rest of the world.

How the law protects brands

WHAT IS A BRAND?

In the absence of a generally accepted definition, it may be helpful to think of a brand as the consumers' impression of a supplier. Trade marks are very important to that image but so too are other things such as the appearance of the supplier's products and their packaging, its presence on the worldwide web, customer connections and so on. Different intellectual property rights therefore protect different aspects of branding. Trade mark and the law of passing off protect the trade mark and other signs by which a trader's goods are identified in the market and that protection is complemented in certain respects by registered design protection. Art work and copywriting for advertising are protected by copyright. Trade connections and customer information are protected by the law of confidence and database right. Web presence is protected by domain name registration as well as by trade mark registration and the law of passing off.

TRADE MARKS

A trade mark is a sign that distinguishes one supplier's goods or services from those of others. Trade marks can consist of words, names, designs, letters, numerals or the shape of goods and their packaging so long as they can be represented in writing or diagrams. They serve two important purposes. First, they provide reference points for marketing and distribution. Secondly, they offer an assurance of origin and quality to consumers. Preventing unauthorized use of a trade mark is therefore important to consumers and suppliers alike. Unauthorized use is prevented by the action for passing off or equivalent rights of action and by the registration of trade marks.

PASSING OFF

A claim for passing off has 3 elements that are sometimes referred to as 'the holy trinity' namely:

1. The complainant must have goodwill or a reputation in the market for the supply of the relevant goods or services by reference to a trade mark or other indicator;

2. The alleged wrongdoer must have misrepresented intentionally or otherwise by adopting the same or similar indicator that his or her goods, services or business are the same as or somehow connected with the complainant's; and

3. As a result of such misrepresentation the complainant has lost sales, suffered damage to his or her reputation or goodwill or suffered some other damage.

I shall discuss each of these elements in turn.

REPUTATION AND GOODWILL

The first of those elements is that the complainant's business, goods or services are recognized in the market by reference to a trade mark or other indicator. Such market recognition is usually referred to as reputation and the *reputation* of a business, product or service is the focus of customer loyalty known as *goodwill*. That is important because goodwill is the interest that the action for passing-off protects. Where a business has a substantial local following, opening a similar business in the same town under a similar name is likely to be actionable. On the other hand, opening a similar business in the same or similar name but in another town where the complainant has no reputation is not actionable. The existence of goodwill or reputation is usually proved by sales and marketing figures supported by samples of the claimant's advertising and promotional literature.

MISREPRESENTATION

The second element of an action for passing off is that the complainant's customers are led to believe that a competitor's goods, services or business are those of, or in some way connected to, the complainant. Such inducement is called misrepresentation and there are many examples. The competitor can trade under the same or similar name as the complainant. He or she may use a similar logo. A shop can be decorated in similar colours. The effect of the misrepresentation must be the deception or confusion of at least one purchaser. The misrepresentation need not be intentional though confusion or deception will be inferred where an intention to mislead can be proved. Among the first signs of confusion are enquiries or complaints in respect of competing goods or services. Confusion or deception is usually proved by the testimony of purchasers who were induced by the misrepresentation to procure the competing goods or services though, increasingly, market research evidence is used by both sides to show the impact of the alleged misrepresentation on the market.

DAMAGE

The third element is that the complainant should have suffered some kind of loss or damage by reason of the misrepresentation. This may take the form of lost sales or erosion of the complaint's goodwill. This third element will be presumed so long as reputation or goodwill and misrepresentation can be established. There are several variants to the action for passing off but this is the classic form of it.

Trade mark registration and passing off compared

The advantage of the action for passing off is that it does not require a trade mark to be registered. Indeed, the remedy often protects signs and other indicators that could never be registered as trade marks. The remedy is therefore useful for established businesses. However, passing off is much less useful for entrants to a market, particularly SME (*small and medium enterprises*). Trade mark registration assists SME businesses because protection may begin long before the mark is used. To understand how such protection works, it is necessary always to remember that trade marks are registered for specified goods.

Trade mark infringement

In the UK and other countries of the EU, there are three ways in which a registered trade mark may be infringed.

USING AN IDENTICAL SIGN IN RESPECT OF IDENTICAL GOODS OR SERVICES

One way is by using a sign that is identical to the registered trade mark in respect of identical goods.[34] 'Use' in this context includes attaching a sign to goods or their packaging, marketing goods or services by reference to the sign or using it on business stationery or in advertising.[35] The question whether an identical sign has been used in respect of identical goods or services is usually determined by comparing the sign complained of with the registered mark as it appears in the complainant's certificate of registration and the goods or services complained of with those in the complainant's specification. There is no need to consider whether there is a likelihood of confusion, whether unfair advantage has been taken of the registered mark or anything else.

USING AN IDENTICAL OR SIMILAR SIGN IN RESPECT OF SIMILAR OR IDENTICAL GOODS OR SERVICES

Secondly, a registered trade mark may also be infringed if there is a likelihood of confusion (including the likelihood of association with the registered trade mark) through the use either of an identical sign in respect of goods or services that are similar to those for which the mark is registered, or of a similar sign in respect of goods or services that are identical or similar to those for which the mark is registered.[36] Again, a comparison is made between the sign and goods or services complained of with those in the certificate of registration. A likelihood of confusion is determined by a global appreciation of all relevant factors as perceived by the average consumer of the goods or services in question.

TAKING UNFAIR ADVANTAGE OF A SIGN HAVING A REPUTATION

Finally, where a registered trade mark has a reputation in the UK[37], yet another way to infringe it is to take unfair advantage of its reputation or damage its distinctive character or repute by using an identical or similar mark without due cause.[38]

---

34   S.10 (1) Trade Marks Act 1994.
35   S.10 (4) Ibid.
36   S.10 (2) Ibid.
37   Or, in the case of a Community trade mark 'reputation in the Community' (see Art 9 (1) (c) Community trade mark regulation).
38   S.10 (3) Ibid.

Geographical indications

A geographical indication is defined as 'a sign used on goods that have a specific geographical origin and possess qualities or a reputation that are due to that place of origin'.[39] Such signs are sometimes referred to as appellations of origin. Well known examples include the sparkling wine from the Champagne region of France known as 'Champagne', whisky from Scotland known as 'Scotch' and ham prepared in Parma known as 'Parma ham'. Such appellations are protected in the UK by the law of passing off and they may often be registered as trade marks laws. There is also specific EC legislation protecting designations of origin,[40] geographical indications[41] and traditional specialities.[42]

Use of design law in branding

Harmonization of registered design law and the adoption of the Community design regulation have extended the opportunities for brand protection in Europe since 2001. It is now possible to register as designs features that could not be registered as trade marks, such as the lines, contours, colours, ornamentation, shape, texture or materials of product and packaging. It is also possible to register as designs many signs that were already capable of registration as trade marks, such as logos and cartoon characters. Since design registration confers the exclusive right to make a product incorporating or applying the design, the practical effect of registering such a mark as a design is to extend the mark's monopoly well beyond the goods or services specified in the trade mark registration.

Use of copyright in branding

Other forms of legal protection are available for specific aspects of branding. For instance, the design of a trade mark may be the result of considerable artistic endeavour. Artwork for such signs is artistic work and as such protected by artistic copyright. The same type of copyright also protects artwork for posters, brochures and stationery. Also to be considered are literary copyright for advertising copy, musical copyright for advertising jingles, dramatic copyright for radio and television commercials and performers' rights for the performances of the actors and singers who make such commercials.

Protecting trade connections

Protecting customer records such as names and contact details, purchases, complaints, maintenance records and feedback is essential for building and maintaining goodwill. Customer lists have long been regarded as confidential information and as such protected

---

39   WIPO 'About Geographical Indications' at http://www.wipo.int/about-ip/en/about_geographical_ind.html.
40   Council Regulation (EC) No 510/2006 of 20 March 2006 on the protection of geographical indications and designations of origin for agricultural products and foodstuffs.
41   Commission Regulation (EC) No 1898/2006 of 14 December 2006 laying down detailed rules of implementation of Council Regulation (EC) No 510/2006 on the protection of geographical indications and designations of origin for agricultural products and foodstuffs.
42   Council Regulation (EC) No 509/2006 of 20 March 2006 on agricultural products and foodstuffs as traditional specialities guaranteed.

by the law of confidence. The protection afforded by the law of confidence has recently been supplemented by database right. Database right protects investment in obtaining, verifying or presenting the contents of a database.[43] Extraction and reutilization of customer records to create a competing customer database would infringe such database right.[44]

Domain names

Since the middle of the 1990s the domain name in the address of a website has been important for branding. The home page of a typical website has at least three components:

1. the server identifier which is usually 'www' for 'worldwide web';
2. the domain name which is usually a trade name or trade mark of the business such as 'WTO', 'WIPO' or 'IPO' for the World Trade Organization, World Intellectual Property Organization and the UK Intellectual Property Office; and
3. a suffix which identifies the nature of the site such as '.com' or '.net' for a company or network or the national or territorial registry such as '.uk' for the UK, '.eu' for the European Union, '.fr' for France, '.de' for Germany, '.cn' for China, '.jp' for Japan and '.sl' for Sierra Leone.

Domain names without a national identifier are known as gTLD (*generic top level domain names*) and those with such an identifier ccTLD (*country code top level domains*).

Generic TLDs are registered by registries accredited by a California company called ICANN (*Internet Corporation for Assigned Names and Numbers*).[45] One of the conditions for accreditation is that the registrar requires every applicant for registration of a gTLD to agree to refer any complaint by a trade mark owner to expert determination before a panellist in accordance with the UDRP (*Uniform Domain-Name Dispute-Resolution Policy*).[46] The panellist is selected from lists maintained by ICANN approved dispute resolution service providers, one of which is the WIPO Arbitration and Mediation Centre.[47] In return for a flat fee of around US$1,500 per domain name, the service provider arranges for the panellist to consider written evidence submitted by the parties, and to deliver his or her decision within a few days.

ICANN also accredits national and regional registries for the country code domains. The registry for the .uk domain (*Nominet UK*) operates a similar dispute resolution scheme known as the DRS (*Dispute Resolution Service*).[48] So too does *EURid* (the '.eu' registry) in conjunction with the Czech Arbitration Court.

While expert determination disposes of almost all domain name disputes it does not displace the jurisdiction of the courts. Indeed, submission to the jurisdiction of a national court is a condition for submitting a dispute for resolution under the UDRP.

---

43   Reg 13 (1) Copyright and Rights in Databases Regulations 1997 (SI 1997/3032) (see http://www.ipo.gov.uk/cdpact1988.pdf).
44   Reg 16 (1) Ibid.
45   http://www.icann.org.
46   http://www.icann.org/dndr/udrp/policy.htm.
47   http://www.wipo.int/amc/en/domains.
48   http://www.nominet.org.uk/disputes/drs.

Further information on the internet

For some good general information on brands and the theory of branding a sound place to start is the website of the British Brands Group at www.britishbrandsgroup.org.uk. Because the BBG is a ginger group campaigning for changes in the law and better enforcement of the existing laws for the benefit of its members, the materials on that site tend to be polemical but they show why branding is important. The Chartered Institute of Marketing has also published an excellent series of downloadable articles on branding written by some leading experts on the topic on its 'Knowledge Hub' at www.cim.co.uk. These cover such topics as defining brands, types of brands, how brands work and brand strategy. Good, basic information on trade mark registration as well as an extensive database of trade mark applications and registrations is found on the 'Trade Marks' page of the UK-IPO website at www.ipo.gov.uk. Similar information on Community trade marks is available on the OHIM website at oami.europa.eu. The WIPO website at www.wipo.int has a good introduction to designations of origin and a wealth of materials on domain names. More information on domain names is to be found on the ICANN and Nominet sites at www.icann.org and www.nominet.org.uk respectively.

How the law protects designs

FUNCTIONAL AND AESTHETIC DESIGNS

In everyday language, *design* may refer to functionality or appearance. A well-designed engine is usually taken to mean an engine that is engineered to maximize fuel efficiency or performance. Designer jeans or a handbag is understood to be an item of clothing or a fashion accessory that is styled to please the eye. There is of course overlap. The aerodynamic shape of a sports car or aircraft may be aesthetically pleasing as well as functionally efficient.

DESIGN PROTECTION REGIMES

In the UK, the law protects both aspects of design. Unregistered design right protects the functionality of a product – that is to say, aspects of shape or configuration of an article or part of an article – for up to 10 years. Design registration under the Registered Designs Act 1949 and Community design registration protect the appearance of a product for up to five renewable periods of 5 years. Just as there is overlap between aesthetics and functionality in everyday experience, so there is in the law. Unregistered design right can be used to protect ornamental as well as functional features of an article while a car body that is new and has individual character may also be functionally efficient. The interface between design registration and branding has already been mentioned. There is also a similar interface between design and technology in that unregistered design right can be used to protect mechanical arrangements or electrical circuitry. In that context, it is important to note that unregistered design right[49] implements the UK government's obligation under the Washington Treaty[50] to protect the topography or layout of semiconductor chips.

---

49   The Design Right (Semiconductor Topographies) Regulations 1989, SI 1989 No. 1100 (http://www.opsi.gov.uk/si/si1989/Uksi_19891100_en_1.htm).
50   Treaty on Intellectual Property in Respect of Integrated Circuits (http://www.wipo.int/treaties/en/ip/washington/trtdocs_wo011.html).

COPYRIGHT IN PROTECTING DESIGNS

For many years the UK and other Commonwealth, common law countries protected both aesthetic and functional designs indirectly by copyright. Every design drawing no matter how simple or pedestrian[51] was treated as an original artistic work in which copyright subsisted automatically for the life of the draughtsman plus 50 years. Copying a substantial part of an article made from such a design drawing infringed that copyright. The remedies for copyright infringement were draconian. Not only could the infringer be injuncted and made to pay damages for infringement of the copyright (including, sometimes, additional damages where the justice of the case so required) but he or she had to pay damages for conversion of every infringing copy deemed to belong to the copyright owner. The protection afforded by copyright for an everyday object like a teapot could be far more valuable than the 20 year monopoly afforded by a patent for an invention that might have cost millions to develop. There were, however, plenty of anomalies in the law. Designers who made their designs directly from a prototype rather than a drawing enjoyed no protection unless their prototype was a sculpture or work of artistic craftsmanship.[52] Some designs, such as electrical circuitry, could not be protected because copyright in a 2-dimensional drawing could only be infringed by making a 3-dimensional object if it was clear to a person not an expert in relation to objects of that description that the object was a reproduction of the drawing.[53] Copyright could not be relied upon to prevent the repair of a product.[54]

Concern over such anomalies and the effect of such protection on the UK, since few other industrial countries protected designs in this way, led to a review of design law which led ultimately to the Copyright Designs and Patents Act 1988. The Act created a new intellectual property right known as unregistered design right and excluded industrial designs from copyright protection. Although these provisions have been in force for nearly 20 years it has taken surprisingly long for them to register with the general public. The public and, as the dialogue with Mr. Pepys illustrates, many of their professional advisors, still appear to believe that designs are protected by copyright. It is not clear why that should be. Perhaps it is because design right has many of the characteristics of copyright in that it arises automatically and is infringed by copying. Maybe it is because copyright still protects surface decoration. Whatever the reason, it is still necessary to correct the misapprehension.

UNREGISTERED DESIGN RIGHT

Design right is defined as a property right that subsists in accordance with Part III of the Copyright Designs and Patents Act 1988 in original designs.[55] 'Design' is defined as design of any aspect of the shape or configuration (whether internal or external) of the whole or part of an article.[56] This covers most things including the design of components but surface decoration is specifically excluded.[57] Thus, the shape of a garment and the configuration of its pockets, buttons and so on may be protected by unregistered design right but the pattern of the fabric from which the garment is made would not. Thus, in the case study at the beginning of this book, the shape of Mr. Aardvark's distelfinks was protected by unregistered design right but the image of the finches by artistic copyright.

---

51   *British Northrop Ltd. v Texteam Blackburn Ltd.* [1974] RPC 1.
52   See *Merlet v Mothercare Ltd.* [1986] FSR 115.
53   S.9 (8) Copyright Act 1956.
54   See *British Leyland Motor Corpo. v Armstrong Patents Ltd.* [1986] AC 577.
55   S.213 (1) CDPA.
56   S.213 (2) CDPA.
57   S.213 (3)(c) CDPA.

Unregistered design right comes into being when a number of conditions are met. One of those conditions is *originality*.[58] The design must be *original* in the sense that it is not copied wholly from an earlier design; [59] but there is an additional requirement that the design should not be commonplace in the design field in question at the time of its creation. [60] Another condition is that the design must be recorded in a drawing, computer assisted design file or other document or, alternatively, it must be embodied in a prototype.[61] Yet another condition is that the design must be created by or for someone in the EC or some other country that affords reciprocal protection to UK designs, or articles made to the design should be first marketed in one of those countries.[62] Except for semiconductor topography designs where the qualification requirements are relaxed, this last requirement excludes from design right protection many designs from such important industrial countries as the USA, Japan, China, India, Russia and South Korea. [63]

Design right confers no monopoly in a design. The right is infringed by making articles to the design,[64] that is to say *copying* the design so as to produce articles exactly or substantially to the design.[65] Absent copying, making articles that are similar or even identical to the design is not enough. Such similarity must result from copying. However, similarity is often an indication of copying. It is usually proved by showing objective similarity between the original design and the alleged copy and an opportunity for the alleged copyist to make a copy. If those facts can be established, copying will be presumed unless the similarity can be explained otherwise. Design right subsists for 15 years or 10 from the end of the calendar year in which articles made to the design are first put on the market if they were made available for sale or hire in the first 4 years of that term.[66] In the last 5 years of the term, anyone in the world, including an infringer, can apply for a licence to do anything that would otherwise infringe the design right as of right.[67]

DESIGN REGISTRATION

In contrast to unregistered design right, design registration protects surface decoration as well as the design of 3 dimensional products. '*Design*' for the purpose of design registration is defined as 'the appearance of the whole or a part of a product resulting from the features of, in particular, the lines, contours, colours, shape, texture or materials of the product or its ornamentation.'[68] Any industrial or handicraft item may be a *product* except a computer program. Specifically included in the definition of '*product*' are packaging, get-up, graphic symbols, typographic typefaces and parts of other products[69] so long as they remain visible during normal use.[70] Thus, registered designs can protect not just the shape and configuration of a garment, but also the colours, print and texture of its material. In that respect, the scope

---

58   S.213 (1) CDPA.
59   *Farmer Build Ltd v Carier Bulk Materials Handling Ltd and Others* [1998] EWCA Civ 1899 (3 Dec 1998) (www.bailii. org/ew/cases/EWCA/Civ/1998/1899.html).
60   S.213 (4) CDPA.
61   S.213 (6) CDPA.
62   S.213 (5) CDPA.
63   See *Mackie Designs Inc v. Behringer Specialised Studio Equipment (UK) Ltd, Ulrich Bernhard Behringer & Behringer Spezielle Studiotechnik GmbH* [1999] EWHC Ch 252 (22nd Feb 1999) (http://www.bailii.org/ew/cases/EWHC/Ch/1999/252. html).
64   S.226 (1) CDPA.
65   S.226 (2) CDPA.
66   S.216 CDPA.
67   S.237 (1) CDPA.
68   S.1 (2) Registered Designs Act 1949 (http://www.ipo.gov.uk/regdesignactchanges.pdf.
69   S.1 (3) Ibid.
70   S.1B (8) (a) Ibid.

of registered design protection is wider than unregistered design right but it is narrower in that it protects only components that are visible during normal use.

Another important difference is that design registration confers a monopoly. A registered proprietor enjoys the exclusive right to make, market, import, export or stock a product that incorporates or applies the registered design.[71] The right is infringed by making, marketing , trading or stocking a product that incorporates or applies the registered design or a design that is so similar to the registered design that it does not produce a different overall impression upon an informed user.[72] There is no need for a proprietor to prove copying. An action will lie even if the products complained of were designed independently, and in ignorance, of the registered design.

This monopoly is, of course, contingent on registration of the design with the Designs Registry of the UK Intellectual Property Office or OHIM. The conditions for registration of a design are *novelty* and *individual character*.[73] A design is new if no identical design (or no design whose features differ only in immaterial details) was previously available to the public.[74] A design has individual character if the overall impression it produces on the informed user differs from the overall impression produced on such a user by any design which was previously available.[75] Having said that, it is significantly cheaper to apply to register a design than it is to apply to register a trade mark and considerably less expensive than an application for a patent. Unlike patent and trade mark applications, registered design applications are not published before grant and again unlike trade marks there is no procedure for opposing design applications. Examination is limited to making sure that the application form has been completed correctly and that the correct fee has been paid. In the case study, the absence of an examination procedure enabled Elsie to register her distelfink even though Mr. Aardvark's were already on the market. Disputes over the validity of a registration arise in invalidity applications to the Designs Registry of the UK IP Office or in counterclaims for invalidity in infringement proceedings. The message to design owners is to register first and ask questions later.

UNREGISTERED COMMUNITY DESIGN AND COPYRIGHT

There are two other rights that have to be mentioned in any discussion of design protection in the UK. The first is automatic European Community wide protection from copying of designs that could have been registered as registered designs under the Registered Designs Act 1949 or as Community designs known as *unregistered Community design right*. This right arises under the Community design regulation and lasts up to 3 years from the date the design was first made available to the public.[76] Unregistered Community design protection is intended to protect designs that have a very short shelf life such as children's toys and games and fashion accessories.[77] The other right that should be mentioned is artistic copyright. Fabric, wall and floor covering and other decorative designs continue to be protected indirectly by copyright so long as the design is first recorded in a drawing or other artistic work. Copyright protection subsists for much longer than design right and there is no provision for licences of right after 5 years.

---

71   S.7 (1) and (2) Ibid.
72   S.7 (1) and S.7A (1) Ibid.
73   S.1B (1) Ibid.
74   S.1B (2) Ibid.
75   S.1B (3) Ibid.
76   Art 11 (1) of the Community design directive.
77   Paragraph (25) of the recitals.

DESIGN PROTECTION OUTSIDE EUROPE

Although there is an obligation under TRIPS to protect new or original, independently created industrial designs, there is very little consistency as to how that obligation is discharged, particularly outside the EU. Some countries, such as Japan,[78] Australia[79] and Canada,[80] provide for design registration. There is an international agreement to facilitate the registration of industrial designs[81] to which the European Union has acceded although Belize, Botswana, Namibia and Singapore are the only English speaking countries that are party to it as at the time of writing. On the other hand, it is possible to obtain a *'design patent'* for a 'new, original and ornamental design for an article of manufacture' in the USA.[82] Such a patent is treated for most purposes as though it were a patent for an invention, but the term is very much shorter.[83] Also, as applications for design patents are examined in much the same way as applications for patents for inventions, the cost of obtaining such a patent is much more than the cost of registering a design. There are now very few countries that provide unregistered design protection for functional designs. Where such protection exists at all, it is generally through registration as a utility model or a local equivalent.

FURTHER INFORMATION ON THE INTERNET

For general information on design, one of the best places to start is probably the Design Council website at www.design-council.org.uk. The Design Council covers not only aesthetic and functional designs but also matters that are not generally associated with design such as services. It is alarming that there is very little direct legal protection for some of those designs. For the law on registered designs and unregistered design rights, the Designs Registry of the UK-IPO at www. ipo.gov.uk is as good as anywhere. The Community Designs page on the OHIM site at oami. europa.eu contains a great deal of material on Community design registration and unregistered Community designs. The WIPO site at www.wipo.int holds the Hague Agreement[84] and the design laws of most countries in its CLEA (Collection of Laws for Electronic Access) database.[85]

HOW THE LAW PROTECTS TECHNOLOGY

For the purpose of this chapter *'technology'* connotes the application of science and engineering to the production and distribution of goods and services. Until the development of the digital computer, technology was concerned with tangible things such as machines and substances. Increasingly it is concerned with the processing and use of information. Traditionally, new products and processes have been protected by patents and the law of confidence. Discussion of this topic is now complicated by the need for separate treatment of ICT (*information and communications technology*) because of the express exclusion from patent protection in the European Patent Convention of programs for computers and methods of doing business 'as such'. There is also the implied exclusion of such protection to a greater or lesser extent in the laws of other countries. This exclusion is perhaps symptomatic of the fact that innovation in services is not protected as well as innovation in products and processes. One of the reasons for this circumstance may

---

78   See 'Procedures for Obtaining a Design Right' on the Japan Patent Office website at http://www.jpo.go.jp/ tetuzuki_e/index.htm.

79   Designs Act 2003 (http://www.austlii.edu.au/au/legis/cth/consol_act/da200391).

80   Industrial Design Act, R.S.C. 1985, c. I-9 (http://www.canlii.org/ca/sta/i-9).

81   Hague Agreement Concerning the International Registration of Industrial Designs ('Hague Agreement') (http:// www.wipo.int/treaties/en/registration/hague).

82   35 USC 171(http://www.law.cornell.edu/uscode/html/uscode35/usc_sec_35_00000171----000-.html).

83   'Patents for designs shall be granted for the term of fourteen years from the date of grant' (35 USC 173).

84   See Footnote 27.

85   http://www.wipo.int/clea/en/index.jsp.

be that the basic concepts of modern patent law were developed in the 19th century when the economies of Western Europe and North America were based on manufacturing. That may no longer be appropriate in economies that are based increasingly on services. Returning to the protection of tangible things, patent protection is reinforced in the UK by unregistered design right. Copyright and the obligation of confidence are the main means of protecting ICT.

THE INVENTOR'S CHOICE

Except for software-related and business method inventions, an inventor has the choice of keeping his or her invention secret and relying on the law of confidence supplemented perhaps by design right, copyright and other IPR to prevent use or disclosure of the invention by employees, collaborators and other confidantes; or publishing it to the world in return for a patent. If a product cannot easily be reverse engineered and security is good, the first option is to usually preferable. There are no patent office, search or professional fees to pay and the technical advantage can be protected indefinitely. The monopolies of the manufacturers of *Chartreuse*[86] and *Coca-Cola* have been maintained for centuries in that way. The problem of relying on the law of confidence is that most products can be reverse engineered once they are put onto the market, or the technology can be acquired through parallel research. Patenting can crystallize that advantage so long as the invention is patentable and the legislative provisions are complied with.

HOW PATENTS WORK

To understand how a patent protects an invention, it is helpful to refer to a *patent specification*. Any one will do and if there is none to hand it may be worth downloading one from any of the online patent databases. A specification describes the invention, explains how to make use of it and marks out the monopoly claimed. The main parts of the document are the description and explanation (which are sometimes called the 'teaching'), and the exclusive rights that are claimed by the inventor which are set out in numbered paragraphs called '*the claims*'. The specification is drafted by the inventor or his or her patent attorney and submitted to the UK or other intellectual property office for examination. If and when the application is approved – possibly with amendments – a monopoly is granted with effect from the application for the claim. A patent is infringed if a third party does things that fall within the scope of one or more of the claims without the patentee's licence. [87] To decide whether a patent has been infringed, it is first necessary to construe or interpret the claim without referring to the alleged infringement and then consider whether the acts complained of fall within the wording of the claim. The words of the claim are given their usual meaning unless it is clear from the context that some technical or other meaning was intended for them. The claim has to be interpreted in the way that it would be understood by someone who might want to make or use the invention.

VALIDITY CAN BE REVIEWED AT ANY TIME

In many cases there is argument not only over the construction of the claim and whether the patent has been infringed but also over the patent's validity. Typically, a claim for infringement is met by a counterclaim for revocation. A reality that comes as a nasty shock to many patentees is that the grant of a patent is not a guarantee of validity. It is no more than an indication that the intellectual property office has examined the application but been unable

---

86   See http://en.wikipedia.org/wiki/Chartreuse_(liqueur).
87   See S.60 (1) Patents Act 1977 at http://www.ipo.gov.uk/patentsact1977.pdf.

to find any reason to refuse it. There will, of course, be searches and members of the public are given an opportunity to make observations on the application, but the time and resources of patent examiners are not unlimited and they rarely make enquiries that are as thorough as those made by a defendant to an infringement claim. Accordingly, patents are challenged successfully in a high percentage of infringement cases.

ICT

Although there is an obligation under Art 27 (1) of TRIPS to make patents available for inventions in all fields of technology without discrimination,[88] computer programs and methods of doing business (both of which are engines of innovation in the modern information-based economy) are specifically excluded from patent protection under both the EPC and Patents Act 1977.[89] However, this exclusion from patentability is not total since it applies only to the extent to which a patent relates to such excluded subject-matter. Ingenious drafting relying on that exception has enabled patents to be granted for at least some software-related inventions[90] in the EPO though recent decisions of the Court of Appeal have[91] greatly reduced that possibility in the UK. Yet another complicating factor in relation to hardware is that the topographies of semiconductor chips are protected primarily by regulations that extend the scope, term and qualifications for unregistered design protection to such articles.[92]

COPYRIGHT IN PROTECTING TECHNOLOGY

The primary protection for software in the UK is copyright. Copyright prohibits reproduction of any substantial part of an original work without the owner's consent. That includes not just a program's source code but also the way in which the code is arranged, screen output, manuals, preparatory materials such as specifications, flow charts and programmers' notes and anything else that is in the package. It is generally believed that software enjoys more extensive copyright protection in the UK than in the USA. If that is the case, it goes a long way towards offsetting the difficulty in patenting software related inventions in this country. UK copyright law is certainly less complicated than American. There is no requirement for registration in the UK. Accordingly, the US concepts of copyrightable and non-copyrightable matter and the ideas/expression dichotomy[93] do not apply here and there is no need for a complex 'filtration test' to separate literal (and hence protected) matter from abstract (and unprotected) matter.[94] In the UK there is a simple prohibition against *copying* and it does not matter whether the reproduction is literal or conceptual so long as it forms a *substantial part* of the original. The reproduction of matter that has been incorporated from an earlier work such

---

88   See http://www.wto.org/english/docs_e/legal_e/27-trips_04c_e.htm#5.

89   See Art 52 (2) (c) EPC at http://www.european-patent-office.org/legal/epc/e/ar52.html and S.1 (2) (c) Patents Act 1977.

90   See T208/84 VICOM OJ 1987 14.

91   See *Macrossan v Comptroller-General Of Patents, Designs And Trade Marks* 2005 [2006] EWHC 705 (Ch) (3 April 2006) [2006] EWCA Civ 1371 (27 Oct 2006) at http://www.bailii.org/ew/cases/EWCA/Civ/2006/1371.html.

92   The Design Right (Semiconductor Topographies) Regulations 1989 SI 1989 No. 1100 at http://www.opsi.gov.uk/si/si1989/Uksi_19891100_en_1.htmhttp://www.opsi.gov.uk/si/si1989/Uksi_19891100_en_1.htm.

93   However S.3 (2) of the CDPA provides that copyright does not subsist in a literary, dramatic or musical work unless and until it is recorded, in writing or otherwise (see http://www.ipo.gov.uk/cdpact1988.pdf).

94   First formulated in *Nichols v. Universal Pictures Corporation*, 45 F.2d 119 (2d Cir. 1930) and applied to software in *Computer Associates International, Inc. v. Altai, Inc.*, 982 F.2d 693 (2d Cir. 1992).

as the transcript of a trial is not substantial[95] but the plot of a play[96] and indeed the structure, sequence and organization of a software package may be.[97]

CONFIDENTIALITY

Source code and other sensitive technical information can be protected by the law of confidence. An obligation of confidence arises whenever sensitive, secret or little known information is communicated to another in confidence. The information must be such that its use or disclosure could harm the person confiding the information (*'the confider'*) or benefit the person to whom the information is confided (*'the confidante'*). It can include technical information, such as chemical formulae, recipes, production methods and source codes; or commercial information, such as budgets, customer lists and marketing plans. Information is communicated in confidence whenever the confidante expressly acknowledges the confidentiality of the information and circumstances of the disclosure in a confidentiality or non-disclosure agreement or where the circumstances are such that any fair minded person would consider the information and disclosure to be confidential. Unless the information ceases to be secret through some act or omission of the confidante, the obligation of confidence subsists only for so long as the information remains secret or not generally known. The obligation of confidence may not be relied upon to conceal wrongdoing. There are circumstances in which judges will release confidantes from a duty of confidence or even order disclosure of confidential information if they consider it to be in the public interest.

PLANT VARIETIES

Art 37 (3) (b) of TRIPS obliges WTO members to protect plant varieties such as seeds for new crops, species of vine and so forth by patents, an effective *sui generis* system or combination of the two. As agriculture is likely to be used increasingly for energy production this area of the law is likely to become increasingly important. In the UK plant varieties are protected by the Plant Varieties Act 1997[98] which establishes a Plant Variety Rights Office[99] within the Department for the Environment, Food and Rural Affairs (DEFRA)[100] to grant rights in distinct, uniform, stable and new plant varieties known as 'plant breeders' rights'.[101] As an alternative to national protection, there is a Community Plant Variety Office which provides plant variety protection throughout the EU pursuant to Council Regulation (EC) No 2100/94 of 27 July 1994

---

95   *Cantor Fitzgerald International and Another v Tradition (UK) Limited and Others* [2000] R.P.C. 95.
96   *Holland v Van Damm Productions Ltd* [1936-1945] McG CC 69.
97   See the discussion in *Navitaire Inc v easyJet Airline Co. and another* [2004] EWHC 1725 (Ch) (30 July 2004) and the cases referred to at http://www.bailii.org/ew/cases/EWHC/Ch/2004/1725.html.
98   http://www.opsi.gov.uk/ACTS/acts1997/1997066.htm.
99   S.2 (1).
100   http://www.defra.gov.uk.
101   S.6 (1) of the 1997 Act provides:
      Plant breeders' rights shall have effect to entitle the holder to prevent anyone doing any of the following acts as respects the propagating material of the protected variety without his authority, namely—
        (a) production or reproduction (multiplication),
        (b) conditioning for the purpose of propagation,
        (c) offering for sale,
        (d) selling or other marketing,
        (e) exporting,
        (f) importing,
        (g) stocking for any of the purposes mentioned in paragraphs (a) to (f) above, and
        (h) any other act prescribed for the purposes of this provision.
(http://www.opsi.gov.uk/ACTS/acts1997/ukpga_19970066_en_2#pt1-pb1-l1g2.)

on Community plant variety rights.[102] In the USA patents known as 'plant patents' are available under the federal patents act for 'distinct and new varieties of plants including cultivated spores, mutants, hybrids, and newly found seedlings.'[103] There is an International Convention for the Protection of New Varieties of Plants[104] which establishes an International Union for the Protection of New Varieties of Plants which is better known by its French initials of UPOV.

FURTHER INFORMATION

Essential reading for any inventor is Graham Barker and Peter Bissell's little book *A Better Mousetrap: The Business of Invention* which may be ordered from the authors' website at www. abettermousetrap.co.uk for a few pounds. That site also contains a good deal of other useful information for inventors. Beyond that, there is so much information on patents on the internet that it is hard to advise where to start. Probably the best resources are the WTO TRIPS Gateway and the websites of the WIPO, European Patent Office and the UK-IPO at www.wto. org, www.wipo.int, www.epo.org and www.ipo.gov.uk respectively. For plant varieties, the best sites are probably DEFRA and UPOV at www.defra.gov.uk and www.upov.int.

How the law protects creative works

OVERVIEW

The creative output of advertisers, broadcasters, composers, entertainers, film makers, musicians, publishers and web designers is protected by *copyright* and a range of intellectual property rights known as *rights related to copyright*. Those rights protect not only such industries as music, publishing and entertainment but also education, research and much of the work of central and local government.

COMMON CHARACTERISTICS

None of the rights mentioned above requires registration in the UK. All come into being automatically as soon as the conditions for subsistence are met. A condition that is common to all those rights is that the creator of the protected matter must be a national or resident of, or have some other connection with, the UK or a state that affords reciprocal protection for British work. None of the rights confers a monopoly. They restrict certain acts to the author, artist or other creator which are infringed by doing one or more of those acts without consent. Some of the rights, such as copyright and design rights have already been discussed in relation to brands, design and technology. Others such as moral rights, publication rights and artists' resale rights apply only to protecting creativity.

COPYRIGHT

Lasting creative output, such as architecture, drawings, films, novels, paintings, plays, sculptures and musical scores, is protected by copyright. Such output is grouped as follows in the UK:

*   original artistic, literary, dramatic and musical works, [105]

---

102   OJ L 227 , 01/09/1994 P. 1–30.
103   36 USC 161.
104   http://www.upov.int/en/publications/conventions/1991/act1991.htm.
105   S.1 (1) (a) CDPA.

- broadcasts, films and sound recordings,[106] and
- typographical arrangements of published editions.[107]

They are protected by Part 1 of the Copyright, Designs and Patents Act 1988. This Act has been updated several times to implement a number of Council directives for the approximation of the copyright laws and laws relating to copyright of the member states. Some of those directives give effect to international agreements to which all EC member states are party.

ORIGINALITY

This has already been touched upon in the context of unregistered design right in Chapter 5. *Originality* in the context of artistic, dramatic, literary and musical works means the application of independent skill and labour. A work is said to be *original* if and in so far as it has not been reproduced from an earlier work.

ARTISTIC WORKS

Artistic works are categorized into those in which copyright subsists irrespective of artistic quality such as collages, diagrams, drawings, engravings, plans, paintings, works of architecture (buildings or models for buildings) and works of artistic craftsmanship.

LITERARY WORKS

A literary work may be anything that can be written, spoken or sung (other than plays or musical scores that are protected by dramatic and musical copyright) and includes computer programs, compilations and databases.

SCOPE OF COPYRIGHT PROTECTION

Copyright confers exclusive right to reproduce, publish, lend, rent, perform, communicate or adapt any of the above works. These rights are infringed by doing any of those things without the owner's permission. The remedies for infringement include injunctions, delivery up and forfeiture of infringing copies, damages (including additional damages where the flagrancy of the case or the benefit to the wrongdoer are such that the justice of the case so requires) or an account of profits and costs.

AUTHOR

The person upon whom those rights are conferred is usually the person who created the work (known as *'the author'*) or his or her employer if he or she created the work in the scope of his or her employment; but special provisions apply to the Crown, Parliament and international organizations. The author must be a national or resident of the UK or a state that affords reciprocal protection for the works of British authors or the work must be published or broadcast in such a state. Since most countries adhere to Berne or to one or more of the other conventions that require reciprocal protection for the works of contracting parties, it is unusual for that condition not to be satisfied.

---

106   S.1 (1) (b) CDPA.
107   S.1 (1) (c) CDPA.

RIGHTS IN PERFORMANCES

An exclusive right to authorize the broadcasting, filming, taping or other recording of a ballet, concert, opera, play or recital is conferred upon each actor, dancer, musician, singer or other performer who participates in such spectacle by Part II of the Copyright, Designs and Patents Act 1988. A similar right is also conferred by that Part upon any film or recording studio or radio or TV station who contracts with those performers for the right to broadcast or record their work. Those rights are known collectively as *'rights in performances'*. Filming or taping a performance without the authority of the performer or of his or her studio or broadcaster infringes that right. That right can be infringed directly with a camera or microphone in the auditorium, or indirectly by filming or taping the playing of a recording of the performance. The remedies for infringement of a right in a performance are much the same as for the infringement of any other intellectual property right. They include injunctions, damages, delivery up of infringing material and costs.

ECONOMIC AND MORAL RIGHTS

Copyrights and rights in performances are often referred to as *'economic rights'* to distinguish them from rights that protect the integrity of certain types of copyright works and the reputations of their authors known as *'moral rights'*. Since 1 Feb 2006 performers have enjoyed moral rights in their performances similar to those conferred on authors.[108] Examples of moral rights include the right to be identified as author of an artistic, dramatic, literary[109] or musical work or director of a film,[110] the right to object to derogatory treatment of the work[111] and the right to prevent false attribution.[112] Authors or performers whose moral rights are infringed have an action for the infringement of those rights.

PUBLICATION RIGHT

Publication right is intended to encourage investment in publishing previously unpublished material in which copyright has expired. It is a right equivalent to copyright that comes into being when a person publishes for the first time a previously unpublished work after the expiry of copyright protection in that work.[113] *'Publication'*, for these purposes, includes making the material available online, lending, renting, performance and broadcasting as well as in print. Most but not quite all of the provisions of Part 1 of the CDPA apply to publication right including the rights and remedies for infringement.[114] Because the incentive provided by this IPR is aimed at European publishers, the first publisher rather than the contributor of the unpublished material is the first owner of the right and first publication must take place either

---

108   The Performances (Moral Rights, etc) Regulation 2006.
109   This right does not apply to computer programs, typefaces or computer generated works (see S.79 of the CDPA).
110   S.77 Copyright, Designs and Patents Act 1988.
111   S.80 Ibid.
112   S.84 Ibid
113   Reg. 16 (1) of The Copyright and Related Rights Regulations 1996, SI 1996 No. 2967 (http://www.opsi.gov.uk/si/si1996/Uksi_19962967_en_1.htm).
114   Reg. 17 (1) Ibid.

in the European Economic Area (that is to say one of the countries of the EU or EFTA)[115] or the publisher must be a national of one of those states.[116]

ARTISTS' RESALE RIGHT

Artists' resale right (also known as *'droit de suite'*) is a royalty for living artists on the resale of their work in the commercial art market.[117] The right was introduced into the UK on 14 Feb 2006 in accordance with the Resale Right Directive.[118] The right only applies to sales of work over €1,000 and the maximum royalty payable on any single sale is €12,500 and can be enforced only through a collecting society.

COPYRIGHT LICENSING

Some IP legislation contains provisions that regulate IP licensing. Chapter VII of Part I of the CDPA, for instance, provides a legal framework for copyright licensing. Typically these include standard terms upon which copyright owners permit the reproduction, publishing, performance or other use of their work. They are often negotiated by collecting societies and associations of users such as schools and universities. Disputes over such terms may be referred to an independent, statutory tribunal known as the Copyright Tribunal.[119] Contracts between collecting societies and other powerful copyright owners are also regulated by EC and UK competition law.

FURTHER INFORMATION ON THE INTERNET

The UK-IPO at www.ipo.gov.uk has extensive information on copyright including an unofficial consolidation of Parts I and II of the 1988 Act and the publication right and database right legislation, relevant Council directives, guidance on copyright in relation to art, computing, films, the internet, music, photographs, TV, theatre and the spoken work and links to collecting societies and the Copyright Tribunal. Probably the best starting point for information on collecting societies is the joint website of the Performing Rights Society and the Mechanical Copyright Protection Society at www.mcps-prs-alliance.co.uk.

---

115   European Free Trade Association, a free trade bloc founded in 1960 by the UK together with Austria, Denmark, Norway, Portugal, Sweden and Switzerland in response to the establishment of the EC. EFTA was subsequently expanded by the accession of Finland, Iceland and Liechtenstein. EFTA's importance as a trading bloc was diminished greatly by the departure of the UK and Denmark in 1972. Those countries were later followed by Austria, Finland, Portugal and Sweden. The EFTA reached agreement with the EU to form the EEA in 1994.

116   Reg. 17 (4) Ibid.

117   Reg. 3 of The Artist's Resale Right Regulations 2006, SI 2006 No. 346 (http://www.opsi.gov.uk/si/si2006/20060346.htm).

118   Directive 2001/84/EC of 27 September 2001 of the European Parliament and of the Council on the Resale Right for the benefit of the author of an original work of art (droit de suite).

119   http://www.ipo.gov.uk/ctribunal.htm.

4 *Dispute Resolution Options*

Essentially an intellectual property right is a right to sue. Except for the very few intellectual property infringements that are also crimes,[1] it is up to the intellectual property owner to take proceedings in the civil courts if his or her right is infringed.

Court proceedings

Court proceedings fall into two phases:

1. determining the rights and remedies of the parties; and
2. enforcing any remedies that the court may grant.

While it is possible for parties to agree alternatives to a court's determination of their rights and remedies (many of which are faster and less formal and expensive than the court's procedures), there is no lawful substitute in a civilized society for the court's powers of enforcement. Only a state can lawfully imprison citizens or deprive them of their property and, even then, only in accordance with generally accepted rules. The courts are the agents by which states exercise those coercive powers.

Determining rights and remedies

In most civilized societies this procedure takes the following course:

* The court satisfies itself that the complainant (usually called a *'claimant'* in England and Wales, *'pursuer'* in Scotland and *'plaintiff'* in most other countries) has a right to sue and the person sued (the *'defendant'*, or *'defender'* in Scotland) is answerable before it.
* If it is satisfied thus, the court then decides whether the right(s) claimed by the claimant subsist(s) and if so whether such right(s) has or have been infringed.
* If it finds that one or more rights have been infringed, the court then determines the remedy for such infringement. That may take place in several stages. For instance, the court may decide on one occasion that the defendant is liable in principle to compensate the claimant in damages and then go on to decide the precise amount of compensation on another occasion.
* The court's decisions may be subject to appeal or review.

---

1   These are listed on the UK-IPO website at http://www.ipo.gov.uk/crime/crime-whatis/crime-whatis-offenceguide. htm.

Remedies and enforcement

If an intellectual property right is infringed, the following remedies may be available to the owner:

*   **Declarations:** a formal statement of the rights or obligations of the parties;
*   **Injunctions:**[2] an order of the court to do or refrain from doing a specified act;
*   **Damages:** an order to pay the injured party a sum of money by way of reparation for the harm done;
*   **Account of Profits:** an order to account for and surrender any profits that a wrongdoer has gained from his or her wrongdoing;
*   **Costs:** an order to contribute to the successful party's expenses of bringing or defending the claim.

The court can compel obedience to its injunctions by punishing disobedience with a fine, seizure of assets or even imprisonment. It can compel payment of a monetary award by authorizing seizure of funds or other assets, deduction of some or all of an income stream, a charge over property or the bankruptcy of an individual or the administration or winding up of a company. Injunctions can be interim (that is to say, temporary) or perpetual (permanent). A court will grant a perpetual injunction after it has determined the rights and liabilities of the parties. It may grant an interim injunction before that determination if it believes that a party could suffer irreparable harm before it has completed its processes.

Civil and common law systems

Most modern industrial countries have legal systems that fall into one or other of the following categories:

*   **Common law systems:** judge-made laws and practices based on or influenced by English law; and
*   **Civil law systems:** codifications of general legal principle that originate in imperial Rome and have been developed by legal scholars over many centuries.

An important difference between the two is that the parties choose the issues and the evidence to be presented in common law systems while the judge acts as referee while in civil law systems the court leads the investigation and calls the evidence.

The significance of the difference between those two systems from the point of view of litigants is that the cost of litigation in common law countries such as England and the USA is much higher than in civil law countries such as France, Germany and the Netherlands. In a report published in November 2003[3] the UK government's high level Intellectual advisory on intellectual property (IPAC) compared patent litigation in England and Wales, France, Germany, the Netherlands and the USA. It found the average cost of a patent infringement claim to be:

*   £1 million in England if brought in the High Court and between £150,000 and £250,000 if brought in the Patents County Court;

---

2   Called 'interdicts' in Scotland and certain other countries.
3   IPAC '*The Enforcement of Patent Rights*' November 2003, which may be downloaded from Mandy Haberman's website at http://www.mandyhaberman.com/media/IPAC-18-11.pdf.

- €30,000 to €50,000 in France;
- €25,000 to €50,000 in Germany;
- €10,000 to €20,000 in the Netherlands for summary proceedings or €40,000 for a simple action;
- between US$2 and 4 million in the USA.

It was not hard to see why. The report found that trials average half a day in France and the Netherlands and a day in Germany compared to 1 to 5 in England and Wales and 2 weeks and upwards in the USA. Teams consisting of an advocate and a patent attorney are typical in the civil law countries. In England, on the other hand it is not unusual to instruct leading and junior advocates, two litigators and a patent attorney in the High Court. Even in the USA where there is no formal distinction between advocates, litigators and patent attorneys, patent litigation is conducted by teams of 4.

The UK legal systems

The first point to note is that there is no such thing as the 'UK legal system'. There are separate legal systems for England and Wales, Scotland and Northern Ireland. Each legal system has its own courts that have developed their own bodies of case or judge-made law over the years. The legal systems of England and Wales and Northern Ireland are very similar. The structures, jurisdictions and even the names of some of the courts are the same and decisions of one jurisdiction's courts tend to be followed by those of the other. However, the legal system of Scotland remains very different despite sharing a common legislature and the House of Lords as final court of appeal with the rest of the UK. It should also be noted in passing that the Isle of Man and Channel Islands are not part of the UK though they are British territory. Each of those islands has its own legislature, executive and court system which has developed its own case law albeit that much of it is modelled on or influenced by UK statutes and English case law.

England and Wales

There are separate courts for civil and criminal proceedings in England and Wales. 'Civil' in this context includes 'family' as well as civil and commercial. The civil courts consist of the *Senior Courts* of England and Wales and a nationwide network of local county courts. The Senior Courts (which used to be called the Supreme Court of England and Wales)[4] consist of the *Court of Appeal*, the *High Court of Justice* and the *Crown Court*. The High Court was formed by the merger in 1873 of several ancient courts that had developed parallel rules and practices known as *'common law'* and *'equity'*. The common law courts awarded damages for breach of contract and other wrongdoing. The courts of equity – also called chancery because the principles of equity were first developed by the Lord Chancellor – granted injunctions and other orders to prevent or undo wrongdoing but they had no power to compensate. The merged court applied both common law and equity but in order to preserve expertise and continuity the judges of that court were organized in separate chancery and common law divisions. Cases that had previously been heard by the chancery courts such as claims for an injunction for

---

4   Renamed by S.59 (1) of the Constitutional Reform Act 2005.

the infringement of an IPR were usually heard by a judge of the Chancery Division whereas claims for damages for injuries suffered in an accident or moneys due under a contract were heard by the common law or Queen's Bench Division. The High Court continues to sit in three Divisions – namely, the Chancery, Queen's Bench and Family Division. Intellectual property cases are now allocated to the Chancery Division by statute[5] and patent and registered design cases assigned to a special panel of judges within the Chancery Division known as the '*Patents Court*'.[6] The county courts are a network of local courts with very wide civil jurisdiction. Intellectual property infringement claims other than patent and design cases are heard in the Preston, Manchester, Mold, Liverpool, Leeds, Newcastle, Bristol, Birmingham, Cardiff and Caernarfon County Courts. Patent and registered design cases as well as other intellectual property claims may be heard in the Central London County Court which is sometimes called '*The Patents County Court*'. In both the High Court and the country courts, intellectual property cases are tried by a judge sitting alone while appeals are heard by panels of three judges (or '*Lord Justices*') of the Court of Appeal.

Scotland

There are three sets of courts in Scotland:

1. The *Court of Session* and the *High Court of Justiciary* which are superior courts of record exercising respectively civil and criminal jurisdiction throughout Scotland;
2. *Sheriffs Courts* having wide civil and criminal jurisdiction within districts known as sheriffdoms; and
3. *District Courts* having local criminal jurisdiction.

The Court of Session sits in two divisions known respectively as the *Inner House* and the *Outer House*. The Inner House is an appellate court and the Outer House is a court of first instance. Intellectual property claims are brought in the Outer House and are handled by a judge appointed by the Lord President, known as '*the Intellectual Property Judge*'.[7]

Northern Ireland

The Northern Irish courts are organized very much like those of England and Wales. The equivalent of the Senior Courts of England and Wales is the *Court of Judicature of Northern Ireland* consisting of the Court of Appeal, High Court and Crown Court of Northern Ireland.[8] There is also a network of county courts. The High Court sits in three Divisions also known as the Queens Bench, Chancery and Family Division. Intellectual property cases are brought in the Chancery Division. There is no special patents court for Northern Ireland. Appeal lies from the High Court and county courts to the Court of Appeal.

---

5   S.61 (1) and Sched.1 para. 1 (h) Senior Courts Act 1981.
6   S.62 (1) Senior Courts Act 1981.
7   Rule 55.2 of the Rules of the Court of Session 1994 (http://www.scotcourts.gov.uk/session/rules/chapter55.asp).
8   Formerly known as the Supreme Court of Judicature and renamed by S.59 (2) of the Constitutional Reform Act 2005.

Law lords

The House of Lords is the upper house of the UK legislature. It consists of individuals who have distinguished themselves in various activities including the law. Members who are appointed to the House in recognition of their judicial service are known as 'the law lords'. They hear appeals from the highest courts of England and Wales, Scotland and Northern Ireland. This is the last remnant of an obsolete constitutional role in which Parliament was a court as well as part of the legislature. The law lords are also members of another ancient institution known as the *Privy Council*. There they form the Judicial Committee which hears appeals from the highest courts of the Isle of Man and Channel Islands, the last remaining British overseas territories, some of the independent members of the Commonwealth, the Scottish courts in devolution issues (including those involving human rights) and a few other British domestic tribunals. As the exercise of judicial functions by part of the legislature is now regarded as anomalous, the House of Lords is about to be replaced[9] by a new *Supreme Court for the United Kingdom*. This new court will perform the same functions as the House of Lords and will have similar but not quite identical jurisdiction. The law lords will become the first members of the new court.[10]

UK Intellectual Property Office

The Comptroller or chief executive of the UK-IPO has jurisdiction to hear and determine a number of intellectual property disputes. These include disputes over title to a patent or patent application,[11] amendment,[12] non-infringement,[13] compulsory licences[14] and revocation[15] of patents, opposition to trade mark applications[16] and invalidity[17] and revocation[18] of trade marks, invalidity of design registrations and licences of right for designs. This jurisdiction is exercised by officials known as hearing officers. Proceedings before a hearing officer are similar to court proceedings except in two important respects. The costs that may be awarded against a party are limited to a few thousand pounds unless a party behaves unreasonably and many proceedings are resolved without a hearing.

European courts and tribunals

The UK is party to several very important European treaties including the Treaty of Rome,[19] the European patent Convention[20] and the European Convention on Human Rights.[21]

---

9   According to a press release from the Ministry of Justice dated 14 June 2007, work had already started on the renovation of the Middlesex Guildhall to house the new Supreme Court and Privy Council and the work is expected to be completed by October 2009 (see http://www.justice.gov.uk/newsrelease140607a.htm).
10   S.24 Constitutional Reform Act 2005.
11   S.8, 12 and 37 Patents Act 1977.
12   S.27 and S.75 Ibid.
13   S.71 Ibid.
14   S.48 Ibid.
15   S.72 Ibid.
16   S.38 Trade Marks Act 1994.
17   S.47 Ibid.
18   S.46 Ibid.
19   http://europa.eu.int/eur-lex/en/treaties/dat/EC_consol.html.
20   http://www.european-patent-office.org/legal/epc/e/ma1.html.
21   Convention for the Protection of Human Rights and Fundamental Freedoms as amended by Protocol No. 11 (http://conventions.coe.int/Treaty/en/Treaties/Html/005.htm).

The Treaty of Rome established a body of law governing relations which applies uniformly throughout the member states of the European Union. These laws govern not only relations between the EU and its member states but also many matters relating to businesses and individuals. As I mentioned above these laws can take the form of 'directives' or instructions to member states to enact legislation or take other measures to bring their laws in line with a common standard and 'regulations' which take effect in each of the states of the EU as though they were national legislation. The ultimate authority for the construction and enforcement of these laws is the European Court of Justice.[22] The Court will hear cases brought before it by the European institutions, national governments and others and also give interpretations on questions of European law that are referred to it by the UK and other national courts under art. 234 of the Treaty of Rome.[23] So far as intellectual property is concerned there are two kinds of cases likely to be of interest: first, actions to annul or amend decisions of the Board of Appeals of OHIM under art 63 of the Community trade mark regulation and the corresponding provision of the Community design regulation and, secondly, references from national courts under art 234 on various provisions of EC intellectual property, competition and trade law. The UK-IPO maintains an up to date table of decided and pending intellectual property cases before the European Court since 1999.[24]

Appeals against decisions of the departments of the European Patent Office lie to Boards of Appeal which are tribunals of legally and technically qualified members under art 21 (1) of the EPC. The precise composition of a Board will vary according to the nature of the appeal. Appeals from the Receiving Section or Legal Division, for example, will be heard by three legally qualified members[25] whereas two technically qualified members and one legally qualified member will hear appeals from the Opposition Division.[26] An Enlarged Board of Appeal will hear questions referred to it by the Boards of Appeal[27] or the President of the Office.[28] There is no court above the Boards of Appeal in matters relating to the EPC. The Boards' decisions cannot be reviewed by the European Court because the EPC is not part of EU Law. Nor, in practice, can they be reviewed by any national court.[29] Considerable work has been done on a European Patent Litigation Agreement[30] which would establish a European patents court but there is not yet any suggestion that such a court should hear appeals from the Boards of Appeal.

The European Convention on Human Rights has now been incorporated into the laws of the United Kingdom by the Human Rights Act 1998.[31] This Convention is construed and

---

22   http://www.curia.europa.eu.
23   The Court of Justice shall have jurisdiction to give preliminary rulings concerning:
          (a) the interpretation of this Treaty;
          (b) the validity and interpretation of acts of the institutions of the Community and of the ECB;
          (c) the interpretation of the statutes of bodies established by an act of the Council, where those statutes so
             provide.
        Where such a question is raised before any court or tribunal of a Member State, that court or tribunal may, if it
        considers that a decision on the question is necessary to enable it to give judgment, request the Court of Justice
        to give a ruling thereon.
        Where any such question is raised in a case pending before a court or tribunal of a Member State against whose
        decisions there is no judicial remedy under national law, that court or tribunal shall bring the matter before the
        Court of Justice.
        (http://europa.eu.int/eur-lex/en/treaties/dat/C_2002325EN.003301.html.)
24   http://www.ipo.gov.uk/about/about-consult/about-ecj/about-ecj-refs.htm.
25   Art 21 (2) EPC.
26   Art 21 (4) (a) EPC.
27   Art 22 (1) (a) EPC.
28   Art 22 (1) (b) EPC.
29   See *R v Comptroller-General of Patents, Designs and Trade Marks, ex parte Lenzing AG* [1996] EWHC Admin 390 at
        http://www.bailii.org/ew/cases/EWHC/Admin/1996/390.html.
30   http://www.epo.org/patents/law/legislative-initiatives/epla.html.
31   http://www.opsi.gov.uk/acts/acts1998/ukpga_19980042_en_3#sch1-pt1.

enforced by the European Court of Human Rights (ECHR) and S.2 (1) of the Act requires courts and tribunals in the UK to take account of that Court's judgments, decisions, declarations or advisory opinions when applying the Act. Very occasionally the ECHR is asked to rule on an intellectual property right. One such occasion was in *Anheuser-Busch Inc. v. Portugal*[32] which was part of the long running struggle between the Czech and American Budweiser brewers over the right to call their beer 'Budweiser' or 'Bud'. Another was *Chappell v UK*[33] when the Court upheld the compatibility of Anton Piller or search orders with the Convention.

The TRIPS obligation

TRIPS requires every WTO member contracting state to provide effective means of enforcing intellectual property rights.[34] Those means must include the right to bring civil proceedings for orders to prevent infringement of those rights and to recover compensation for any loss or damage arising that may result from such infringement.[35] Remedies must be expeditious and sanctions sufficient to deter infringement.[36] Procedures for obtaining civil remedies must be fair and equitable.[37] They should not be unnecessarily complicated or costly. They should not entail unreasonable time limits or unwarranted delay. They may not to be applied in such a manner as to impede legitimate trade. There should be safeguards against abuse of the processes described above.[38]

Commonwealth countries with legal systems modelled on England

The legal systems of Australia, Canada, Hong Kong, India, Ireland, Jamaica, Malaysia, New Zealand, Nigeria and Singapore are modelled on that of England and Wales. As in England, a single judge considers evidence called by one party and challenged by the other. Appeals lie to a three judge bench and thereafter to a local supreme court or to the Privy Council in London. One significant difference is that there are separate federal and state or provincial courts in Australia, Canada and other federations. In such countries, cases concerning federal legislation, such as patent, trade mark and copyright claims, tend to proceed in the federal courts while breach of confidence and passing off cases proceed in the state or provincial courts.

USA

There are also separate state and federal courts in the USA. The federal courts consist of *District Courts* with wide civil and criminal jurisdiction, 11 regional or *Circuit Courts of Appeals* and one national *Supreme Court*. As in Australia and Canada, the federal courts hear patent, copyright

---

32   73049/01 [2007] ECHR 40 (11 January 2007) URL: http://www.bailii.org/eu/cases/ECHR/2007/40.html.
33   10461/83 [1989] ECHR 4 (30 March 1989) URL: http://www.bailii.org/eu/cases/ECHR/1989/4.html.
34   Art 41 (1) TRIPS (http://www.wto.org/english/docs_e/legal_e/27-trips_05_e.htm#1).
35   Art 42 TRIPS.
36   Art 41 (1) TRIPS.
37   Art 41 (2) TRIPS.
38   See the 'Index of Disputes Issues' on the WTO website at http://www.wto.org/english/tratop_e/dispu_e/dispu_ subjects_index_e.htm#patents.

and trade mark cases. The procedure of the District Courts is similar to that of the English High Court with the important difference that it is not uncommon for civil claims, including intellectual property infringement cases, to be tried by jury. There is no patents court as such but the judges of the District Court for the District of Columbia, the District of Columbia Circuit Court and the Court of Appeals for the Federal Circuit have developed considerable expertise in intellectual property. The US Supreme Court hears appeals from federal circuit courts and petitions for the review of decisions of the state courts on issues of public importance.

Common law jurisdictions influenced by England

The court structures of South Africa, its English speaking neighbours, Mauritius and Sri Lanka are similar to those of Commonwealth countries with legal systems modelled on that of England, but the substantive laws, legal terminology and procedure are often derived elsewhere.

France

At first sight the French legal system resembles that of England and Wales in structure and even in nomenclature. There is a supreme court known as the *Cour de Cassation*, regional courts of appeal (*Cours d'Appel*), superior courts of first instance (*Tribunaux de Grande Instance*) having civil jurisdiction and assize courts (*Cours d'Assises*) in the main cities as well as lower courts of civil and criminal jurisdiction; but closer examination quickly reveals some important differences. First there are separate systems of public and private law. Public law governs relations between citizens and the state while private law governs relations between citizens. Secondly, the administration of justice is decentralized. There are courts of appeal in each of the main regions which hear appeals from the courts of first instance in their area. The *Cour de Cassation* operates very differently from the House of Lords. It gives rulings on points of law which can be sought at any stage. Most importantly, evidence and legal submissions are usually presented in writing and cases are decided by benches of three judges. There is rarely anything like a common law trial. Hearings are brief and costs low. Patent and other intellectual property infringement claims may be brought in any one of several regional specialist superior courts of first instance where there are specialist patent judges but in practice most claims are brought in Paris.

Germany

German is a federal state with a federal supreme court (*Bundesgerichthof*), regional courts of appeal (*Oberlandsgericht*) and district courts of general civil and criminal jurisdiction (*Landsgerichte*). The distinctions between public and private law and between commercial and civil law mentioned above also exist in Germany. One of the consequences is that the validity and subsistence of an IPR is a public law issue which is determined by the Patent Court in Munich while infringement is private law for determination by the *Landsgericht*. The upshot is that the invalidity of a patent cannot be pleaded as a defence to infringement in Germany. All that can be done is to launch a revocation action in Munich. Claims may be brought in a number of designated *Landsgerichte* though in practice most cases are brought in Dusseldorf and Munich. As in France, there is no trial in the English sense. Hearings are very short, evidence and submissions are usually in writing and costs are recovered on a sliding scale.

Japan

Japan modelled its legal system on Germany's and the structure of its courts, substantive law and civil procedure are very similar. As in Germany, claims are brought in the district court. Most actions are brought in Tokyo though some are brought in Osaka. Invalidity is not a defence. Applications for revocation may be brought only in the Patent Office. Evidence tends to be in writing. Appeal lies to a regional court of appeal and a Supreme Court. One distinguishing characteristic of Japanese litigation is that there is so little of it. Japanese society discourages confrontation. Thus a very high proportion of disputes are resolved without recourse to litigation.

China

Contrary to popular prejudice, China takes intellectual property infringement very seriously and provides criminal sanctions and inexpensive administrative as well as civil remedies. Criminal proceedings can be initiated by a complaint to the police, procurator or court. Regional state intellectual property offices have power to restrain an infringement but not order compensation. Claims for monetary relief have to be brought in the civil courts. Chinese procedure resembles that of Japan in that invalidity is no defence and in the encouragement of conciliation. As in Japan and Germany, revocation proceedings have to be brought by separate action. Claims are brought in a district court of general jurisdiction known as the Intermediate Peoples' Court. As in other civil law countries there is no trial in the English sense. Evidence and submissions are mainly in writing. Appeal from the Intermediate Peoples' Court lies to a regional appeal court known as a Higher Peoples' Court.

Alternatives to litigation

Although the courts underpin all other ways of resolving dispute in that they alone have power to compel compliance with a settlement, parties are free to resolve their differences in other ways. They may do so through negotiation, either face to face or facilitated by a mediator. If that is not possible, they can refer their dispute to arbitration or some form of expert determination. The UK-IPO encourages both methods of dispute resolution. It offers mediation by its own officials and also lets out space in its offices for mediation by other mediators. It also provides expert opinions on whether patents are valid or whether they have been infringed. Probably the most successful method of dispute resolution is domain name dispute resolution offered by the WIPO, Nominet and other service providers.[39]

---

39   These are discussed in detail in Chapter 13.

5 *Woolf Rules, OK!*

Overview

On 26 April 1999 a new procedural code[1] came into force known as the *Civil Procedure Rules* (the CPR). The CPR provided a uniform code for civil litigation in the Senior Courts and county courts in place of the *Rules of the Supreme Court* which governed the procedure of what we now call the 'Senior Courts' and the *County Court Rules* which governed procedure in the county courts.

The code was, however, intended to be much more than a replacement for the existing rules of court. Lord Woolf, who was then the Master of the Rolls or presiding judge of the Court of Appeal in England and Wales had carried out an extensive review of civil justice in England and Wales in which he detected the following defects:

> *'The defects I identified in our present system were that it is too expensive in that the costs often exceed the value of the claim; too slow in bringing cases to a conclusion and too unequal: there is a lack of equality between the powerful, wealthy litigant and the under resourced litigant. It is too uncertain: the difficulty of forecasting what litigation will cost and how long it will last induces the fear of the unknown; and it is incomprehensible to many litigants. Above all it is too fragmented in the way it is organised since there is no one with clear overall responsibility for the administration of civil justice; and too adversarial as cases are run by the parties, not by the courts and the rules of court, all too often, are ignored by the parties and not enforced by the court.'[2]*

The new procedural code was intended to change the landscape of civil litigation in England and Wales. The features of this new landscape were to be as follows:

- litigation would be avoided wherever possible;
- litigation would be less adversarial and more cooperative;
- litigation would be less complex;
- the timescale of litigation would be shorter and more certain;
- the cost of litigation would be more affordable, more predictable, and more proportionate to the value and complexity of individual cases;
- parties of limited financial means would be able to conduct litigation on a more equal footing;
- there would be clear lines of judicial and administrative responsibility for the civil justice system;
- the structure of the courts and the deployment of judges would be designed to meet the needs of litigants;
- judges would be deployed effectively so that they could manage litigation in accordance with the new rules and protocols; and
- the civil justice system would be responsive to the needs of litigants.[3]

---

1   CPR 1.1 (1) (http://www.justice.gov.uk/civil/procrules_fin/contents/parts/part01.htm#rule1_1).
2   Access to Justice – Final Report (http://www.dca.gov.uk/civil/final/contents.htm).
3   Ibid. para 9 'Overview' at http://www.dca.gov.uk/civil/final/overview.htm.

While there may be very few signs that litigation is less adversarial, less complex or more affordable the CPR have had an effect on dispute resolution in England and Wales. Complainants do think twice before going to law, if only because the fees for issuing proceedings have increased and rather more work now has to be done before launching an action than was required under the old rules. Parties are more inclined to explore alternatives to litigation such as expert determination and mediation – again, because litigation is expensive. There has been a wholesale change of terminology. Latin tags and Norman French have almost disappeared and age old terms like *'plaintiff'* and *'motion'* have given way to 'claimant' and 'interim application'. Most importantly, Pre-Action Protocols and provisions encouraging early settlement[4] concern out of court dealings as well as litigation. The upshot is that the CPR are important regardless of the method of dispute resolution.

The statutory framework

The CPR were established pursuant to S.1 (1) of the Civil Procedure Act 1997 which provided for there to be rules of court (to be called 'Civil Procedure Rules') governing the practice and procedure to be followed in the Court of Appeal, the High Court, and county courts. Those rules are made by a committee known as the *'Civil Procedure Rule Committee'* consisting of the Master of the Rolls, Chancellor and others appointed by the Lord Chancellor.[5] The power to make rules has to be exercised with a view to securing that the civil justice system is accessible, fair and efficient.[6] The CPR are to be supplemented by practice directions[7] which may amplify any matter set out in a rule.[8] The Act authorizes the Civil Procedure Rule Committee to make rules by statutory instrument – that is to say legislation made under the authority of an Act of Parliament.[9]

The structure of the CPR

The CPR are divided into a number of Parts each of which deals with an aspect of civil procedure. For instance, Part 1 addresses the *'Overriding Objective'* or policy of the Rules,[10] Part 2 their application and interpretation, Part 3 case management and so on. Each Part is divided into a number of rules many of which are subdivided into sub-divisions and some into numbered, lettered and occasionally Roman numbered paragraphs and sub-paragraphs. When referring to a Part it is appropriate to cite the abbreviation 'CPR' followed by the relevant 'Part' and (if desired) the topic that the Part addresses. Thus the conventional citation for the first Part is 'CPR Part 1'. The word 'Part' can be omitted when referring to a rule. Thus, CPR 1.3 refers to the obligation of parties to help the court to further the overriding objective and CPR 1.1 (2) (c) (i) to the provision that 'dealing with a case justly includes, so far as is practicable, dealing with the case in ways which are proportionate to the amount of money involved'.

---

4   Such as CPR Part 36.
5   S.2 (1) Ibid.
6   S.1 (3) Ibid.
7   S.5 (1) Ibid.
8   Para. 6, Sched. 1 Ibid.
9   S.3 (1) (b) Ibid.
10   This will be discussed later.

Nearly all the CPR are amplified by further sets of directions known as 'Practice Directions'. The conventional abbreviation for a Practice Direction are the initials PD followed by the number of the rule which it supplements followed by a dash and the topic that it addresses. Thus 'PD2 – Court Offices'[11] refers to the Practice Direction supplementing CPR Part 2 on court offices and 'PD2b – Allocation of Cases to Levels of Judiciary'[12] to the second Practice Direction supplementing CPR Part 2 on allocation of cases to particular levels of judges. There are also a number of free standing practice directions which do not relate to any particular rule such as 'PD – Protocols' on pre-action protocols[13] and pre-action behaviour[14] and 'PD – Competition Law' on claims relating to arts. 81 and 82 of the Treaty of Rome and to Chapters I and II of the Competition Act 1998.[15] Each practice direction is divided into numbered paragraphs and sub-paragraphs. It is conventional to refer to a direction by the initials or name of the practice direction followed by the paragraph number. Thus 'PD3 para. 1.1' refers to the direction that CPR 1.4 (2)[16] includes as an example of active case management, the summary disposal of issues which do not need full investigation at trial,[17] and 'PD – Protocols para. 4.1' the direction that in cases not covered by any approved protocol, the court will expect the parties to act reasonably in exchanging information and documents relevant to the claim and generally in trying to avoid the necessity for the start of proceedings.[18]

Many of the former Rules of the Supreme Court and County Court Rules that I have mentioned in the first paragraph survive as Schedules to the CPR. Schedule 1 preserves the old Rules of the Supreme Court (usually abbreviated to 'RSC') and Schedule 2 the old County Court Rules (CCR). The old rules are subdivided into 'Orders' and 'Rules' which are referred to by the initial 'O' (always in upper case) followed by the number of the Order and 'r' (always in lower case) followed by the rule number. Thus, 'RSC O45 r1' in Schedule 1 relates to the rule that 'references to any writ shall be construed as including references to any further writ in aid of the first mentioned writ'[19] and 'CCR O17 r7 (1)' in Schedule 2 to interpleader proceedings under an execution which are ordered to be transferred to a county court from the High Court.[20] Several of the RSC and CCR are now supplemented by practice directions.

Court guides

The application of the CPR and practice directions is further amplified in a series of court guides which are invaluable to practitioners and litigants alike. Those that are most relevant to intellectual property litigation are the *'Patents Court Guide'*[21], the *'Chancery Guide'*[22] and the *'Admiralty and Commercial Courts Guide'*. The Patents Court Guide supplements the Chancery Guide with regard to intellectual property claims and chancery practitioners refer to the

---

11   http://www.justice.gov.uk/civil/procrules_fin/contents/practice_directions/pd_part02.htm.
12   http://www.justice.gov.uk/civil/procrules_fin/contents/practice_directions/pd_part2b.htm.
13   This will be discussed later.
14   http://www.justice.gov.uk/civil/procrules_fin/contents/practice_directions/ pd_protocol.htm.
15   http://www.justice.gov.uk/civil/procrules_fin/contents/practice_directions/ competitionlaw_pd.htm.
16   'Active case management includes ...
            (c) deciding promptly which issues need full investigation and trial and accordingly disposing summarily of
            the others.'
(See http://www.justice.gov.uk/civil/procrules_fin/contents/parts/part01.htm#rule1_1.)
17   http://www.justice.gov.uk/civil/procrules_fin/contents/practice_directions/ pd_part03.htm#IDAGSPFD.
18   http://www.justice.gov.uk/civil/procrules_fin/contents/practice_directions/ pd_protocol.htm#IDARGVMG.
This provision is also important and will also be discussed later.
19   http://www.justice.gov.uk/civil/procrules_fin/contents/schedule1/ rscorder45.htm#ruleIDAGDBTG.
20   http://www.justice.gov.uk/civil/procrules_fin/contents/schedule2/ccrorder16.htm.
21   http://www.hmcourts-service.gov.uk/infoabout/patents/crt_guide.htm.
22   http://www.hmcourts-service.gov.uk/cms/files/chancery_guide_2005.pdf.

Commercial Guide on topics that are not addressed in the Chancery Guide. Other guides that may be consulted occasionally include the *'Queen's Bench Guide'*, *'Mercantile Court Guide'* and *'Technology and Construction Court Guide'* all of which can be downloaded from HM Courts Service website.[23]

Forms

Many practice directions require and others permit the use of specified forms known as *'Practice Forms'*. For instance, para. 3.1 of PD7[24] requires claimants to use practice form N1[25] or practice form N208[26] to start a claim and paragraph 2.1 (5) of PD23 – Applications provides that Practice Form N244 may be used for applications.[27] These forms can be downloaded from the Ministry of Justice website.[28] Some of those forms (the *'General Forms'*) apply to all kinds of civil proceedings. There are also special forms for Commercial Court, Technology and Construction Court, arbitration, insolvency, directors' disqualification and other proceedings.

Two important forms for intellectual property litigation that are not found on that website are the draft orders for a search order and a freezing injunction. These are to be found in the Annexe[29] to PD25 – Interim Injunctions[30] and there are alternative drafts at Appendix 5 of the Commercial Court Guide.[31] Shortly before the CPR came into force the judges of the Chancery Division and Commercial Courts published several forms for interim injunctions and undertakings in everyday language which practitioners were required to use. These slipped from view when the CPR were introduced but they are in keeping with the spirit of the CPR and may (and perhaps should) still be used. It is also worth referring to Part II of the 1999 edition of The Supreme Court Practice[32] for prescribed and Queen's Bench and Chancery Masters' Forms which may easily be adapted for modern use.

The overriding objective

At the beginning of this chapter I wrote that the CPR were intended to change the landscape of civil litigation in England and Wales. The instrument of that change was to be CPR 1.1 (1) which established 'the overriding objective of enabling the court to deal with cases justly'. 'Dealing with a case justly' was to include so far as practical:

(a) ensuring that the parties are on an equal footing;
(b) saving expense;
(c) dealing with the case in ways which are proportionate –
    (i)   to the amount of money involved;
    (ii) to the importance of the case;

23   http://www.hmcourts-service.gov.uk.
24   http://www.justice.gov.uk/civil/procrules_fin/contents/practice_directions/ pd_part07.htm#IDAYOHKD.
25   The claim form.
26   The Part 8 claim form.
27   http://www.justice.gov.uk/civil/procrules_fin/contents/practice_directions/ pd_part23.htm#IDANCFLD.
28   http://www.justice.gov.uk/civil/procrules_fin/menus/forms.htm.
29   http://www.justice.gov.uk/civil/procrules_fin/contents/practice_directions/ pd_part25.htm#IDAPTCKD.
30   http://www.justice.gov.uk/civil/procrules_fin/contents/practice_directions/ pd_part25.htm.
31   http://www.hmcourts-service.gov.uk/docs/admiralcomm/Commercial%20Court%20Guide%20 December%2020 06%20rev1%20rh%20clean.pdf.
32   If one can be found.

  (iii) to the complexity of the issues; and

  (iv) to the financial position of each party;

(d) ensuring that it is dealt with expeditiously and fairly; and

(e) allotting to it an appropriate share of the court's resources, while taking into account the need to allot resources to other cases.[33]

Every rule and practice direction of the CPR including the RSC and CCR that are preserved in Schedules 1 and 2 is supposed to be interpreted to give effect to the overriding objective.[34] The court is required to seek to give effect to the overriding objective when it exercises any power given to it by the CPR.[35] Parties are required to help the court to further the overriding interest.[36] The intention was for the overriding interest to run through every rule, practice direction and order like the world 'Blackpool' through a stick of Blackpool rock.

Pre-action protocols

The first of the features of the new landscape that Lord Woolf mentioned in his Final Report was that Litigation would be avoided wherever possible.[37] He hoped to achieve that by the following means:

(a) People will be encouraged to start court proceedings to resolve disputes only as a last resort, and after using other more appropriate means when these are available.

(b) Information on sources of alternative dispute resolution (ADR) will be provided at all civil courts.

(c) Legal aid funding will be available for pre-litigation resolution and ADR.

(d) Protocols in relation to medical negligence, housing and personal injury, and additional powers for the court in relation to pre-litigation disclosure, will enable parties to obtain information earlier and promote settlement.

(e) Before commencing litigation both parties will be able to make offers to settle the whole or part of a dispute supported by a special regime as to costs and higher rates of interest if not accepted.[38]

The protocols referred to in paragraph (d) are now supplemented by pre-action protocols for the Construction and Engineering Disputes (which include computer supply disputes), defamation, professional negligence, judicial review and possession claims based on rent arrears.[39] The objectives of these protocols are to:

(1) encourage the exchange of early and full information about the prospective legal claim,

(2) enable parties to avoid litigation by agreeing a settlement of the claim before the commencement of proceedings, and

---

33   http://www.justice.gov.uk/civil/procrules_fin/contents/parts/part01.htm#rule1_1.

34   CPR 1.2 (b) which is now, alas, subject to the qualification introduced by CPR 76.2 in the current hysteria of the so-called 'war on terror' and the slavish surrender of national interests to the dictates of a discredited and isolated partisan president of a foreign power.

35   CPR 1.2 (a) (http://www.justice.gov.uk/civil/procrules_fin/contents/parts/part01.htm#rule1_2).

36   CPR 1.3.

37   Woolf 'Access to Justice' Final Report, para 9 'Overview' at http://www.dca.gov.uk/civil/final/overview.htm.

38   Ibid.

39   http://www.justice.gov.uk/civil/procrules_fin/menus/protocol.htm.

(3) support the efficient management of proceedings where litigation cannot be avoided.[40]

The courts expect parties to abide by those protocols[41] and they may penalize non-compliance by disallowing costs[42] or interest[43] that would otherwise be due to the party in default, ordering such party to pay such costs[44] or costs and interest at a higher rate.[45]

Pre-action protocols for Intellectual Property

As I explained to Mr. Aardvark and Mr. Pepys in conference there is no pre-action protocol for intellectual property as such though a committee of intellectual property practitioners and experts chaired by Michael Skrein of *Richards Butler*[46] proposed several draft protocols for different types of intellectual property litigation. Work on these was suspended for several months pending consultations by the Lord Chancellor's Department[47] on a general pre-action protocol.

The result of that consultation was that paragraph 4 of PD – Protocols was expanded to require complainants to submit detailed letters of claim48 and defendants a detailed and reasoned response[49] before resorting to litigation. Paragraph 4.7 of the practice direction reminds parties that they are required to consider whether some form of alternative dispute resolution procedure would be more suitable than litigation, and if so, endeavour to agree which form to adopt. Indeed, the paragraph adds that they may be required by the court to provide evidence that alternative means of resolving their dispute were considered and that the courts take the view that litigation should be a last resort, and that claims should not be issued prematurely when a settlement is still actively being explored. They are warned that if this paragraph is not followed then the court must have regard to such conduct when determining costs.[50] The Practice Direction does not prescribe any particular form of ADR but suggests discussion and negotiation, early neutral evaluation by an independent third party (for example, a lawyer experienced in that field or an individual experienced in the subject matter of the claim) and mediation.[51] However, it expressly recognises that no party can or should be forced to mediate or enter into any form of ADR. [52]

Following such revision of paragraph 4 of PD – Protocols Mr. Skrein's committee has produced a *Code of Practice for Pre-Action Conduct in Intellectual Property Disputes*.[53] The code sets out the steps which parties should follow where litigation is being considered.[54] Its aim is to encourage

---

40   PD-Protocols para 1.4 at http://www.justice.gov.uk/civil/procrules_fin/contents/practice_directions/pd_protocol. htm#IDAXBVMG.
41   Para 2.2 Ibid.
42   Para 2.3 (1) Ibid.
43   Para 2.3 (3) Ibid.
44   Para 2.3 (1) Ibid.
45   Para 2.3 (2) and (4) Ibid.
46   The other members were David Attfield (Lovells), Geoff Bayliss (Boult Wade Tennant), Liz Coleman (UK-IPO), Marcus Dalton (SmithKline Beecham), Susan Davey (BBC), Bridget Doherty (Lord Chancellor's Department for Ministry of Justice), Carolyn Jones (Clerk to the Committee, Richards Butler), Sir Hugh Laddie (then a Patents Court judge), Tom Mitcheson (Barrister), Jonathan Rayner James QC, (Barrister), Judith Sullivan (UK-IPO), Clive Thorne (Denton Wilde Sapte) and Jeff Watson (UK-IPO).
47   The Department which was then responsible for the administration of justice in England and Wales.
48   Paras. 4.2 and 4.3.
49   Paras. 4.4, 4.5 and 4.6.
50   Para. 4.7 Ibid.
51   Ibid.
52   Ibid.
53   http://www.cipa.org.uk/download_files/code_of_practice.pdf.
54   Para. 1.1.

parties to exchange information with each other prior to issuing proceedings to ascertain whether proceedings can be avoided and if not, to ensure that the parties understand the issues sufficiently to ensure that any litigation is dealt with proportionately and in keeping with the overriding objective.[55] The code echoes the requirement in paragraph 4.1 of PD – Protocols that the parties should behave reasonably at all times. The code makes recommendations for letters of claim and response for each type of intellectual property claim and suggests alternative methods of resolving disputes in each case. It therefore complements PD – Practice Directions and both should be referred to by litigants and their professional advisors.

Where to find the CPR

Before the CPR came into force every practitioner had to buy two very expensive text books every year:

- the *Supreme Court Practice* published by Sweet & Maxwell for the RSC which was known as 'the white book' because it had a white cover; and
- the *County Court Practice* published by Butterworths for the CCR which was known as 'the green book' because it had a green cover.

These were the only publications in which those rules were conveniently displayed and they tended to be used by judges and advocates in court. Successors to the white and green

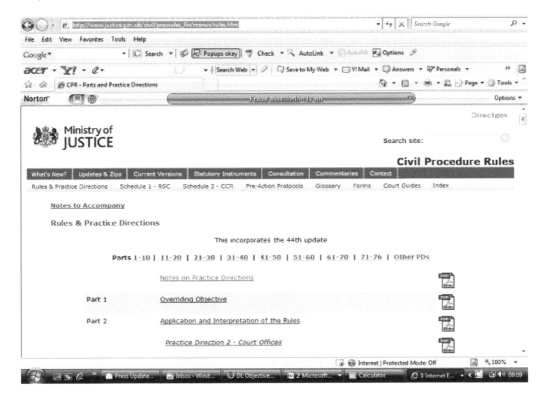

Figure 5.1   Screen shot from Ministry of Justice's website

---

55   Para 1.2.

books are still published and indeed there are now competing compilations and commentaries on the rules but as there are no longer two sets of rules it is no longer essential to invest in both. Moreover, since the CPR are updated several times a year, the best point of reference is probably the Ministry of Justice's website at:http://www.justice.gov.uk/civil/procrules_fin/menus/rules.htm, a screen dump of which appears in Figure 5.1. This screen links to each rule, practice direction, protocol, form, court guide and several commentaries. The white and green books are still worth consulting for their commentary and case citations but relevant authorities can also be found by keyword searches of the BAILII[56] and other legal databases.

---

56   www.bailii.org.

6 *So You Want to Sue Somebody*

In the 1970s and 80s almost every intellectual property case seemed to be launched by a 'without notice' application for a search order, freezing injunction or other interim injunction. Although those remedies remain available, they are much less likely to be resorted to. That is because the courts expect parties to a dispute to make a genuine effort to resolve their dispute without recourse to litigation and, where that is not possible, to conduct proceedings as cost-effectively, expeditiously, proportionately and transparently as possible.

Question to be considered

Before threatening proceedings a complainant should consider the following questions:

- What are the prospects of success?
- Are the benefits of litigation likely to outweigh the costs and, if so, by how much?
- Is there sufficient funding to take the claim to trial or even appeal, and, if necessary, pay the other side's costs?
- Is there anything to prevent the issue of proceedings?

What are the prospects of success?

The outcome of litigation is notoriously difficult to forecast. The merits of a case always count for something but rarely for everything. A perfectly good case may be abandoned for all sorts of reasons. Usually it is because a litigant runs out of money. Sometimes a change of management or ownership leads to a reconsideration of litigation. Even when a case is prosecuted, it may be lost because a witness dies, an important point may be missed or a judge falls into error. Counsel can never guarantee the outcome of litigation but an experienced barrister or solicitor advocate can usually estimate accurately in terms of percentages a party's prospects of success. If litigation is to be covered by insurance the insurer will insist on such an assessment. A litigant who is funding his own litigation probably needs one just as much and possibly more.

Will the benefits outweigh the costs?

This will always be a subjective matter because different people can take different views on the value of an outcome. For some litigants this is a straightforward monetary exercise. If the damages and costs likely to be recovered amount to so many pounds and the estimated costs so many more, then the benefits of litigation can be said to outweigh the costs if the amount of the likely recovery exceeds the likely costs. Others may look beyond the monetary value of the amount likely to be recovered. Where litigation removes a dangerous competitor from the market or deters infringement an action may still be worthwhile even if nothing is recovered from the other side. To decide whether the costs of litigating are likely to outweigh the benefits a litigant must value the benefits that he or she hopes to gain including such intangibles as the effect of an injunction or the determination of a point of law. Next the litigant should discount any tangible benefit and/or the value of any intangible benefit by the percentage prospects of success. In estimating the likely costs it is prudent to prepare for the worst possible scenario. Although it is so obvious as to go without saying, the litigant must find out as much as he or she can about the means of his or her opponent. At the very least he or she should order a company search or Dun & Bradstreet report.

Funding

Unless you are insured or rich or both, or have very good reason to think you will be one or the other by the time you have to pay your lawyers, you should hesitate long and hard before threatening proceedings. It is rarely wise to bluff. Your opponent may capitulate on receiving a solicitor's letter but he or she is just as likely to order a company search or Dun & Bradsteet report on you. Often I get enquiries about patents or intellectual property rights from business people through *Business Link* or an inventors' club who seem to think that I am a patent agent. I usually take their call to explain what barristers do in the course of which we discuss the law and their enquiry. During such conversations I usually ask them how they would fund litigation were their intellectual property right to be infringed. Many reply that they would seek a 'no win, no fee' deal or after-the-event insurance. US style contingency fee retainers where the lawyer shares the client's recovery are not permitted for litigation in this country and even if they were they would not be very attractive because there would remain the risk of paying the other side's costs. A type of 'no win, no fee' deal called a *'conditional fee agreement'* or 'CFA' is available here but there are very few intellectual property cases that are suitable for them. As for after-the-event insurance, underwriters will accept the risk only if they are advised by experienced counsel or solicitor-advocate that there is a very good prospect of success. Even then, the premium will be one third of the sum insured.

Impediments to litigation

Many circumstances can prevent the issue or prosecution of proceedings in England. A claim may be stayed if the parties have agreed to refer disputes to arbitration[1] or to the courts of some other country. It must be stayed if substantially the same dispute is already before the courts of some other EU state.[2] If the defendant is not within and has no substantial contacts

---

1   S.9 of the Arbitration Act 1996 (http://www.opsi.gov.uk/acts/acts1996/ukpga_19960023_en_2#pt1-pb3-l1g9)
2   Art 27 (1) of Council Regulation (EC) No 44/2001 of 22 December 2000 on jurisdiction and the recognition and enforcement of judgments in civil and commercial matters (OJ L 012 , 16/01/2001 P. 1 – 23 at http://eur-lex.europa. eu/LexUriServ/LexUriServ.do?uri= CELEX:32001R0044:EN:HTML) provides:

> Article 27:
>> 1. Where proceedings involving the same cause of action and between the same parties are brought in the courts of different Member States, any court other than the court first seised shall of its own motion stay its proceedings until such time as the jurisdiction of the court first seised is established.

with England or Wales, he or she may argue that the English courts do not[3] have or should not exercise[4] their jurisdiction to determine the dispute. Also, a defendant may be dead, bankrupt or under some other disability or, in the case of a company, in liquidation.

Initiating the claim

If after considering those questions the complainant still wishes to proceed he or she should write, or better still, instruct specialist solicitors or other authorized litigators to write, a *letter of claim* in accordance with para 4 of PD-Protocols[5] and the *Code of Practice for Pre-Action Conduct in Intellectual Property Dispute*[6] unless there are special reasons not to do so. Paragraph 2.2 of the code gives the following examples of circumstances where a departure from the code and Protocol would be justified:

- where it is reasonable for the claimant to apply for an interim injunction within a time scale or in a manner which does not reasonably allow full compliance with this code;
- where there is a reasonable and urgent need to issue proceedings to found jurisdiction;
- where the limitation period is about to expire;
- where a claim for unjustified threats might arise; or
- where it would clearly be unreasonable to expect a party to comply with the Code as a result of matters arising from the parties' previous dealings.

A decision to depart from the protocol should not be taken lightly because the court has extensive powers to penalize what it considers to be unreasonable behaviour by, for example, ordering a party to pay or forego costs or interest on damages.

Interim injunctions

The court will usually expect parties to act reasonably in exchanging information and documents relevant to the claim and generally in trying to avoid the necessity for the start of proceedings,[7] but there are circumstances in which it will countenance a departure from that course of conduct. Where, for example, there is reason to believe that a respondent will hide or destroy evidence or remove his or her assets from the reach of the courts as soon as he or she learns that a claim has been or is likely to be brought, the court will not require an applicant to warn the respondent of an application for an order to permit a search of the respondent's premises or restrictions on the use and movement of the respondent's assets. Similarly, the court will not expect an applicant to allow a respondent 28 days in which to respond to a request for undertakings if the applicant is likely to suffer irreparable damage during that time.

---

2. Where the jurisdiction of the court first seised is established, any court other than the court first seised shall decline jurisdiction in favour of that court.

3   CPR 11(1) (a) at http://www.justice.gov.uk/civil/procrules_fin/contents/parts/part11.htm.
4   CPR 11 (1) (b) Ibid.
5   See Chapter 9.
6   Ibid.
7   Para. 4.1 PD-Protocols (http://www.justice.gov.uk/civil/procrules_fin/contents/parts/part01.htm#rule1_1).

Founding jurisdiction

This exception requires more explanation than the others. Put simply, there are some disputes that can be contested in more than one legal system. In such cases, different parties may want to litigate in different forums. An intellectual property owner, for instance, is likely to favour a jurisdiction that disposes of disputes quickly while an alleged infringer would prefer the dispute to linger somewhere that processes cases more slowly. If essentially the same dispute is proceeding before the courts of different EU member states, art. 27 (2) of Council Regulation (EC) No 44/2001 requires the courts other than the one first seised to refuse to hear the case. It follows that if a party wants to make sure that a dispute will be litigated in England that party must issue in that country before the other side issues proceedings elsewhere. A table comparing patent litigation in England, France, Germany and the Netherlands appears in Chapter 8.

Move quickly

The danger of delay is illustrated by *Molins Plc v. G.D SpA*.[8] This was a dispute between an English patentee and its Italian licensee over the terms of a patent licence. The patentee claimed minimum royalties under the licence which the licensee refused to pay on the ground that the licence was voidable for misrepresentation or mistake. The following chronology is taken from the judgment of Mr. Justice Pumfrey:

> [2] The effect of Clause 5 of the agreement is that minimum royalties due under the licence agreement since 1994 have been of the order of £100,000-£150,000, G.D never having given notice to make the licence non-exclusive. In mid-1994, G.D requested that the 1994 royalty payment be deferred, and Molins agreed to this subject to the payment of an additional consideration of £30,000. In 1995, 1996 and 1997 no royalty payments were, it would seem, made by G.D, and a suggestion by Molins that a similar deferment of royalty to that which had taken place in 1994 (for a similar consideration) was not accepted. On 14th August 1998, Molins wrote to G.D formally requesting payment of the minimum royalties due under the agreement. After some correspondence which I have not seen, G.D wrote to Molins on 30th March 1999 in the following terms:
>
>> *'Further to our letter dated September 8th 1998 and the letter signed by Mr Chris Horton dated March 30th 1999, we have now been able to take legal advice on your request for payment of outstanding royalties under the above licence.*
>>
>> *As mentioned in our previous letters dated September 8th 1998 and June 11th 1997, we entered into the licence in reliance on representations by Molins plc that:*
>>
>>> *"(a) The patented invention covered by the licence disclosed the Rejection Device which enabled rejection of single cigarettes and so eliminated the need for a group expeller.*
>>>
>>> *(b) By using a device as patented, we would be able to develop a commercially marketable packing machine for which no group expeller would be required."*

---

8   [2000] EWHC Patents 170 (2 Feb 2000) (http://www.bailii.org/ew/cases/EWHC/Patents/2000/170.html.

It is now clear that these representations were untrue.

We understand from our lawyers that in these circumstances G.D S.p.A. is entitled to the rescission of the licence and to the refund of the royalties already paid under the licence.'

Without prejudice discussions took place at the offices of the English solicitors instructed by G.D, Linklaters.

[3] On 22nd June 1999, Molins' solicitors, Bristows, wrote a letter before action to Linklaters. On 30th June 1999, Linklaters replied to this letter saying that they would seek instructions, and on 6th July 1999 Bristows chased them for a reply. The reply from Linklaters on 7th July was that instructions were still awaited from G.D.

[4] On 13th July Bristows issued a claim form seeking payment of £523,600 and interest. The case as set out in the particulars of claim accompanying the claim form is that this sum is the total of the unpaid minimum royalties due and owing to Molins under the provisions of the agreement. On 13th July 1999, Bristows wrote to Linklaters informing them that the claim form had been issued and asking whether Linklaters had instructions to accept service in the United Kingdom, in order to avoid the expense of serving in Italy. The reply to this letter which is dated 15th July 1999 merely says that Linklaters are awaiting instructions, and on 21st July 1999 Linklaters wrote to Bristows saying that they had no instructions to accept service. Two days earlier, on 19th July 1999, G.D had issued proceedings in the civil court of Bologna against Molins seeking to terminate the agreement on the grounds that the agreement was invalid for a mistake under English law, and was entered into pursuant to a misrepresentation made by or on behalf of Molins, the misrepresentation in question being sufficient so it is alleged, to entitle G.D to rescind the agreement.

[5] By an application to the President of the Court in Bologna, G.D sought authorisation to serve the proceedings so issued on Molins by fax. The certified translation of this application is as follows:

'G.D SpA. (hereinafter, for the sake of brevity, referred to as "G.D") with its registered office located in Bologna, via Pomponia n. 10, in the person of its present legal representative, Mr Gian Carlo De Martis, acting in his capacity as Managing Director; represented and defended – according to the power of attorney attached hereto marginally – by the lawyers Gian Paolo di Santo from the Court of Milan and Pier Antonio Mareschi from the Court of Bologna; electively domiciled at the latter's office, located in Bologna, Via D'Azeglio n.21.

WHEREAS
– the aforesaid company intends to start legal proceedings against Molins plc – an English company having its registered office located in Blakelands, Milton Keynes – with the purpose of obtaining the rescission of a licence agreement entered into by the applicant and by Molins on 18th May 1992, which has finally turned out to be inevitably vitiated by a mistake, and to be therefore voidable;

– in spite of all the efforts repeatedly made by G.D in order to settle the controversy amicably, Molins has recently escaped any contact with the applicant;
– the judicial paper being examined is to be translated into English;
– specially during the holidays it would be extremely easy for Molins to try and prevent the execution of the service of process according to the methods provided for by the international Agreements;

All this stated, first
G.D, represented and defended as referred to herein in the caption,

Asks
for Your Excellency The Presiding Judge of this Court to authorise serving the writ of summons attached hereto in copy, together with the respective sworn translations into the English language, to Molins plc, 11 Tanners Drive, Blakelands, Milton Keynes, Buckinghamshire MK14 5LU, by faxing it to the latter company's fax number 0044-1908-218499.'

The application is dated 19th July 1999 and signed by the two lawyers. The authorisation is endorsed on the application in the following words:

"After having taken note of the above-stated request, the needed authorisation is hereby granted."

The authorization is dated 20th July 1999 and is signed by the Clerk of the Court and by the President.

[6] The fax transmission to Molins of the process thus authorised had, it would seem, been completed by about 4.00pm on 20th July 1999. Molins served the claim form on G.D on 3rd August 1999.'

The Italian licensee applied to Mr. Justice Pumfrey to stay the English proceedings on the ground that the Italian court was first seised of the dispute. Though making clear that he did so without any satisfaction[9], the judge found that he had no alternative but to stay the claim for unpaid minimum royalties. The court will not require a party to comply with the code or PD-Protocols if the consequence is to oust the jurisdiction of the English court.

Expiry of the limitation period

Most legal systems impose a time limit in which civil proceedings must be brought. That is usually called *'the limitation period'* and the legislation imposing such limits is called *'the statute of limitation period'*. Limitations vary considerably from country to country and often from claim to claim. The statute of limitations for England and Wales is the Limitation Act 1980. The Act provides a limitation period of 6 years from the date upon which the cause

---

9   He said at paragraph [34]: 'It is one of the objects of the Convention to prevent concurrent proceedings, and I do not think that to mark my disapproval of G.D's activities by refusing to accede to their application to stay these proceedings would be desirable. Accordingly I do not think that I should refuse this application for a stay on the grounds that the Italian proceedings are an abuse of process.'

of action accrues in the case of claims founded on tort which includes most intellectual property infringements[10] and contract.[11] However, there are a number of important exceptions including claims for slander of title, slander of goods or other malicious falsehood which must be brought within one year of accrual of the cause of action.[12] It goes without saying that no claimant will be expected to delay issuing proceedings where the claim is about to expire.

Unjustified threats

This topic was raised in my conference with Mr. Aardvark and Mr. Pepys in Chapter 1 and it will be explored in more detail later. Very briefly, intellectual property law in the UK differs from intellectual property law in most other countries and indeed other grounds of civil liability within the UK in that it can be actionable merely to threaten certain types of infringement proceedings if there is no justification for the threat. Provisions to that effect occur in the Patents,[13] Registered Designs,[14] Copyright Designs and Patents[15] and Trade Marks Acts[16] and in regulations implementing the Community design[17] and trade mark[18] regulations and Madrid Protocol[19] in the UK. Since a letter of claim could contain an actionable threat the court will expect modified adherence to the code and protocol to obviate that risk.

Previous dealings

In addition to matters already covered by one or more of the other exceptions, the court will not require rigid compliance with the code or protocol where there have already been extensive negotiations and the parties' positions are clear. A very good example is *Halifax Financial Services Ltd. v Intuitive Systems Ltd*,[20] where the court refused to enforce a complex dispute resolution protocol as there had already been lengthy correspondence between the parties. Another but very different situation which would be covered by this exception would be a domain name dispute where the parties will have agreed already to refer any dispute between them to expert determination under the UDRP, Nominet DRS or some other scheme.

---

10   Section 2. Time limit for actions founded on tort:
An action founded on tort shall not be brought after the expiration of six years from the date on which the cause of action accrued.
11   Section 5. Time limit for actions founded on simple contract:
An action founded on simple contract shall not be brought after the expiration of six years from the date on which the cause of action accrued.
12   S.4A Ibid.
13   S.70 Patents Act 1977 as amended.
14   S.26 Registered Designs Act 1949 as amended
15   S.253 of the Copyright, Designs and Patents Act 1988.
16   S.21 Trade Marks Act 1994.
17   Reg. 2 The Community Design Regulations 2005, SI 2005 No. 2339 at http://www.opsi.gov.uk/si/si2005/20052339.htm.
18   Reg. 6 of the Community Trade Mark Regulations 2006 (SI 2006 No. 1027) at http://www.opsi.gov.uk/si/si2006/20061027.htm.
19   Ref 4 of the Trade Marks (International Registrations) Order 1996 as amended by reg. 10 of The Trade Marks (International Registrations Designating the European Community, etc.) Regulations 2004 SI 2004 No. 2332 at http://www.opsi.gov.uk/si/si2004/20042332.htm.
20   [1999]1 All ER 664 at http://www.cedr.co.uk/library/edr_law/Halifax_financial_services.pdf.

Letter of claim

A letter of claim is what Americans call a *'cease and desist'* letter. English lawyers used to call them *'letters before action'* before the CPR[21] came into force. Though the main reason for sending such letters is that the courts expect them to be sent and may penalize complainants who fail to comply with that requirement, there is also the incentive to do so in that a comprehensive, reasoned and well documented letter offers the best opportunity to persuade the other side to accept the claim and so resolve the case quickly and with minimal cost. Letters of claim are therefore very important documents and very great care should be taken in drafting them. That is one of the reasons why it is always wise to instruct a specialist solicitor or other authorized litigator or specialist counsel for this kind of work. Such a specialist will be alert to the groundless threats provisions of the patents, designs and trade mark legislation mentioned above and he or she will make sure that the case is presented in a compelling but not overbearing manner.

Letters of claim should never be regarded as a prelude to inevitable litigation. [22] They should give sufficient details to enable the other side to understand and investigate the claim without extensive requests for further information. [23] At the very least that should:

- indentify the claimant,[24]
- state the remedies that he or she seeks,[25] and
- provide details of any funding arrangements such as a CFA or after-the-event insurance that the claimant may have entered into.[26]

If, for instance, patent infringement is alleged, the letter should identify the activities complained of. It should specify the claims[27] and state why the other side has infringed, or appears about to infringe them.[28] The letter should enclose copies of any essential documents relied upon [29] such as the patent specification and evidence of infringing use such as a photograph, drawing, brochure or description of an offending product.[30]

The letter should request prompt acknowledgement to be followed by a full written response within a reasonable period.[31] *PD-Protocols* suggests one month for most claims[32] and the *Code of Practice for Pre-Action Conduct in Intellectual Property Disputes* 14 days.[33] A complainant should state whether court proceedings will be issued if the full response is not received within the stated period.[34] If the complainant needs any documents in the other side's possession, the letter should identify them and ask for copies.[35] If the complainant is willing to enter into mediation or another alternative method of dispute resolution, you should say so.[36] The letter should state that it follows the practice direction and code and that any reply should

---

21   http://www.justice.gov.uk/civil/procrules_fin/index.htm.
22   Para 4.2 PD-Protocols.
23   Para 4.3 (a) PD-Protocols.
24   Para 3.2 (c) Code.
25   Para 3.2 (d) Code.
26   Para 3.2 (e) Code.
27   Para 3.2D (j) Code.
28   Para 3.2D (i) Code.
29   Para 4.3 (b) PD-Protocols.
30   Para 3.2D (f) Code.
31   Para 4.3 (c) PD-Protocols.
32   Ibid.
33   Para 4.1 Code.
34   Para 4.3 (d) PD-Protocols.
35   Para 4.3 (e) PD-Protocols.
36   Para 4.3 (f) PD-Protocols.

also do so. [37] It should draw attention to the court's powers to impose sanctions for failure to comply with PD-Protocol.[38] Unless the complainant knows that the other side has instructed a solicitor or other professional intermediary, the letter should enclose copies of the practice direction [39] and code. [40] A draft letter of claim appears in the *Appendix*.

The response

Turning now to the respondent, how should he or she respond to such a *letter of claim*? The decision is easier to make than it was before the CPR came into force in April 1999 because claims made after that date are much less likely to be frivolous. In those days, letters before action tended to be peremptory and even provocative and were often sent before the claim had been investigated properly. Although there are still some litigants who push their luck, the culture has changed. The amount of work necessary to prepare a letter of claim in accordance with the PD-Protocols and code requires a considerable upfront investment from the claimant. It is not likely to incur those costs unless it believes that it will recover them from the other side.

If a respondent is advised that he or she will have to settle the claim eventually, the time specified in the *letter of claim* for a reply is likely to be his or her best opportunity to get out of the dispute with minimum cost and delay. Once a claim is issued costs start rising remorselessly as on a taxi meter. If, on the other hand, the respondent genuinely believes that he or she is in the right, a courteous, reasoned, well documented and perhaps sympathetic and co-operative *response* is the best opportunity to persuade the other side that it is wrong and to give it an opportunity to back down gracefully. Whatever the decision, the reply should be clear, courteous and concise. If the respondent's case is weak, a party that has spent many thousands of pounds investigating a claim is unlikely to be impressed by defiance and bluster. If the respondent is in the right, the objective must be to persuade the other side that it is in its interests to withdraw. An aggressive or cantankerous response is hardly likely to help.

If the justice of the other side's case is clear, if it has the will and resources to go to trial and if the respondent can afford to settle, then it is probably in the respondent's interests to admit the claim and pay the amount due without more ado. If the respondent concedes the justice of the case but cannot afford to settle in full, it is usually better to negotiate time than lodge a defence that everybody knows to be hopeless. It is now possible to offer to settle a money claim without depositing the full sum in court.[41] If the court considers that the offer was reasonable and that the claimant should have accepted it, it may disallow some of the claimant's costs or even order the claimant to pay any costs that may accrue from 21 days after the communication of the offer.[42] If the respondent concedes at least part of the claim he or she should set out any undertakings that he or she is prepared to give[43] and any compensation that he or she is prepared to pay together with an explanation as to how that sum has been computed. [44]

---

37   Para 3.2 (a) Code.
38   Para 4.3 (g) PD-Protocols.
39   Para 4.3 (g) PD-Protocols.
40   Para 3.2 (b) Code.
41   CPR Part 36 at http://www.justice.gov.uk/civil/procrules_fin/contents/parts/part36.htm#rule36_2.
42   CPR 36.14 at http://www.justice.gov.uk/civil/procrules_fin/contents/parts/part36.htm#rule36_14.
43   Para 4.2 (b) of the Code.
44   Para 4.2 (c) of the Code.

If the respondent decides to contest part or the whole of the claim, the response should state which part is accepted and which is denied.[45] The response should therefore give detailed reasons why a claim is not accepted. The letter should enclose copies of any important documents upon which the respondent relies.[46] For instance, if he or she contends that the complainant's patent was obvious having regard to the prior art or indeed anticipated the letter should give full details of the publications or other evidence relied upon.[47] Similarly, if a respondent disputes that a work has been copied, the response should explain any objective similarities between the alleged copy and the copyright owner's.[48] The response should also enclose copies of any documents requested by the claimant wherever possible. If it is not possible, the response must explain why the documents are not enclosed. If a respondent needs any documents from the other side, he or she should ask for them in the letter.[49] If a respondent has a counterclaim he or she should set it out giving the same details as would be required of a complainant.[50] The response must also give details of any insurance or other funding arrangements that may have been made.[51] If the other side has offered mediation or some other alternative method of dispute resolution the letter must state whether or not the offer is accepted and, if not, it must explain why it has not been accepted.[52] A draft letter of response also appears in the *Appendix*.

Breaking the deadlock

The imperatives of avoiding litigation if at all possible and resolving the dispute with minimal cost and delay should always be at the forefront of the minds of both parties. Accordingly, not even a comprehensive denial of a party's case should necessarily lead to litigation. An exchange of well reasoned letters and evidence between competent and experienced litigators should identify the points of dispute and possibly even point to the solution. If, for instance, the outcome of a dispute hangs on a point of law, the construction of a patent claim or other complex issue, the solution may lie in referring the matter for expert neutral evaluation by experienced specialist counsel, a retired or even serving judge under Section G2 of the *Admiralty and Commercial Court Guide*.[53] Similarly, if face to face negotiations prove fruitless, the logjam may be broken by the intervention of an experienced mediator. Expert neutral evaluation, mediation and other forms of alternative dispute resolution will be discussed in the following chapters. If the parties are still in dispute after all other means of resolution have been tried litigation remains as a last resort.

---

45   Para 4.6 (a) PD-Protocols.
46   Para 4.6 (b) PD-Protocols.
47   Para 4.2D (h) Code.
48   Para 4.2B (h) Code.
49   Para 4.6 (c) PD-Protocols.
50   Para 4.2 (f) Code.
51   Para 4.2 (g) Code.
52   Para 4.6 (d) PD-Protocols.
53   http://www.hmcourts-service.gov.uk/docs/admiralcomm/Commercial%20Court%20Guide%20December%202 006%20rev1%20rh%20clean.pdf.

7 *What Happens if Neither Side Gives in*

Overview

There are really only two ways of resolving disputes. The parties can negotiate terms of settlement (*'negotiation'*) or a third party can determine them (*'adjudication'*). Mediation looks a lot like a hybrid or *'third way'*[1] because of the involvement of the third party but the role of that third party is quite different from that of a judge, arbitrator, expert panellist or other adjudicator. In mediation, the neutral guides the parties towards settlement, chairing joint discussions, discussing the issues from every angle with each side individually, raising and testing possible solutions and generally facilitating agreement. Mediation can therefore be considered as a refinement of negotiation.

Negotiation

This is a consensual process with four possible outcomes. The first is that the claimant drops some or all of its demands. The second is that the respondent gives in to such demands. The third is that each side trades advantages for concessions from either side until they reach a compromise. The fourth is that they develop a solution that had not been in the contemplation of either side. In their well-known book, *Getting to Yes: Negotiating Agreement without Giving in,*[2] Roger Fisher and William Ury of Harvard Law School drew a distinction between *'positional negotiation'* and *'principled negotiation'*. Positional negotiation is where the parties make demands and trade concessions. By contrast, principled negotiation is looking for solutions based on shared interests. It involves separating people from problems, focussing on interests rather than positions, inventing options for mutual gain and insisting on objective criteria. Positional negotiation generates the first three outcomes but not the fourth. Principled negotiation sometimes brings forth the fourth outcome as well as one of the other three. In everyday life, some bargains can only be struck by accepting the terms of the other party in full while others can develop through offer and counter-offer. A bus fare is a trite example of the first category. Negotiating the price of a house is a commonplace example of the second. Much the same is true of litigation. The paper setting out HM Revenue & Customs litigation policy observes:

> *Some disputes have an all-or-nothing character, involving a single point of law that would be decided one way or the other by the courts, with no middle ground. Such disputes should be settled on all-or-nothing terms.*[3]

---

1   The Wikipedia article on 'the third way' describes it as 'a centrist political philosophy of governance that embraces a mix of market and interventionist philosophies. The Third Way rejects both socialism and laissez-faire approaches to economic governance, but chiefly stresses technological development, education, and competitive mechanisms to pursue economic progress and governmental objectives.' (See http://en.wikipedia.org/wiki/Third_Way_(centrism)#_note-2.)

2   The current edition which includes input from Bruce Patton was published in 1994 by Houghton Mifflin Books ISBN 0395631246.

3   Para 14 of HMRC 'Litigation and Settlement Strategy' (http://www.hmrc.gov.uk/practitioners/lss.pdf).

Officials are advised not to split the difference or offer any discount for an agreement not to litigate but also not to seek 'low value settlements' in cases where HMRC are not prepared to litigate.[4]

However, most disputes are amenable to settlement through principled negotiation. The techniques through which that may be achieved will be discussed further in the chapter on mediation.

Adjudication

The rest of this chapter deals with adjudication whether by judges, administrative tribunals, arbitrators or otherwise. Adjudicators decide cases by applying *law* to *facts* in accordance with an agreed or otherwise pre-determined *procedure*. This can best be illustrated by an example. Suppose the composer of a piece of music complains that he has lost revenue from sales of copies of his work because someone has printed and distributed copies of a very similar work without his consent. The UK Copyright, Designs and Patents Act 1988 confers upon the owner of copyright in a work in which copyright subsists the exclusive right to copy that work and distribute those copies in the UK.[5] That right is infringed by doing or authorizing any of those things in the UK without the owner's consent.[6] If that right is infringed, the owner can claim damages, injunctions or other relief for such infringement from a court.[7] The job of the court is to determine whether the circumstances for the grant of those remedies apply. To do that job it needs to make findings of fact such as whether and to what extent the complainant's work was original, whether the complainant was a citizen or resident of the UK or of some other country whose works are protected, whether the work was copied and do forth. Often such facts are admitted or at least not disputed. If nothing is disputed the court can usually grant a remedy without more ado. Where a fact is disputed, the court has to listen to, and evaluate, the testimony of witnesses. Where one side contradicts the other, the contradiction may be resolved by a document such as a mobile phone record or a letter or even some physical phenomenon which tends to support one party's account, such as paper containing a fragment of the alleged copy that has been jammed in a printer. The finder of fact – in this case a judge – has to weigh up those indications and come to a conclusion as to which side is more likely to be right on each point at issue. Having drawn those conclusions the judge applies the law.

Evidence

Indicators as to what has happened such as the testimony of witnesses and documents are known as '*evidence*'. In most cases there are four types of evidence:

1. Oral Testimony: statements of witnesses to an event as to what they saw, heard, did or otherwise experienced;
2. Documents: records of information of all kinds in any medium including letters, bookkeeping entries, photographs, emails and even SMS texts;

---

4   Ibid.
5   S.16 (1) Copyright, Designs and Patents Act 1988 (see http://www.ipo.gov.uk/cdpact1988.pdf).
6   S.16 (2) Ibid.
7   S.08 (2) Ibid.

3. Material Evidence: physical objects such as an item of machinery and merchandise; and
4. Expert Evidence: the findings or opinions of experts.

Not all evidence can be relied upon or given equal weight. Witnesses may be confused, mistaken, forgetful or even mendacious. Documents that appear to relate to one matter may turn out to relate to quite another. Some documents may even be forged. That is also true of material evidence. There may be more than one school of thought on a particular topic. Some experts may be better than others as practitioners of their discipline. In common law countries like England and Wales, evidence may be tested for clarity, comprehensiveness, consistency and credibility by questions from the opposing party known as *'cross-examination'*. Cross-examination, as every young barrister is told by more experienced counsel, does not mean examining crossly. The adjective 'cross' used to refer to the relative positions in the court room of the witness and advocate not to the mood of the cross-examiner. A view on the credibility of a witness can be gained from his or her demeanour in the witness box, the consistency of his or her answers under cross-examination with earlier statements or with information derived from documents that were made before the action began. Often such view governs the conclusion that the court reaches on a disputed fact.

Court procedure in England and Wales

To minimize the risk of reaching a false conclusion on incomplete or unreliable evidence or wasting time and resources on unproductive enquiry, most courts and tribunals have a procedure for the production, exchange and evaluation of evidence. In England and Wales the process starts with the exchange of *'statements of case'*. These set out the facts that each side intends to prove, accept or dispute thereby identifying the factual issues in dispute. The next stage is for each side to draw up and exchange lists of documents relating to the disputed issues which are or have been in its possession or otherwise available to it. This process is called *'disclosure'*. Each party has a right to inspect or request copies of the documents on the other side's list. The inspection or delivery of copies of the other side's documents is called *'inspection'*. The third stage is the exchange of statements of the witnesses that each party intends to call. These statements are verified by an attestation known as a *'statement of truth'* in the following form:

'I believe that the facts stated in this witness statement are true.'[8]

Knowingly making a false statement may be a contempt of court.[9] Such statements may be verified on oath or affirmation and tested by cross-examination at trial. If one party or the other intends to call an expert witness such expert must set out his or her evidence in writing. The written testimony of an expert witness is known as *'an expert's report'*. Experts' reports are usually exchanged at the same time as or shortly after the exchange of witness statements. The process by which evidence is tested and evaluated is known as a *'trial'* in England.[10] Shortly before the trial, the parties paginate, index and copy bundles of the documents that are most likely to be read or referred to by the court and exchange written summaries of their submissions

---

8   Para 2.2 of PD-Part 22 at http://www.justice.gov.uk/civil/procrules_fin/contents/practice_directions/pd_part22.htm#IDAACDKD.
9   CPR 32.14 at http://www.justice.gov.uk/civil/procrules_fin/contents/parts/part32.htm#rule32_14.
10   In Scotland the equivalent procedure is called a 'proof'.

known as '*skeleton arguments*'. Courts in England and Wales sit to hear witnesses and argument between 10:30 and 16:15 with an hour's adjournment for lunch at 13:00 every working day of the year. Extempore judgments may be delivered immediately after a hearing but nowadays judges tend to set out their decisions with reason in writing. If a court finds in favour of the defendant the case is dismissed. If it finds in favour of the claimant it will consider the remedy. Parties who are dissatisfied with a decision may apply for permission to appeal. If permission is refused they may renew their appeal to the court of appeal. If permission is granted the appeal court will review the decision of the court below and consider the evidence and arguments on which it was based. If they disagree with it they may substitute their own order or remit the case possibly with guidance or instructions to the court below.

OTHER TRIBUNALS IN THE UK

A similar procedure albeit with some modifications is followed by administrative tribunals in the United Kingdom such as hearings before officers appointed by the Chief Executive of the Intellectual Property Office and the Copyright Tribunal. Parties exchange statements of case, witness statements and skeleton arguments but disclosure and cross-examination are usually limited or dispensed with altogether. Where the parties' cases can be presented adequately in writing an oral hearing can be avoided altogether. Arbitrators also proceed in much the same way in the United Kingdom though there are wide variations in rules and practice between arbitral forums and indeed between individual arbitrators. Some proceedings take place entirely on paper with a minimum of formality while others resemble the civil courts in almost every detail. So, too, do some ADR procedures such as domain name dispute resolution proceedings before expert panellists appointed under the Nominet Dispute Resolution Service Policy.[11] Procedural fairness requires each party to be given an opportunity to be heard and to make submissions and to produce evidence in support of his or her case.

Other countries

Courts and administrative and arbitral tribunals in other English speaking countries follow similar procedures though they may retain the terminology that used to be used in England before the Civil Procedure Rules. For instance, 'statements of case' are still called '*pleadings*' and 'disclosure' is still known as '*discovery*'. Discovery in the USA tends to be more extensive than in England and there are often wide-ranging pre-trial hearings where witnesses are cross-examined under oath and recorded in documents in a process known as '*taking depositions*'.[12] US lawyers also make extensive written submissions known as '*briefs*' which tend to be longer and more detailed than English skeleton arguments. The fact finding procedure of civil law countries is very different though there are similar notions of procedural fairness. The investigation is led by the court rather than by the parties. Judges identify the issues in dispute and direct the production of evidence. Parties' legal representatives assist the process by making supplementary evidence available to the court or tribunal and offering written and oral submissions on the materials but they do not direct the process in the way that parties' legal representatives do in common law countries.

11　　http://www.nominet.org.uk/disputes/drs/policy/?contentId=3069.
12　　Rule 30 Federal Rules of Civil Procedure at http://www.law.cornell.edu/rules/frcp/Rule30.htm.

Implementing remedies

The remedies usually sought in intellectual property infringement claims were listed in Chapter 4. They include declarations, injunctions, damages or accounts of profit and costs. Declarations, being determinations of the rights and obligations of the parties, do not require implementation but the other remedies do. Disobedience to an injunction is a contempt of court punishable in England and other common law jurisdictions by fine, imprisonment, seizure of assets or other sanctions and in civil law countries by a financial penalty known as an *'astreinte'* which is fixed when the order is made and levied automatically until the order is complied with.[13] Awards of damages, accounts and costs require one party to pay another. Such payments can be compelled if not made voluntarily. For instance, an order to pay money can be enforced in England by:

- *'execution'* – seizing and realizing some or all of the debtor's goods;
- *'attaching earnings'* – stopping money from the debtor's pay;
- *'third party debt orders'* – freezing funds in a debtor's bank account or other moneys due to the debtor;
- *'charging order'* – securing payment of the debt by charging the defendant's real property with a compulsory mortgage; and
- *'insolvency'* – taking possession of, and realizing, the debtor's property and distributing the proceeds fairly among his or her creditors.

The European Judicial Network pages on the EU website contain detailed information on the methods of enforcing judgment which are available in each of the EU member states.[14]

Interim injunctions

Chapter 4 referred to *'interim'* as well as *'perpetual'* injunctions and observed that a court will grant an interim injunction 'if it believes that a party could suffer irreparable harm before it has completed its processes'. An example of the circumstances in which a court might grant an interim injunction is where the expected market appeal of a product that is said to be protected by an intellectual property right is very much shorter than the interval between issue of the claim form and trial, and the defendant would be unlikely to compensate the claimant adequately for damage to its rights, either because the nature and extent of such damage would be impossible to calculate or because the defendant would be unable to afford such compensation. Decisions on whether or not to grant an interim injunction have to be made very quickly and on incomplete materials. The principles developed by the English courts[15] are as follows:

1. An applicant for an interim injunction has to satisfy the court that he or she *can* win the case at trial. It is no longer necessary in England and Wales to show that the applicant is likely to win, though, obviously, the stronger the claim the more likely it is that the courts

---

13   L'astreinte est une mesure de nature à assurer l'exécution d'une décision de justice ayant condamné une partie à faire ou à ne pas faire quelque chose. Elle consiste à devoir payer une certaine somme d'argent en cas de retard par la partie condamnée dans l'exécution de la condamnation. (see Wikipedia at http://fr.wikipedia.org/wiki/Astreinte). The European Commission works in this way when it levies a fine of so many euros per day for non-compliance with one of its orders.
14   See 'Enforcement of Judgements – General Information' European Judicial Network in civil and commercial affairs at http://ec.europa.eu/civiljustice/enforce_judgement/enforce_judgement_gen_en.htm.
15   See *American Cyanamid Co v. Ethicon Ltd* [1975] AC 396 HL(E) at http://www.justis.com/titles/iclr_s7540015.html.

will want to help. Some courts require a good *prima facie* case. That is not the standard for England and Wales. If the claim is clearly hopeless the application fails. If not, the court considers the next question.

2. The court considers whether the applicant could be compensated adequately in damages were the claim to succeed. If the court believes that the nature and extent of the loss can be assessed accurately from records that the defendant is likely to keep and that the damages likely to be awarded are within the respondent's means, the application will fail. If not, the court proceeds to the next question.

3. The court considers whether the respondent will be injured irrevocably should the claim fail after an interim injunction has been granted. Interim injunctions are always conditional upon a promise by the applicant to compensate the respondent for any loss or damage that he or she may suffer as a result of the order should the court subsequently decide that the injunction should never have been made. Such a promise is known as *'a cross undertaking as to damages'* and as it can be very onerous it is not to be offered lightly. If the court believes that the respondent could be compensated adequately by the applicant on his cross-undertaking as to damages it will incline towards granting an injunction unless there is a good reason why it should not do so. These are matters that are considered in the final stage.

4. The last stage is to weigh all relevant factors such as the conduct of the parties, whether there has been appreciable delay and which decision would be more likely to avoid injustice. As the dialogue in Chapter 1 illustrates, the failure of a party to apply for an injunction at the earliest possible moment can be fatal for all sorts of reasons. One reason is that if an applicant can live with an infringement for a few weeks while he or his solicitor takes a holiday, the court will ask itself why he cannot put up with it until trial. Another reason is that the alleged infringer may have invested time, money and effort into making or marketing the allegedly infringing article and he or she would suffer hardship were an injunction to be granted. This weighing of such factors is sometimes called *'the balance of convenience'*. It is an exercise in judicial discretion which appellate courts are very reluctant to second guess.

Because perpetual injunctions are granted after the rights and obligations of the parties have been determined they can be broad and general. For instance, once the court has found that copyright subsists in a certain work and the defendant has infringed it, the judge will simply order the defendant not to infringe the claimant's copyrights. Such an order would cover not just the infringing acts that provoked the litigation such as copying a particular work and selling the copies but also acts that the defendant has not yet done. Protection would also extend to all the claimant's copyrights including those in works the copyright owner has yet to create for so long as those copyrights subsist. By contrast, interim injunctions have to be much more limited in scope because they are granted before the parties' rights and obligations have been established. A typical order would be:

'.... the Defendant is restrained until judgment or further order in the meantime from doing or authorizing the following acts:

> (a) *making the game or puzzle known as "Maize Maze" photographs of which are annexed to this Order ("the Maize Maze");*
> (b) *advertising the Maize Maze or offering it for sale;*
> (c) *stocking the Maize Maze ....'*

The cross-undertaking as to damages is also extracted until trial. Either party may apply to the court to be relieved from some or all of its obligations at any time if it believes that circumstances have changed since the order was made. More information on the procedure is available below.

Search Orders and Freezing Injunctions

It will be remembered from the dialogue in the first chapter that my instructing solicitor, Mr. Samuel Pepys and his client, Mr. Aardvark, came to see me about getting an *'Anton Piller Order'* in order to close down one of Mr. Aardvark's competitors. When I asked him why he wanted to do that Mr. Pepys replied:

> *'Because it would force them to let me and members of my staff into their offices and search their computers and filing cabinets. Possibly even their homes and cars. It holes them up in their offices for hours preventing them from talking to anybody else, except perhaps their solicitor so long as they are quick about it. Since solicitors with experience of these orders tend to be few and far between it will cost them a pretty penny to take legal advice. So we can knock the stuffing out of them before they have even started.'*

Mr. Pepys continued that it would be even better if we could combine the *Anton Piller* with a *Mareva orde*r because such an order would prevent the other side from transferring funds abroad or even spending it on anything other than legal advice and day to day necessaries and he was about to add that as lawyers cost money the other side would quickly exhaust their resources. *Anton Piller* and *Mareva* orders (or search orders and freezing injunctions as they are now called) certainly had the effect of quickly bringing competitors to their knees but that was never the courts' intention when they began to grant those orders. Search orders are supposed to preserve vital documentary or other evidence that would otherwise have been hidden or destroyed by an unscrupulous defendant on learning that he was being or was about to be sued. Similarly, freezing injunctions are intended to keep within the power of the court sufficient assets to satisfy a judgment, if they would otherwise have been removed or just spent by such a defendant. Both orders are at the extreme of the courts' jurisdiction and numerous safeguards have been introduced to prevent abuse. Those safeguards, including in particular the appointment of an independent supervising solicitor for search orders, make such orders extremely expensive but they are still used frequently as they remain an important tool for the enforcement of intellectual property rights. Again, more information on the procedure is available below.

Security for costs

In England and Wales as in most countries the unsuccessful party usually pays or contributes towards the successful party's costs. If a wealthy defendant believes that the claimant cannot afford to pay his costs if he wins, he may be inclined to settle a less than meritorious claim for more than it is worth. A safeguard against such pressure is to require certain types of claimant to secure payment of the defendant's costs. Such security can take any form that is satisfactory to the defendant or the court and usually takes the form of a deposit of funds into court or other bank account or a bond by a financial institution, director or other third party. If a claimant fails to give such security within the period agreed by the parties or ordered by the court, the claim will be stayed. The usual reason for seeking security for costs is that the claimant is a company or other body and there is reason to believe that it will be unable to pay the defendant's costs if ordered to do so[16] but there a number of other claimants against whom such an order may be made.[17]

Weeding out non-starters

In Chapter 4 I referred to some research by the government's own high level advisory committee on intellectual property which showed that the average cost of a patent infringement claim in England is £1 million if brought in the High Court and between £150,000 and £250,000 if brought in the Patents County Court.[18] In Chapter 5 I wrote that one of the reasons for introducing the CPR was to make the cost of litigation more affordable, more predictable, and more proportionate to the value and complexity of individual cases.[19] Courts in England and Wales now have 'the overriding objective of enabling the court to deal with cases justly'[20] which connotes:

'(b)   saving expense;

(c)   dealing with the case in ways which are proportionate –
       (i)   to the amount of money involved;
       (ii)   to the importance of the case;
       (iii) to the complexity of the issues; and
       (iv)   to the financial position of each party;

(d)   ensuring that it is dealt with expeditiously and fairly.'[21]

The court is required to seek to give effect to the overriding objective by 'actively managing cases'.[22] Active case management includes identifying issues at an early stage[23] and deciding promptly which issues need full investigation and trial and accordingly disposing summarily of the others.[24]

---

16   CPR 25.13 (2) (c) at http://www.justice.gov.uk/civil/procrules_fin/contents/parts/part25.htm#rule25_13.
17   CPR 25.13 (2) lists the following:
      (a) the claimant is –
          (i) resident out of the jurisdiction; but
          (ii) not resident in a Brussels Contracting State, a Lugano Contracting State or a Regulation State, as defined in
              section 1(3) of the Civil Jurisdiction and Judgments Act 1982 (7); ...
      (d) the claimant has changed his address since the claim was commenced with a view to evading the consequences
      of the litigation;
      (e) the claimant failed to give his address in the claim form, or gave an incorrect address in that form;
      (f) the claimant is acting as a nominal claimant, other than as a representative claimant under Part 19, and there
      is reason to believe that he will be unable to pay the defendant's costs if ordered to do so;
      (g) the claimant has taken steps in relation to his assets that would make it difficult to enforce an order for costs
      against him.
18   IPAC 'The Enforcement of Patent Rights' November 2003 which may be downloaded from Mandy Haberman's
website at http://www.mandyhaberman.com/media/IPAC-18-11.pdf.
19   See para. 9 of the 'Overview' of Lord Woolf's final report at http://www.dca.gov.uk/civil/final/overview.htm.
20   CPR 1.1 (1).
21   http://www.justice.gov.uk/civil/procrules_fin/contents/parts/part01.htm#rule1_1.
22   CPR 1.4 (1).
23   CPR 1.4 (2) (b).
24   CPR 1.4 (2) (c).

The court has two powers to implement that obligation. First, it may *strike out* a statement of case that discloses no reasonable grounds for bringing or defending the claim,[25] constitutes an abuse of the court's process or is otherwise likely to obstruct the just disposal of the proceedings.[26] If the defect in the statement of case can be cured by amending or replacing the defective statement of case, the strike-out may not be fatal. The party whose statement of case is struck out may be allowed to carry on provided he or she corrects the defect and pays any costs that may be awarded. If, on the other hand, the claim or defence is hopelessly flawed because it is wrong in law or because it is frivolous, vexatious or otherwise wrong to let it continue, the claim or defence may be struck out altogether. Secondly, the court may summarily give judgment without a full trial where it considers that the claimant or, as the case may be, defendant has no real prospect of succeeding on the claim or issue and there is no other compelling reason why the case or issue should go to trial.[27]

---

25   CPR 3.4 (2) (a) at http://www.justice.gov.uk/civil/procrules_fin/contents/parts/part03.htm#rule3_4.
26   CPR 3.4 (2) (b) Ibid.
27   CPR 24.2 at http://www.justice.gov.uk/civil/procrules_fin/contents/parts/part24.htm#rule24_2.

8 *How to Prepare Your Case*

Introduction

There is a widely held view that cases are won and lost by counsels' eloquence. As a barrister I suppose I have an interest in encouraging that belief but the truth is that far more cases are won through careful preparation than compelling oratory. As often as not cases are won or lost well before anyone enters the court room. Advocates have to do the best with the briefs they are given. If the evidence they require is not there or does not stand up to judicial scrutiny, there is a limit to what they can do.

The starting point

Ideally, preparation should start long before any dispute arises. The optimum legal protection for the brand, product, process or other advantage in which the business wishes to invest should be identified and obtained. This is not necessarily the most extensive type of protection. A 20-year patent, for example, is quite unnecessary for a product with a shelf-life of a few years. Legal protection must extend to the countries where the product is likely to be sold in significant quantities as well as in the countries in which it is to be made. Once legal protection is in place, sufficient funding should be available to enforce such protection. A large business or institution should be able to afford litigation. A smaller business is likely to require specialist intellectual property insurance. Funding is crucial because far more cases fail for lack of money than for lack of merit. It is sometimes possible to secure after-the-event cover or legal representation under a conditional fee agreement but lawyers and insurers will take such risks only in the strongest possible cases. Finally, the market should be monitored closely so that actual and potential challenges can be detected early. A patent or trade mark watch service should be considered. Staff should be trained to look out for tell tale signs of infringing activities such as a sudden and unexplained drop in demand for a previously successful product or communications about products that have nothing to do with your business. These must be reported, investigated and documented since they will constitute the basis of any claim.

Choosing the right jurisdiction

'*Jurisdiction*' can refer to a national or regional legal system or to a court or tribunal within a legal system. Both can be important to the success of your case. The first topic has already been considered in Chapter 6. Table 8.1 compares patent litigation in England and three of its civil law neighbours.

Table 8.1   Patent litigation: Comparative table

Source: IPAC (Intellectual Property Advisory Committee) 'The Enforcement of Patent Rights' (Nov 2003).

Jurisdiction	England and Wales	France	Germany	The Netherlands
Average cost of an action per party (£)*	Patents Court: 1,000,000 Patents County Court: 150–250,000	20,700–34,500	Typically 17,250–34,500	Summary proceedings: 6,900 Simple action: 27,500
Average Length of Trial or Dispositive Hearing	1–5 days	2 hours	1 day	½ day
Typical Representation	Patents Court: 5 (leading and junior advocates, senior and assistant litigator and one patent attorney Patents County Court: 2–3 (advocate, litigator and/or patent attorney)	1 lawyer and/or 1 patent attorney	1 lawyer and/or 1 patent attorney	1 lawyer and/or 1 patent attorney
Disclosure and inspection of documents	Automatic	Only when ordered by the court	Only when ordered by the court	Only when ordered by the court
Injunctions	Available in appropriate cases	Available in appropriate cases	Available in appropriate cases	Available in appropriate cases
Time to Trial	Patents Court: 9 to 15 months Patents County Court: 8 months	Fast Track: 2–3 months First Instance: 12–18 months	District Court: 9–18 moths Federal Patents Court (Validity Action): 2–3 years	Full procedure: 12–18 months Accelerated procedure: 10–12 months Summary procedure: 1 day to 2–3 months
Specialist Tribunal	Yes	Paris only	Yes in principal district courts of Dusseldorf, Mannheim and Munich and also in Federal Patents Court	Yes
Availability of Costs	Loser contributes about 75 per cent of successful party's expenses	No	Loser pays costs on a fixed scale of roughly 5 per cent of value of claim	Loser pays court fees of between £1,400–7,000

*   Computed at the rate of £1,00 = €1.43

If you decide to litigate in the UK you may have a choice of tribunals. Generally, the courts have exclusive jurisdiction in infringement and threats actions and Intellectual Property Office hearing officers have exclusive jurisdiction in disputes over pre-grant such as appeals form examiners[1] and oppositions to trade mark applications[2]. Courts and hearing officers share jurisdiction over a whole range of other disputes such as whether or not a product or process would infringe a patent[3] and the invalidity[4] and revocation of registered trade marks.[5] In England and Wales, court proceedings relating to patents, registered designs, registered Community designs and semiconductor topographies must be launched in the Patents or Patents County Court.[6] All other intellectual property[7] proceedings must be brought in the Chancery Division of the High Court or the Central London, Preston, Mold, Manchester, Liverpool, Leeds, Newcastle, Birmingham, Bristol, Cardiff or Caernarfon County Courts.[8]

Statement of case

Perhaps the most important documents in a case are the *'statements of case'* or *'pleadings'*. These were mentioned briefly above. The reason why they are important is that they set out each party's case. They identify the facts that each party intends to prove or dispute at trial as well as the legal principles that he or she intends to invoke. Very great care must be taken in preparing them because a party can call evidence only on the facts that appear in his or her statement of case. For that reason they should be settled or drafted by the advocate who is likely to present the case. Those facts must contain all the ingredients for a successful action. If they do not, the statement of case may be struck out and judgment given to the other side. The practice is to *plead* (that is to say, write) the facts in numbered paragraphs with supplementary paragraphs known as 'particulars' for points that require detail such as the circumstances in which a contract was made or the similarities between a copyright work and an alleged copy. A claimant's statement of case usually concludes with the words 'AND THE CLAIMANT CLAIMS' followed by the specific relief sought such as an injunction, damages, an account of profits, costs or other relief as the case may be. Such conclusion is known as 'the prayer'. A defendant's statement of case must identify the paragraphs that he or she knows to be true[9] as well as those that he or she believes to be untrue[10] and those that the defendant can neither accept nor deny but requires the claimant to prove.[11] It is conventional to respond to each numbered paragraph of the particulars of claim with a parallel numbered paragraph admitting, denying or not admitting the claim. If the defendant has a defence that raises a point not covered by the particulars of claim, he or she should plead it in the defence.

---

1   Under S.8 and S.12 Patents Act 1977.
2   S.27 (1) Ibid.
3   S.71 Patents Act 1977.
4   S.47 Trade Marks Act 1994 (http://www.ipo.gov.uk/tmact94.pdf).
5   S.46 Ibid.
6   Para. 2.2 PD-Part 63 Patents and Other Intellectual Property Claims (http://www.justice.gov.uk/civil/procrules_fin/contents/practice_directions/pd_part63.htm#IDAFLBMF).
7   That is to say copyright, rights in performances, rights conferred under Part VII of the Copyright, Designs and Patents Act 1988, design right, unregistered Community designs, Olympic symbols, plant varieties, moral rights, database rights, unauthorized decryption rights, hallmarks, technical trade secrets litigation, passing off, geographical indications, registered trade marks and Community trade marks.
8   CPR 63.13 and para. 18.1 PD-Part 63 (http://www.justice.gov.uk/civil/procrules_fin/contents/practice_directions/pd_part63.htm#IDAGZQGF).
9   CPR 16.5 (1) (c).
10   CPR 16.5 (1) (a).
11   CPR 16.5 (1) (b).

If the defendant has a claim against the claimant as well as a defence, it can be raised as a counterclaim in the same document as the defence. That should also be set out in numbered paragraphs following in sequence from the defence and should begin with the words 'AND THE DEFENDANT COUNTERCLAIMS' followed by the relief sought. In England and Wales each statement of case must be verified by a statement of truth such as 'I believe that the facts stated in this statement of case are true.'[12] Verifying a statement of truth without an honest belief in its truth is a contempt of court.[13] Statements of case can usually be amended at any time[14] by consent of all parties or permission of the court[15] but such consent is usually conditional upon paying any costs that the other side incurs as a result of such amendment. Examples of two statements of case, namely particulars of claim and a defence for an unregistered design rights case appear in the Appendix.

Gathering evidence

In the absence of a successful strike out application or summary judgment, the next stage of the process is to gather evidence relating to the points at issue between the parties that are identified by their *statements of case*. It will be recalled that the following types of evidence are used in court:

- documentary evidence: letters, photographs, records, emails, texts and other written materials in any medium;
- oral testimony: statements of witnesses usually under oath;
- material evidence: physical objects such as an item of machinery and merchandise; and
- expert evidence: the findings or opinions of experts.

To ensure that nobody is taken by surprise, the parties are expected to make their evidence available to each other. Sometimes this requires an order of the court but it usually takes place by agreement. It generally proceeds in phases starting with disclosure and inspection of documents followed by an exchange of statements of witnesses of fact and experts' reports.

Disclosure

Unless the parties agree, or the court orders otherwise, every party to litigation has a duty to make a reasonable search for[16] and disclose to the other parties any document which is or has been in his or her physical possession,[17] any document that he or she is entitled to possess[18] or any document that he or she has a right to inspect and copy[19] that relates to the case. This process is called *'disclosure'*. A party has a duty to disclose not just the document that he or she relies upon but also any document that adversely affects his or her own case,[20]

---

12   Para 2.1 PD-Part 22.
13   CPR 32.12 (1).
14   CPR 17.1 (1).
15   CPR 17.1 (2).
16   CPR 31.7 (1) at http://www.justice.gov.uk/civil/procrules_fin/contents/parts/part31.htm#rule31_7.
17   CPR 31.8 (2) (a) Ibid.
18   CPR 31.8 (2) (b) Ibid.
19   CPR 31.8 (2) (c) Ibid.
20   CPR 31.6 (b) (i).

adversely affects another party's case[21] or supports another party's case.[22] *'Documents'* for this purpose mean 'anything in which information of any description is recorded.'[23] They include but are not limited to paper records. The definition extends to electronic records such as e-mails and other electronic communications, word processing files and databases.[24] Disclosure is a very serious obligation. A party may not rely on any document which he or she fails to disclose without the court's permission[25] and a false disclosure statement may be prosecuted as a contempt of court.[26]

Lists of documents

Documents are disclosed in a list of documents in form N265.[27] This form consists of 3 pages and starts with a 'disclosure statement' which is signed by the party concerned. The statement indicates the extent of the search and states whether any computers, mobile phones or other electronic devices had been searched. If any such devices have been searched, the statement identifies them and also the files that are the subject of the search. Finally, there is a certificate that the party making the statement understands the duty of disclosure and has complied with it. The actual list is in three parts. The first part lists the documents in the party's control which he or she does not object to showing to the other side. The second part consists of documents in his or her control that he or she does object to showing and there is space to set out the reasons on the form. The last part lists documents that are no longer in a witness's control. Such lists should be exchanged on a date agreed by the parties which is normally a few days after the delivery of the last statement of case.

Inspection

A party to whom a document has been disclosed has a right to inspect that document except where the document is no longer in the control of the party who disclosed it;[28] the party disclosing the document has a right or a duty to withhold inspection of it[29] if inspection would be disproportionate to the issues in the case.[30] A party who has a right to inspect a document must give the party who disclosed it written notice of his or her wish to inspect it.[31] The party who disclosed the document must permit inspection not more than 7 days after the date on which he or she receives the notice.[32] The party seeking disclosure may request a copy of the document provided he or she also undertakes to pay reasonable copying costs. The party

---

21   CPR 31.6 (b) (ii).
22   CPR 31.6 (b) (iii).
23   CPR 31.4 Ibid.
24   Para. 2A1 of PD-Part 31 at http://www.justice.gov.uk/civil/procrules_fin/contents/practice_directions/pd_part31. htm#IDAKLVLD.
25   CPR 31.21.
26   CPR 31.23 (1).
27   This form may be downloaded from HM Courts Service website at http://www.justice.gov.uk/civil/procrules_fin/ menus/forms.htm.
28   CPR 31.3 (1) (a).
29   CPR 31.3 (1) (b).
30   CPR 31.3 (1) (c) and (2).
31   CPR 31.15 (a).
32   CPR 31.15 (b).

disclosing the document must then supply a copy not more than 7 days after receiving the request.[33] The consequences of failing to allow inspection of a document are the same as for failing to disclose it.[34]

Oral testimony

In England and other common law countries oral evidence is given in three stages:

1. Evidence in chief: the witness's story in his or her own words given at a party's request;
2. Cross-examination: the witness's response to questions put by parties other than the party calling the witness to test the witness's memory, understanding or truthfulness; and
3. Re-examination: questions put by the party calling the witness to correct a false impression that the witness may have given in response to questions in cross examination.

Occasionally, the judge or tribunal chair asks supplementary questions to clarify points that he or she believes to have been missed by the advocates.

Witness statements

Until the early 1990s evidence in chief in civil trials was given in the witness box as it still is in criminal cases. Coaxing evidence in chief from a witness required special skills. It had to be elicited by questions that did not indicate the desired answer to the witness. At the same time, a witness had to be kept to the point otherwise he or she would repeat what he or she had already said, digress into irrelevancies or omit something important. It had already been the practice for some years to exchange statements of the witnesses of fact.[35] Gradually courts began to order such statements to stand as a witness's evidence in chief. Nowadays, evidence in chief is confined to asking a witness to confirm his or her statement and whether he or she wishes to add to it or amend it in any way. Witness statements have to be prepared with very great care, particularly for proceedings before the Intellectual Property Office or interim injunction applications where there is no opportunity for cross-examination. Ideally, they should be edited by the advocate who will present the case. So far as possible, a witness statement should be in the witness's own words.[36] It must contain the truth, the whole truth and nothing but the truth. No pressure of any kind should be placed on a witness to give other than a true and complete account of his or her evidence.[37] On the other hand, a witness statement must be as concise as the circumstances of the case allow and present the evidence in an orderly and readily comprehensible manner.[38] Documents and other material evidence upon which a witness relies may be exhibited to the statement. Exhibiting a document to a witness statement can often confer a double benefit by clarifying, explaining and enhancing the significance of the document and corroborating the evidence of the witness. A witness statement is verified by the statement: 'I believe that

---

33   CPR 31.15 (c).
34   CPR 31.21 provides: 'A party may not rely on any document which he fails to disclose or in respect of which he fails to permit inspection unless the court gives permission.'
35   RSC O38 r2A.
36   Para 1, Appendix 9, Chancery Guide at http://www.hmcourts-service.gov.uk/cms/files/chancery_guide_2005. pdf.
37   Para 6 Ibid.
38   Para 2, Ibid.

the facts stated in this witness statement are true.'[39] As with statements of case, verifying a statement of truth for a witness statement without an honest belief in its truth is a contempt of court.[40]

Expert evidence

The duty of an expert is to help the court on the matters within his or her expertise.[41] He or she should assist the court by providing objective, unbiased opinion on matters within his or her expertise.[42] At no time should he or she assume the role of an advocate.[43] Expert evidence should be independent and uninfluenced by the pressures of litigation.[44]

Expert evidence is often used in intellectual property cases. In patent actions, for instance, an expert in the relevant technical field can help the court construe a claim by outlining the background information of the persons to whom the patent is addressed and the terminology that such persons are likely to use. In copyright and unregistered design claims, an expert can help the court decide whether a work has been copied by identifying similarities and dissimilarities between the copyright work and putative copy and explaining the significance of such similarities and dissimilarities. Upon an inquiry as to damages or account of profits a forensic accountant can help the court to quantify a claimant's loss or a defendant's profits. Though an expert is usually engaged by one or more of the parties, his or her duty to the court overrides any obligation to the person paying the fee or sending instructions.[45] Expert witnesses are expected to deliver a written report unless the court directs otherwise.[46] Such report must:

1. give details of the expert's qualifications;
2. give details of any literature or other material which the expert has relied on in making the report;
3. contain a statement setting out the substance of all facts and instructions given to the expert which are material to the opinions expressed in the report or upon which those opinions are based;
4. make clear which of the facts stated in the report are within the expert's own knowledge;
5. say who carried out any examination, measurement, test or experiment which the expert has used for the report, give the qualifications of that person, and say whether or not the test or experiment has been carried out under the expert's supervision;
6. summarize any range of opinion on the matters dealt with in the report and give reasons for the expert's opinion on such matters;
7. contain a summary of the conclusions reached;
8. state any qualification to the report if the expert is not able to give an opinion without qualification, and

---

39   Para 2.2 PD-Part 22.
40   CPR 32.12 (1).
41   CPR 35.3 (1).
42   Para 1.3, PD-Part 35).
43   Ibid.
44   Ibid.
45   CPR 35.3 (1).
46   CPR 35.5 (1).

9. contain a statement that the expert understands his or her duty to the court, and has complied and will continue to comply with that duty.[47]

The report must be verified by a statement of truth in the following words:

'I confirm that insofar as the facts stated in my report are within my own knowledge I have made clear which they are and I believe them to be true, and that the opinions I have expressed represent my true and complete professional opinion.'[48]

An expert should consider all material facts, including those which might detract from his or her opinion. [49] He or she should make it clear when a question or issue falls outside his expertise and when he or she is not able to reach a definite opinion because of insufficient information or for some other reason. [50] If, after producing a report, an expert changes his or her view on any material matter, such change of view should be communicated to all the parties without delay, and when appropriate to the court. [51]

Case management

Managing the progress of a case is called 'case management' and it is one of the responsibilities of the court or tribunal. Patent and registered design cases are managed differently from other intellectual property cases in the civil courts of England and Wales. Patent and design cases are managed by the trial judge while other intellectual property cases are managed by procedural judges known as 'masters' in the Royal Courts of Justice in London and 'district judges' everywhere else.[52] In the UK IP Office cases are managed by hearing officers in accordance with Patents, [53] Trade Marks[54] or Registered Design Rules[55] and Tribunal Practice Notices.[56] Arbitrations are managed by arbitrators in accordance with rules agreed by the parties. Often these incorporate standard rules that apply to all arbitrations before the arbitrator's panel. For instance, the WIPO arbitration Rules[57] apply to all arbitrations before members of the WIPO panel. It is usually necessary to have at least one case management hearing (usually known as *'a case management conference'*) to determine disputes over disclosure, applications for security for costs and the like. For more complex cases in the High Court, it may be necessary to have a second case management hearing before the trial judge known as the 'pre-trial review' to make sure that the trial proceeds smoothly.

Skeleton arguments

Immediately before a hearing on any matter of substance, the court or tribunal will require the parties to exchange and lodge written summaries of their submissions known as *'skeleton*

---

47   Para 2.2, PD-Part 35.
48   Paras 2.3 and 2.4, PD-Part 35.
49   Para 1.4, PD-Part 35.
50   Para 1.5, PD-Part 35.
51   Para 1.6, PD-Part 35.
52   CPR Part 63.
53   The Patents Rules 1995 as amended. The URL of the Patents Rules 2007 is http://www.ipo.gov.uk/patentrules2007.pdf
54   The Trade Marks Rules 2000 as amended (see http://www.ipo.gov.uk/tmrules2000.pdf).
55   The Registered Designs Rules 2006, SI 2006 No 1975 at http://www.opsi.gov.uk/si/si2006/20061975.htm.
56   http://www.ipo.gov.uk/patent/p-decisionmaking/p-law/p-law-tpn.htm.
57   http://www.wipo.int/amc/en/arbitration/rules/index.html.

arguments'. A skeleton argument is intended to identify the points that are not in issue and the nature of each party's argument in relation to such points. It is not intended to be a substitute for oral argument.[58] A skeleton argument should therefore identify concisely the nature of the case generally, and the background facts insofar as they are relevant to the matter before the court, the propositions of law relied on with references to the relevant authorities and the submissions of fact to be made with reference to the evidence.[59] It should therefore be as brief as the nature of the issues allows. It should not normally exceed 20 pages of double-spaced A4 paper and in many cases it should be much shorter than that.[60] Arguments should be set out in numbered paragraphs. Abbreviations such as 'C ' for claimant and 'D' for defendant and the British numerical format for dates such as 11.09.2001 for September 11, 2001 should be used wherever possible. Failure or delay in lodging or exchanging skeletons in good time can result in the adjournment of the hearing, disallowance of costs or even an order for a defaulting legal representative to pay wasted costs.[61]

Bundles

Whenever more than 25 pages of written material are likely to be referred to at a hearing, they must be numbered, indexed and filed in a loose leaf binder. The binder or set of binders is known as 'the bundle'. The efficient preparation of bundles of documents is very important. When done properly, the case will be easier to understand and present and time and costs are likely to be saved.[62] The party seeking the hearing takes the initiative but the legal representatives for all of the parties must co-operate. Bundles should be delivered well before the hearing and the consequences of failure or delay in delivering bundles are the same as for failure or delay in delivering skeleton arguments.

Preparation of cross-examination

As I have mentioned earlier, oral evidence is tested for clarity, comprehensiveness, consistency and credibility by questions from the opposing party known as 'cross-examination'. The best cross-examinations are those that are prepared well in advance. There are no hard and fast rules. My practice is to read a witness statement several times, the first time to take it in, the second to identify bits that are helpful, those which are best left alone and the usually more extensive bits that are not helpful. I compare the bits of a statement that are not helpful to other parts of the document to detect inconsistency. Next I compare it to other documented facts to see whether the statement can be undermined. It is, of course, possible for the other side to be right and for my evidence to be wrong so I always test my own evidence in the same way. If there are any nasty surprises it is better to meet them before going to court in order to take counter precautions.

---

58   Para 1, Appendix 7, Chancery Guide at http://www.hmcourts-service.gov.uk/cms/files/chancery_guide_2005. pdf.
59   Para 2 (1), Appendix 7, Chancery Guide at http://www.hmcourts-service.gov.uk/cms/files/chancery_guide_2005. pdf.
60   Para 2 (2), Appendix 7, Chancery Guide at http://www.hmcourts-service.gov.uk/cms/files/chancery_guide_2005. pdf.
61   Para 7.30, Chancery Guide at http://www.hmcourts-service.gov.uk/cms/files/chancery_guide_2005.pdf.
62   Para 7.9, Chancery Guide at http://www.hmcourts-service.gov.uk/cms/files/chancery_guide_2005.pdf.

9 *What Happens on the Big Day*

Unless you can resolve your dispute through negotiation, the time will come when you have to argue the toss before a third party. That could be a trial or other court hearing, arbitration, proceedings in the IP Office, domain name dispute resolution proceedings or other adjudication. It could also be mediation or other form of ADR. These may be categorized as follows:

- paper only proceedings;
- hearings without oral evidence;
- hearings with oral evidence; and
- mediation.

This chapter covers all four types of proceedings.

Paper only proceedings

The best known examples of paper only proceedings are probably domain name dispute resolution proceedings under the UDRP[1] and Nominet's DRS[2] but many proceedings in the UK Intellectual Property Office are also conducted without a hearing as are many arbitrations.

UDRP PROCEEDINGS

This jurisdiction arises from the standard accreditation agreement[3] that every generic top level domain name[4] registrar enters with ICANN.[5] Clause 3.8 of that standard agreement requires each registrar to comply with ICANN's UDRP.[6] Every registrar is therefore required to incorporate the UDRP into every agreement it makes with an applicant for the registration of a generic top level domain name.

Paragraph 4 (a) of the UDRP contains the following provision:

You are required to submit to a mandatory administrative proceeding in the event that a third party (a 'complainant') asserts to the applicable Provider, in compliance with the Rules of Procedure, that:

    (i)   your domain name is identical or confusingly similar to a trademark or service mark in which the complainant has rights; and

---

1   Uniform Domain-Name Dispute-Resolution Policy at http://www.icann.org/udrp/udrp.htm.
2   Dispute Resolution Service at http://www.nominet.org.uk/disputes/drs/policy.
3   http://www.icann.org/registrars/ra-agreement-17may01.htm#1.
4   Examples include domain names ending in '.com', '.org', '.net' and '.info'.
5   'Internet Corporation for Assigned Names and Numbers', a California non-profit, public benefit corporation, the California company that governs the international domain name system pursuant to a memorandum of understanding with the US government dated 26 Nov 1998 (see www.icann.org).
6   http://www.icann.org/general/icann-mou-25nov98.htm.

(ii)   you have no rights or legitimate interests in respect of the domain name; and

(iii)   your domain name has been registered and is being used in bad faith.

In the administrative proceeding, the complainant must prove that each of these three elements are present.

The 'applicable Provider' means one of the following dispute resolution service providers: the ADNRC (Asian Domain Name Dispute Resolution Centre),[7] the Czech Arbitration Court,[8] the NAF (the National Arbitration Forum)[9] and the WIPO (World Intellectual Property Organization).[10] Each of those service providers maintains a panel of neutrals to hear and determine complaints by proprietors or others with interests in trade marks that a generic top level domain name is identical or confusingly similar to their trade mark. If a panellist decides in the complainant's favour the registrar is bound by its agreement with ICANN to transfer the domain name registration to the complainant or cancel the domain name. Service providers process complaints and refer them to panellists who must decide the dispute within 14 days. Service providers charge a non-refundable fee of around US$1,500 for those services of which US$1,000 is paid to the panellist.

The process begins by lodging a complaint with a service provider. If the complainant wants to complain to the WIPO, he or she can download a partially completed form from the WIPO website.[11] The complainant is required to insert his or her name and address, the name and address of the domain name proprietor (who is known as 'the respondent') and the name of the disputed domain name or names. He or she must give his or her contact details and those of any legal representative and state his or her preferred method of communication.

The complainant must identify the registrar and show that its agreement with the respondent incorporated the UDRP. In the substantive part of the form, the complainant must prove that:

• the domain name is identical or confusingly similar to a trade mark in which the complainant has rights;
• the respondent has no rights or legitimate interests in respect of the domain name; and
• the domain name has been registered and is being used in bad faith.

A complainant usually satisfies the first probandum by exhibiting a trade mark registration certificate. Para 4 (a) (i) of the UDRP does not actually require the complainant to own the trade mark. It is enough that he or she has some sort of right in the mark such as an exclusive licence or a controlling shareholding in a registered trade mark proprietor. Nor is it necessary for the trade mark to be registered. A right to bring an action for passing off to restrain the use of the mark will suffice for this purpose. As to whether the respondent has any rights or legitimate interests in respect of the domain name, the best that most complainants can say is that the respondent has nothing to do with them, they have never licensed nor authorized the respondent to use the domain name and that they are not aware of any ground upon which respondent can claim rights or legitimate interests in the disputed domain name. If the respondent has used the domain name as a URL[12] the complainant may exhibit some or all of its pages to the complaint. The last probandum is usually the most difficult because it is

---

7   http://www.adndrc.org/adndrc/index.html.
8   http://www.adreu.eurid.eu.
9   http://domains.adrforum.com.
10   http://www.wipo.int/amc/en/domains.
11   http://www.wipo.int/amc/en/domains/complainant/index.html.
12   Universal resource locator or the address of the website.

necessary to prove not only that the domain name is being used in bad faith but also that it has been registered in bad faith. Complainants are, however, assisted by paragraph 4 (b) of the UDRP which provides:

For the purposes of Paragraph 4 (a) (iii), the following circumstances, in particular but without limitation, if found by the Panel to be present, shall be evidence of the registration and use of a domain name in bad faith:

(i) *circumstances indicating that you have registered or you have acquired the domain name primarily for the purpose of selling, renting, or otherwise transferring the domain name registration to the complainant who is the owner of the trademark or service mark or to a competitor of that complainant, for valuable consideration in excess of your documented out-of-pocket costs directly related to the domain name; or*

(ii) *you have registered the domain name in order to prevent the owner of the trademark or service mark from reflecting the mark in a corresponding domain name, provided that you have engaged in a pattern of such conduct; or*

(iii) *you have registered the domain name primarily for the purpose of disrupting the business of a competitor; or*

(iv) *by using the domain name, you have intentionally attempted to attract, for commercial gain, Internet users to your web site or other on-line location, by creating a likelihood of confusion with the complainant's mark as to the source, sponsorship, affiliation, or endorsement of your web site or location or of a product or service on your web site or location.*

Those who register domain names on a commercial scale with a view to ransoming them to a trade mark proprietor or its competitor are usually sufficiently astute to avoid overt offers to sell but their intention is usually clear enough. The complaint concludes with a statement of the remedies required, the election of a single or three member panel, submission to the jurisdiction of at least one court which would be able to determine the dispute, and confirmation that the respondent has been served with the proceedings and that the fee has been paid and that the complaint is proper and made in accordance with the law.

The complaint and any exhibits are checked by the service provider's staff and if found to be in order they will be forwarded to the respondent. If not, the complainant will be required to put right any deficiency before a copy of the complaint can be sent. The WIPO encloses with the complaint a notice headed 'Notification of Complaint and Commencement of Administrative Proceeding' which summarizes the history of the complaint, requires the respondent to respond within 20 days and explains how he or she can do so, sets out the consequences of failure to respond and invites the respondent to choose between a single member and a three member panel. The party that chooses a three member panel must pay a non-refundable supplemental fee of around US$2,000 and each side must select up to three candidates from any of the service providers' lists of panellists.

Respondents can download a partly completed model response from the service provider's website.[13] The respondent must insert the names and addresses of the parties and the disputed domain name. It must acknowledge service of the complaint and the relevant deadlines, set out its contact details and those of any legal or other representative. If it wishes to challenge a submission that the domain name is identical or confusingly similar to a trade or service mark in which the complainant has rights, a respondent can contest the validity of the registration,

---

13   http://www.wipo.int/amc/en/domains/filing/udrp/index.html.

the complainant's title or the allegation of identity or confusing similarity. It can show that it has rights or a legitimate interest in the domain name by using or preparing to use the domain name in connection with a bona fide offering of goods or services. It can also show that it has rights or a legitimate interest if it is or has been commonly known by the disputed domain name.

Yet another defence is for the respondent to show that it is making a legitimate non-commercial or fair use of the domain name. The domain name of a website set up to criticize an organization that alludes to or even incorporates a name by which the organization is known can sometimes satisfy the rights and legitimate interest criteria provided that there is no intention to make commercial gain, misleadingly to divert consumers or to tarnish a trade or service mark.[14] The provisos make this exception a very narrow one but an example of an occasion when it did apply is *Dorset Police v Coulter*.[15] The respondent used the names 'dorsetpolice.com' and 'dorsetpolice.net' to direct to an active website which discusses a grievance between Respondent and Complainant. The grievance involved Mr. Coulter's allegations that the Dorset Police failed to recover his stolen car, and further allegations of corruption in the police force. Respondent uses the Domain Names to briefly explain a grievance that he has with the Complainant, which will be further explained at a later date. The site also contains a link to a recent article critical of the Complainant regarding another matter. Moreover, the Domain Names, until very recently, automatically redirected traffic (after a brief wait) to a third party website at www.vomit.co.uk which contains further discussion of Respondent's grievance, but appears primarily devoted to vitriolic commentary concerning freemasons and various government entities and employees including the Complainant.'

The complainant argued that the respondent's criticism was offensive to 'a point beyond libellous'. The panellist disagreed finding that the web site had been maintained as a genuine criticism site. Dismissing the complaint, he said:

> *Complainant is a governmental entity. The Panel finds that there is a general, legitimate interest in allowing citizens to use descriptive domain names to publish criticism about their government. The Panel finds that the reasoning of the aforementioned decisions is even more poignant in this case involving a governmental entity. There has been no evidence that the Domain Names have been used for any commercial purpose. Therefore, the Panel finds that Respondent does have a legitimate interest in the Domain Names.*

It has to be stressed that there are two views on this exception and most WIPO panellists incline to the view that the right to criticize does not extend to registering a domain name that is identical or confusingly similar to the owner's registered trade mark or conveys an association with the mark.[16]

Readers will recall that complainants must certify that their complaint is proper and made in accordance with the law. Abusing the UDRP wrongly to deprive a registered proprietor of its domain name is called 'reverse domain name hijacking'. The phrase seems to have been coined by the panellist Dawn Osborn in Case No. D2000-0518 *Maruti Udyog Limited v. Tella Rao*[17] where it was alleged that the complainant had attempted several times to change

---

14   Para 4 (c) of the UDRP.
15   http://www.disputes.org/decisions/0942.htm.
16   See WIPO Overview of WIPO Panel Views on Selected UDRP Questions at http://www.wipo.int/amc/en/domains/search/overview/index.html#24.
17   http://www.wipo.int/amc/en/domains/decisions/html/2000/d2000-0518.html.

the administrative contact of the domain name from the respondent's NIC handle to the complainant's. It has, however, been extended to other circumstances such as applying for the transfer of a domain name which was registered before the complainant company was even incorporated.[18] The UDRP provides no sanction for reverse domain name hijacking beyond the panel's censure and scepticism in future applications which is always embarrassing and can sometimes be damaging.

NOMINET DRS

These are equivalent proceedings for disputes over registrations in the .uk country code top level domain name space. *Nominet UK*[19] used to be the only registrar for second level domain names available to the general public[20] such as '.co.uk' and '.org.uk'[21] but it now accredits others to register such names. A condition of accreditation is that every '*registrant*'[22] must submit disputes over his or her domain name registration to mediation and expert determination in accordance with Nominet's Dispute Resolution Service policy (DRS).[23] The DRS resembles the UDRP in many ways but there are some important differences. First, Nominet provides for informal mediation[24] which disposes of about 55 per cent of the complaints brought before it.[25] If the case does not settle the complainant is invited to refer the case to expert determination upon payment of a fee of £750 + VAT. A second major difference is that there is a sanction for reverse domain name hijacking and other applications brought in bad faith.[26] Nominet complaints and responses are made online without the option of a downloadable hard copy though it is, of course, possible to print them out at the end of the process. Unlike the UDRP, there is a right of appeal to a panel of three in the Nominet system.[27]

UK INTELLECTUAL PROPERTY OFFICE HEARINGS

A large and increasing number of proceedings before UK IP Office hearing officers are disposed of without an oral hearing. Many oppositions to trade mark applications are compromised upon a hearing officer's preliminary indications which are given at a very early stage.[28] Other proceedings commence in the usual way with the exchange of statements of case, witness statements, statutory declarations or affidavits and exhibits. If the parties and the hearing

---

18   As in D2005-0309, Jazeera Space Channel TV Station v AJ Publishing at http://www.wipo.int/amc/en/domains/decisions/html/2005/d2005-0309.html.

19   A private company limited by guarantee in England and Wales under company number 3203859.

20   Others include '.me.uk', '.ltd.uk', '.plc.uk', '.net.uk' and '.sch.uk' for schools.

21   Other registration authorities deal with central and local government (.gov.uk), academic (.ac.uk) and police sites (.police.uk).

22   An applicant or registered proprietor of a '.uk' top level domain name.

23   http://www.nominet.org.uk/disputes/drs/policy/?contentId=3069.

24   Para 5 of the Policy.

25   http://www.nominet.org.uk/disputes/drs/mediation.

26   Para 16 (d) of the DRS procedure ('the Procedure') provides: 'If, after considering the submissions, the Expert finds that the complaint was brought in bad faith, for example in an attempt at Reverse Domain Name Hijacking, the Expert shall state this finding in the Decision. If the Complainant is found on three separate occasions within a 2-year period to have brought a complaint in bad faith, Nominet will not accept any further complaints from that Complainant for a period of 2 years.'

27   Para 18 of the Procedure.

28   Rule 13B (2) Of the Trade Marks Rules 2000 as amended provides:
       After considering the statement of the grounds of opposition and the counter-statement the registrar shall notify the parties whether it appears to her that the mark should or should not be registered in respect of the goods and services listed in the application. (See http://www.ipo.gov.uk/tmrules2000.pdf.)
The practice is now set out in TPN3/2007 (see http://www.ipo.gov.uk/patent/p-decisionmaking/p-law/p-law-tpn/p-law-tpn-2007/p-law-tpn-2007-tpn32007.htm).

officer agree, the case can be decided on the parties' written submissions and documentary evidence. Hundreds and sometimes thousands of pounds can be saved by a documents only proceeding.[29] Further information on IP Office proceedings appears later in this chapter.

Hearings without Oral Evidence

These are hearings in which all the evidence is given in writing. This would include most of the remaining hearings before the UK Intellectual Property Office as well as many applications to the court for interim remedies and even some trials. The following paragraphs will consider 'with' and 'without notice' applications to judges, applications to a master in the Royal Courts of Justice or district judges elsewhere, IP Office proceedings and the streamlined procedure of the Patents Court.

INTERIM APPLICATIONS TO THE JUDGE

These are applications to judges for relief that only a judge can order such as an interim injunction or the committal of a person who disobeys an injunction to prison for contempt of court. Although the practices of the different divisions of the High Court and the county courts have been harmonized there remain important differences between the practice of the Chancery Division and that of the other courts. Since most interim injunction applications are made to the Chancery Division in intellectual property cases it is the chancery practice that will be described. Within the Chancery Division there are slight differences between the practice in London and that in Preston, Manchester, Mold, Liverpool, Leeds, Newcastle, Bristol, Birmingham, Cardiff and Caernarfon and the practice of the Patents Court differs again.

Applications to judges are made to an *'interim applications judge'* and the court in which such judge sits is known as *'the Chancery Interim Applications Court'*. Before the CPR came into force applications to chancery judges in open court were known as *'motions'* to distinguish them from all other applications for interim relief which were known as *'summonses'* and the old less wordy terminology is still in use. An application to a judge is launched by filing an applications notice in form N244[30] and delivering a copy of that document together with a draft minute of order and any evidence relied upon to the appropriate court office[31] and paying the court fee. Those documents must be served on the respondent not less than 3 working days before the hearing not counting the date of service or the date of the hearing.[32] Thus, if an application was to be heard on Monday 5 Nov 2007 the respondent should have received the papers not later than 17:00 on Tuesday, 30 October. The date of hearing is known as 'the return day'.

A wise respondent will use those 3 working days to decide whether or not it wishes to contest the application. If the respondent does not wish to contest it the respondent should give undertakings to the court substantially in the terms of the draft order. The parties are usually excused from attending court where an order signed by both sides can be delivered to the clerk to the Chancery interim applications in sufficient time. If the respondent decides to contest

---

29   See Tribunal Practice Notice (TPN 2/2000) at http://www.ipo.gov.uk/tm/t-decisionmaking/t-law/t-law-tpn/t-law-tpn-2000/t-law-tpn-2000-tpn22000.htm.
30   A copy of which appears in the Appendix. The form can be downloaded from http://www.hmcourts-service.gov.uk/courtfinder/forms/n244_0400.pdf.
31   In London that is the Chancery Judges' Listing Office in Room WG4. In a chancery district registry it is the chancery listing officer.
32   Para 5.7 of the Chancery Guide at http://www.hmcourts-service.gov.uk/cms/files/chancery_guide_2005.pdf.

the application, the respondent must decide whether it can deliver evidence to the applicant in sufficient time for the applicant to deal with such evidence and also whether the application can be dealt with comfortably within 2 hours. Should the answer to either question be no the respondent should try to agree terms with the applicant for the application to be stood over to an appointment known as an 'application by order'.[33] Such terms will usually provide a timetable for the exchange of evidence and perhaps limited undertakings over the hearing of the application by order and the standing over of the application either to a fixed date or a date to be agreed between the parties and the court. Again, if these terms can be recorded in an agreed order the day before, the judge may release at least one or both of the parties from attending court on the return day.

Applications are usually heard at the start of the return day. Judges and advocates are no longer robed for such hearings. The practice is for the list of cases that have not been disposed of by agreement to be read out to the court and for the judge to ask the applicant or his advocate in each case to state simply whether the application is 'effective' or 'ineffective' (that is to say, whether there will be an argument) and the estimated length of the hearing. Anything more than 'effective' or 'effective, my lord, 20 minutes' risks wasting the time of the court. The judge notes the answers and calls the cases in order of brevity, that is to say the shortest first.

If an application is to be heard by order there is usually a frantic rush to meet a very tight timetable. A typical order will require the applicant to serve all its evidence within a week of the return day, the respondent to serve its evidence in reply within 14 days thereafter and the applicant to serve any evidence in response within 7 days after that. The applicant will be expected to prepare a bundle for the use of the judge and advocates and the parties will be expected to have exchanged skeleton arguments one working day before the hearing.

On the day of the hearing the applicant or its counsel will introduce himself and his opponent to the judge with the following words:

> *My lord, I appear for the applicant. My learned friend Mr Frederick Bloggs appears for the respondent. This is an application for an interim injunction to restrain the defendant from making and selling the [blunderbuss] until judgment.*

He or she will then outline the claimant's argument referring to particular points on the skeleton and the case law and statutes upon which the applicant particularly relies. After that he or she reads the evidence relating particular passages or exhibits to points in the skeleton. He or she concludes with a short summary of the main points of the applicant's case and then sits down unless the judge has further questions. The respondent's advocate highlights the main arguments in response and then reads the witness statements in support of his or her case. Should the respondent raise any point which exposes flaws in the applicant's case, its advocate gets an opportunity to reply. The judge will either deliver judgment at the conclusion of the argument or reserve it to a later date. After judgment, the winning party claims summary assessment of its costs.

WITHOUT NOTICE APPLICATIONS

These are applications of which 3 working days notice has not been given to the other side. There are several good reasons for not giving such notice to the other side. It may be that the harm that the applicant seeks to restrain may be done within those days. For instance, a senior member of a research and development team may be about to take up an appointment with a

---

33   Formerly 'motion by order'.

competitor disregarding a restrictive covenant in his contract of employment, or an allegedly infringing article is about to be displayed at a trade show. In those circumstances, the problem is just lack of time and there is no reason why the intended respondent should not be given notice of the hearing as soon as possible. Those applications can usually be heard with the listed 'with notice' applications on an ordinary interim applications day.

There are, however, some applications for which no notice can be given in case the other side takes steps to frustrate any order that the court may make. For instance, a party with damaging evidence in its possession may try to hide or destroy it if it believes it may be forced to disclose that evidence. Similarly, a party with assets in the UK may transfer abroad, hide or even spend those assets rather than risk their seizure by judgment creditors. Applications for orders requiring delivery up or searches to be made, or the freezing of assets, are therefore made without warning before judges sitting in private.

Because of their draconian nature, the courts make a number of special requirements. First, evidence in support of such applications is given by *affidavit* or *affirmation* rather than by a simple *witness statement*. An affidavit or affirmation is sworn on the deponent's scriptures or solemnized before a solicitor or commissioner of oaths. Lying on oath or affirmation is perjury punishable by a heavy custodial sentence and not a mere contempt of court. Secondly, a party who addresses the court in the absence of his or her opponent is bound to disclose all material facts that could affect the exercise of the court's discretion, whether favourable to his side or not. He or she has to put before the court anything that might reasonably have been put by the absent party had it been there. Should any matter not disclosed subsequently come to the applicant's attention, he or she must promise to return to court immediately to correct the error. Search and delivery up orders are usually executed by supervising solicitors who represent the court at the respondent's premises. These are experienced litigators, not connected with either of the parties or their law firms, who ensure that the order is carried out fully but fairly. The independent solicitor is required to report on the execution of the search in writing and his or her report is considered by the court together with any further evidence or argument that either party may wish to present at another hearing before the judge on the return day. Delivery up, search and freezing orders are made for very short periods. They can be discharged or varied at any time and they will in any case be reviewed on the return day.

The paperwork for these applications usually consists of an application notice, draft minute of order and the affidavit evidence upon which the applicant relies. These should be filed with the court at least 2 hours before the hearing[34] preferably with a skeleton argument and copy of the claim form and any statement of case. Usually the only persons present in court will be the judge, his or her clerk, an associate and shorthand writer, counsel for the applicant, his or her instructing solicitor and perhaps a lay client. Some judges lead the proceedings, indicating the points upon which they require counsels' assistance, particularly if they have read the papers. Others allow counsel to open and present the case as the advocate thinks fit. If the judge is minded to make an order, he or she will correct counsel's draft requiring the applicant to draw up a fair copy and present it for sealing before he or she leaves court. If not, the suitors slink away from court, the other side none the wiser.

If you are on the receiving end of a search or delivery up order the first you will hear of it is when the supervising solicitor appears at your premises. He or she will appear alone with the applicants' solicitors and any accompanying expert outside. The supervising solicitor will say that he or she has come to serve a search order. He or she will hand you a copy of the order

---

34   Para 4.3 (1) of PD-Interim Injunctions.

together with copies of the evidence and explain its terms and effect in everyday language. [35] He will tell you that you have a right to seek legal advice so long as you do so immediately and that you can also apply to vary or discharge the order. He will advise you that any instructions you give or advice you receive from your legal advisors may be privileged and of your general right against self-incrimination. Your problem if you try to exercise any of those rights is that you will find it expensive, particularly if you require a specialist solicitor to drop what he or she is doing to attend your premises. There is not usually much point in trying to vary or discharge an order because judges are very reluctant to change their minds once made up. If you think that the other side has overstepped the mark you can make that submission on the return day. On the other hand, you are vulnerable without some representation on site. Your best bet in most circumstances is to call your solicitor and ask him or her to arrange for a junior solicitor, legal executive or even a local agent to attend the search to take a full note of what happens and to make representations to the supervising solicitor if he or she thinks the other side is taking liberties.

Between the search and the return day you should think long and hard about what you want to do. If you can prove that you are the victim of manifest injustice, you can apply for variation or even discharge of the order and an inquiry as to damages on the applicant's cross-undertaking. If not, then it is probably best to delay your application to discharge the order until after trial. If the application was in fact justified the longer you resist the claim the more expense you will incur.

APPLICATIONS TO A MASTER OR DISTRICT JUDGE

Masters and district judges are procedural judges. They sit in offices known as 'chambers' rather than in courtrooms. Their rooms tend to be furnished with a desk at the head of a table with chairs on each side for the parties and their representatives. Typical proceedings before a master or district judge include *case management conferences*, summary judgment proceedings, and applications for a claimant to give security for the defendant's costs or for a party to be given extra time. Proceedings before masters and district judges are almost conversational. Advocates address masters as *'Master'* and district judges as *'Sir'* or *'Madam'* and make their submissions from their seats. Applications are launched by issuing applications notices out of the appropriate court office and serving them together with the supporting evidence not less than 3 working days before the appointment. There is usually quite a long interval between issue and hearing. That enables the respondent to lodge evidence in response and if necessary for the applicant to reply. Judgements are usually given extemporarily at the end of the hearing though occasionally they are reserved. Appeal usually lies to a single judge of the High Court or, as the case may be, a circuit judge in the county court.[36]

HEARINGS IN THE INTELLECTUAL PROPERTY OFFICE

Proceedings in the UK Intellectual Property Office are heard by officials known as *'hearing officers'* on behalf of the Chief Executive Officer who is referred to confusingly as *'the comptroller'* in patents and unregistered design right cases but as the *'registrar'* in respect of trade marks

---

35   Para 7.4 (4) of PD-Interim Injunctions.
36   Para 2A (1) of PD-Part 52 at http://www.justice.gov.uk/civil/procrules_fin/contents/practice_directions/pd_part52.htm#IDA4DNTD.

and registered designs. The practice of the IP Office was reviewed extensively following the implementation of the CPR and is now summarized in paragraph 6 of TPN 1/2000:[37]

- The Office and parties should endeavour to complete with notice proceedings within 18 months. (Paragraph 7.)
- The periods for filing a counterstatement and evidence in patents, registered designs and design right proceedings has been shortened from two months to six weeks except when lodging an opposition, e.g. opposition to amend a patent specification under rule 40(2). (Paragraph 8.)
- The periods for filing a counterstatement and evidence in trade marks revocation (on grounds other than non use), invalidation and rectification proceedings has been shortened to six weeks. However, the period will remain at three months in opposition and revocation on grounds of non use proceedings though an additional "cooling-off" period of three months at the start of opposition proceedings will be granted when sought by both parties. (Paragraph 9.)
- Hearing Officers will have discretion to shorten prescribed periods. (Paragraph 10.)
- The Office will set a period within which a preliminary (interlocutory) hearing should take place and give parties 14 days to agree a date in that period. The Office will fix a date if after 14 days the parties do not agree a date within this period, although Hearing Officers may override the 14 days if there are genuine difficulties. (Paragraph 13.)
- At the commencement of the final evidence round, the Office will aim to fix a date for a substantive hearing for approximately four months later. (Paragraph 14.)
- The party commencing action should provide a statement of case which properly sets out the grounds on which the case against the other side is to be based. If a party fails to provide sufficient information, the Patent Office may challenge the statement. Until the statement of case is in order the proceedings will not be progressed. (Paragraphs 15 to 19.)
- The Office has provided broad guidelines on how to set out a statement of case. (Paragraphs 20 to 25.)
- A declaration of the truth of the information in claims and defences is required for trade marks proceedings and encouraged in other proceedings. (Paragraph 27.)
- The Office will accept a witness statement in evidence although Hearing Officers are authorised to require the filing of an affidavit or statutory declaration if they consider it necessary. (Paragraph 30.)
- Exceptionally the Office is prepared to accept unsigned witness statements or unsworn statutory declarations or affidavits as meeting time deadlines provided a proper version of the evidence is filed within a specified period. The Hearing Officer may impose a cost penalty if, in the event, the formal evidence is different from that originally filed. (Paragraph 31.)
- Where a party adduces evidence of a statement made by another person and does not call that person as a witness, the Hearing Officer may permit the other party to call that person and cross examine them. (Paragraph 32.)
- In deciding whether to grant specific disclosure, Hearing Officers will generally follow principles which mirror those applied by the courts. (Paragraphs 33 to 37.)

---

37   http://www.ipo.gov.uk/patent/p-decisionmaking/p-law/p-law-tpn/p-law-tpn-2000/p-law-tpn-2000-tpn12000. htm.

- The Office intends issuing questionnaires on a selective basis prior to evidence rounds. (Paragraph 38.)
- Hearing Officers will adopt the selective use of 'case management conferences' taking into account the circumstances of the case, eg the need to clarify issues, the degree of complexity, any related actions and any wider public interest issues. (Paragraphs 39 and 40.)
- Hearing Officers are also empowered to call a 'pre-hearing review' prior to a hearing which will give them the opportunity to clarify matters and issue directions on the conduct of the hearing. (Paragraph 41.)
- The Office will routinely ask parties if they have considered Alternative Dispute Resolution (ADR) and Hearing Officers will be prepared to stay proceedings where ADR is being used or seriously considered. They may also take into account a party's unreasonable refusal to consider ADR when awarding costs. (Paragraph 42.)
- In patents revocation hearings the applicant will be invited to open proceedings while in trade marks opposition hearings the opponent will be invited to open. (Paragraph 43.)
- Hearing Officers will retain discretion to deal with excessively long speeches and cross examination. (Paragraph 44.)
- Parties will generally be expected to supply skeleton arguments and authorities at least two days before a hearing. (Paragraph 45.)
- Adducing new evidence during a hearing will be discouraged and will only be allowed after the other party has had sufficient time to digest it. As a rule, documents will only be allowed to be introduced in cross examination which are designed to test the honesty and reliability of a witness. (Paragraph 46.)
- The Office will encourage parties to hold hearings, case management conferences and pre-hearing reviews using telephone conferencing arrangements and video links in suitable cases. (Paragraph 47.)
- Hearing Officers will offer parties the opportunity for proceedings to be decided without the need for a hearing. (Paragraph 48.)

Save that hearing officers sit in hearing rooms resembling courtrooms, a hearing before a hearing officer is very similar to a hearing before a master or district judge. There is minimal formality. Hearing officers are addressed as 'Sir' or 'Madam' and it is customary for the parties to rise when they enter and leave the room. Advocacy tends to be conversational rather than declamatory.

STREAMLINED PROCEDURE

The Patents Court and Patents County Court offer a 'streamlined procedure' whenever appropriate for the just disposal of a case.[38] A 'streamlined procedure' is one in which:

(i)   all factual and expert evidence is in writing;
(ii) there is no requirement to give disclosure of documents;
(iii) there are no experiments;
(iv) cross-examination is only permitted on any topic or topics where it is necessary and is confined to those topics; and
(v)   the total duration of the trial fixed is and will normally be not more than one day.

---

38   Para 10 (b) Patents Court Guide at http://www.hmcourts-service.gov.uk/infoabout/patents/crt_guide.htm.

Legal advisors have a professional duty to draw their clients' attention to the availability of this procedure in suitable cases.[39] The trial takes place in open court and proceeds very much like an application by order. The trial is opened by the claimant's advocate who summarizes his or her client's case by reference to the skeleton argument. He or she reads or points the judge to the evidence if, as is likely, it has already been read, deals with any questions that the judge may raise and sits down. The defendant's counsel responds to the claim by reference to his or her own skeleton and arguments. The claimant has an opportunity to respond after which the trial closes. Although there is rarely any oral evidence this is just as much a trial as the proceedings described in the next paragraph.

Hearings with oral evidence

The way in which courts in England and other common law countries resolve conflicts of fact is by evaluating the performance of witnesses under cross-examination. Cross-examination is intended to test the observation, memory, understanding and in some cases veracity of witnesses. It should be challenging but not threatening, persistent but not repetitive and thorough but not pedantic. The ability to extract evidence from a witness who is or has come to court at the request of the opposite side is a skill at which only a few intellectual property counsel excel.[40] Cross-examination is used mainly at trials but it can be required on other occasions such as applications to commit a contemnor to prison, in arbitrations and IP Office or other tribunal proceedings. The evidence is usually introduced by the counsel for the party calling or inviting the witness to give evidence. In court, the witness is asked by the usher to take an oath on his or her scriptures or make an affirmation to tell the truth, the whole truth and nothing but the truth. The witness is presented with his or her witness statement. He or she is asked to look over it, to confirm that he or she made and signed the statement, whether there is anything that the witness wishes to add or change and if so what, and whether he or she is happy for the statement with any changes to stand as that witness's evidence in chief. The advocate who introduced the witness then sits down and the cross-examination begins. The length and nature of the cross-examination will vary greatly depending on the importance of the evidence, the degree to which it conflicts with other evidence, the length of the statement and the witness's age, health, intelligence and interest in the case. Questions may relate to the subject matter of the testimony, its credibility or both.

A hearing with oral evidence begins in very much the same way as any other hearing. The party having the burden of proof (usually the claimant) opens his or her case pointing to the key points of the argument. He or she takes the judge through the statements of case and skeleton arguments pointing out the factual and legal issues in dispute. He or she indicates the facts that he or she hopes to prove and the legal consequences. Occasionally he or she may have to deal with questions from the judge or objections from other counsel. Having developed his or her case, the advocate calls the first witness of fact, introduces the witness statement into evidence and allows the witness to be cross-examined. If damage has been

---

39   Para 10 (e) Patents Court Guide at http://www.hmcourts-service.gov.uk/infoabout/patents/crt_guide.htm.
40   I wish I could say I was of the few but I cannot. I have never really done enough court work in my career to learn how to do it well. Excellence at cross-examination is gained through experience. It cannot really be taught though there are some tips and tricks that pupil supervisors pass on to their trainees. I learned the importance of keeping a good note and carrying at least 2 pens with different coloured inks: one for recording particular questions or challenges to a witness and the other for his or her reply. There is no such thing as a born cross-examiner but there are some advantages of birth like quick repartee and charm or an attractive build.

done to the witness's evidence which can be repaired at least in part by re-examination, counsel will ask such questions as may be necessary. If not, or after such re-examination is complete, the advocate calls the next witness and the process is repeated. The last witness is often his or her expert and it is often that witness who is subjected to the most rigorous cross-examination, which goes some way towards justifying some experts' fees. Once the last witness is called the advocate for the claimant or other party with the burden of proof says words to the effect 'This is my case' or 'My evidence is complete' and sits down. The other side's advocate then calls his or her first witness and the process is reversed. At the end of the opposing evidence the responding counsel makes his or her oral submissions to the judge on the evidence that has been heard, the conclusions to be drawn from it and the legal consequences of those conclusions. The opening counsel responds to the submissions in his or her opponent's speech and emphasizes the main arguments of his or her own. Judgment may be given immediately after the final speeches but it is usually delivered in writing a few days later. Drafts of the judgment are usually circulated to the parties' legal advisors shortly before the court resumes and counsel are invited to point out any stylistic, grammatical or other errors that appear to need correction. If judgment is given to the claimant an injunction against future infringements of the intellectual property right will usually be granted together with consequential relief such as orders for delivery up of infringing articles and costs. If the claimant has suffered loss and the defendant is worth pursuing further, directions may be given for an inquiry as to damages or account of profits. Costs may be agreed but they are more likely to be referred to a costs judge for detailed assessment. Applications for permission to appeal have to be made to the trial judge in the first instance and it has to be said that once the judge has taken a view of the case it is rarely easy to persuade him or her that there are grounds of appeal.

Proceedings before arbitrators, IP Office and other tribunals in which evidence is adduced follow much the same course. The big difference between trials and arbitrations is that trials (like most other court and tribunal proceedings) take place in public while arbitrations are held in private. Awards are not usually published to the world. The parties are notified that the arbitrator has come to a decision and the text of the award is delivered to whichever party settles the arbitrator's fee. Robes are worn in some but by no means all civil trials. Where robes are worn, counsel wear wigs and gowns and judges and solicitor advocates robes but no wigs.

Mediation

Superficially, mediation looks very like arbitration. The parties are gathered or represented on either side of a long table often with their solicitors and counsel. There is a presiding figure known as '*the mediator*' who directs the proceedings. The process begins very much like arbitration with each party being called in turn to present its case. It is only after those initial presentations that mediation proceedings take a different course. The mediator sends the parties to separate rooms which he or she visits in turn to discuss the case. These discussions, known as 'caucuses', are very important because they help the mediator understand what the dispute is really about. They can uncover fears and animosities which brought the parties into conflict in the first place and get in the way of settlement. However, such discussions can also reveal interests upon which a solution can be built. Everything discussed in caucus is confidential. The mediator can never disclose the information that he or she learns in these discussions but he or she can and in fact is expected to use it. After gathering information the mediator assesses whether the dispute is soluble through his or her good offices. If so the mediator devises possible options which he discusses with the parties in caucus. Through such discussions a settlement may begin to emerge which can be refined and tested. Eventually, it may be appropriate to call back into joint session where the plan is further developed. If everyone can live with the plan the terms are reduced into a settlement agreement or perhaps minute of order. A signing ceremony takes place and the parties go their separate ways.

Read on

Dispute resolution is not easy and requires special skills and training. The next chapter discusses the professional help that is available.

CHAPTER **10** *Where to Get Help*

You can write your own patent application and represent yourself before the UK and other intellectual property offices just as you can write your own will, convey your own house and represent yourself in court. There are folk who try to do all those things. Some manage to do a good job. But it can be risky and it will certainly be time consuming. Hence it will not usually be cost-effective. In an increasingly complex world, it is usually better for an inventor or entrepreneur to concentrate on what he or she does best and leave the complexities of IP law to those who make a living from it.

Patent attorneys

The professionals who apply to the UK-IPO for patents for inventions on behalf of the public are called *'patent attorneys'*. For 124 years they were known as *patent agents* and that title is still used in relation to the register of patent agents, but they changed the name of their professional body from the Chartered Institute of Patent Agents to *Chartered Institute of Patent Attorneys* (CIPA) in 2006[1]. Why they did so is not altogether clear because the title 'patent agent' had been reserved to them by law[2] but the press release announcing the change noted that 'with the passage of time members have adopted the term patent attorney which is the title used by patent practitioners throughout the rest of the English-speaking world.'[3] At least part of the explanation may be that a distinction is drawn in the USA between *patent attorneys*

---

1   'Patent agents change name after 124 years' published: 2 June 2006, by Ted Blake on the CIPA website (see http://www.cipa.org.uk/pages/press/article?6EE509B8-5BF4-450A-8B27-25C711B3C3E5).

2   S.276 of the CDPA provided:

    (1) An individual who is not a registered patent agent shall not—

      (a) carry on a business (otherwise than in partnership) under any name or other description which contains the words 'patent agent' or 'patent attorney' or

      (b) in the course of a business otherwise describe himself, or permit himself to be described, as a 'patent agent' or 'patent attorney'.

    (2) A partnership shall not—

      (a) carry on a business under any name or other description which contains the words 'patent agent' or 'patent attorney' or

      (b) in the course of a business otherwise describe itself, or permit itself to be described as, a firm of 'patent agents' or 'patent attorneys', unless all the partners are registered patent agents or the partnership satisfies such conditions as may be prescribed for the purposes of this section.

    (3) A body corporate shall not—

      (a) carry on a business (otherwise than in partnership) under any name or other description which contains the words 'patent agent' or 'patent attorney' or

      (b) in the course of a business otherwise describe itself, or permit itself to be described as, 'patent agent' or 'patent attorney', unless all the directors of the body corporate are registered patent agents or the body satisfies such conditions as may be prescribed for the purposes of this section.

However, that provision was qualified by S.278 (1) which enabled the term 'patent attorney' to be used in reference to a solicitor, and a firm of solicitors to be described as a firm of 'patent attorneys', without any contravention of S.276.

3   'Patent agents change name after 124 years' published: 2 June 2006, by Ted Blake on the CIPA website (see http://www.cipa.org.uk/pages/press/article?6EE509B8-5BF4-450A-8B27-25C711B3C3E5).

who are lawyers[4] and *patent agents* who are not[5] and it may be that patent agents thought that the change of name would impress US clients. Another explanation may be that patent agents who practise before the EPO have called themselves 'European patent attorneys' for many years. Whatever the reason for the change, the consequence is probably unimportant. The word 'attorney' is interchangeable with 'agent' and is used to refer to persons who are not necessarily lawyers in the context of 'power of attorney'. Conversely, solicitors are sometimes referred to as 'agents' in Scotland.

Patent attorneys are trained in IP law and practice and offer legal advice, representation and other legal services in respect of registered and unregistered designs, trade marks and copyrights as well as patents. Persons registered on the register of patent agents can appear as advocates in the Patents County Court while fellows of the CIPA can apply for the right to appear and conduct litigation in intellectual property matters in the High Court. Nearly all patent attorneys have first, and many have higher, degrees in the natural sciences, technology or engineering or related disciplines. Many are entitled to practise in the EPO and OHIM. Several are also qualified to practise in foreign IP offices.

Patent attorneys are pretty well indispensable when it comes to a patent application. It is possible for a reasonably well informed and intelligent member of the public to apply successfully to register a design or even a trade mark, but it is very difficult for such a person to procure a patent. The difficulty lies in the precision with which the specification of a patent must be drafted, particularly the claims. These must delineate clearly and unambiguously the monopoly that the applicant desires. They must be prepared with one eye on the past – that is to say, everything previously known in the relevant field – and the other eye to the future, that is to say possible technical and commercial challenges to the invention. If those challenges are not anticipated the claims may be circumvented and the viability of the invention undermined. If it is drawn to narrowly, the claim may be circumvented. If it is drawn too broadly or too vaguely the claim may be found to be invalid. That is why an intimate understanding of the relevant technology is vital and why patent attorneys have to be scientifically or technically qualified.

It is also a good idea to use a patent attorney if you wish to challenge competitors' IPR. They know the sort of argument and evidence that impresses officials in the UK and other IP offices and the attorneys are likely to be known and trusted by the attorneys. They are also in the best position to advise on patent directory or trade mark and design registry practice. Where they are perhaps a little less well qualified is where IP issues are intertwined with other difficult legal issues since their legal training is so specialized. Also, while many patent attorneys are qualified to conduct litigation in the Chancery Division or county courts they are not as used to handling large volumes of documentation as solicitors. Nor do they go into court as often as counsel. To make up for some of those relative weaknesses, some firms of patent attorneys have set up or acquired associated law firms.

There are about 3,000 patent attorneys in the UK. Some work in-house for large companies and other institutions. The remainder offer their services to the general public either on their

---

4   §11.6 (a) of the US Patent Rules provides:
         Attorneys.   Any   citizen   of   the   United   States   who   is   an   attorney   and   who   fulfills   the
         requirements   of   this   part   may   be   registered   as   a   patent   attorney   to   practice   before   the   Office.'
Provision is also made for non-citizens who are qualified as 'attorneys' and reside lawfully in the USA to register as 'patent attorneys' (see http://www.uspto.gov/web/offices/pac/mpep/documents/appxr_11_6.htm).
5   §11.6 (b) provides:
         (b) Agents. Any citizen of the United States who is not an attorney, and who fulfills the requirements of this part
         may be registered as a patent agent to practice before the Office.
There is corresponding provision for non-citizen residents to be registered as 'patent agents.'
http://www.uspto.gov/web/offices/pac/mpep/documents/appxr_11_6.htm.

own account as sole practitioners or in partnership with, or as employees of, other patent attorneys. The register of patent agents[6] and the directory of patent attorneys[7] are on the CIPA website. If you consult those databases to look for a patent attorney, you should bear in mind that some patent attorneys offer advice on just about every type of IP in respect of every kind of product while others specialize. If you live a long way from London and need a patent attorney to handle a hearing there, it may be better to instruct one who practises near the UK-IPO since he or she will not have to travel and maybe stay overnight in the capital. Since professional fees are sometimes lower in other European countries than they are here, it is worth remembering that you can instruct a European patent attorney from any contracting party to handle your application for a European patent. If you want patent or other IP protection in the USA you will need a US attorney who may well charge less than his or her British counterpart and there is no reason why she cannot manage the international phase of a PCT application at least as well. Finally, if you want a trade mark or design registration rather than a patent a trade mark attorney can also act for you.

Trade mark attorneys

Trade mark attorneys offer advice and representation before the UK-IPO and OHIM in respect of registered trade marks, registered designs and every other type of IP except patents. Their professional body is the *Institute of Trade Mark Attorneys* (ITMA) which also changed the 'A' in its name from *Agents* to *Attorneys*, though slightly earlier than CIPA. Similarly, *trade mark attorneys* were also formerly known as *trade mark agents* and indeed still are in the context of the register of trade mark agents which was established pursuant to Reg. 3 of The Register of Trade Mark Agents Rules 1990.[8] Only those on the register may describe themselves as *'trade mark agents'*[9] though that does not preclude solicitors being referred to as *'trade mark attorneys'*. Many if not most patent attorneys are also trade mark attorneys but there are a sizeable number of trade mark attorneys who are not also patent attorneys. There are some firms made up exclusively of trade mark attorneys and some trade mark attorneys practise in law firms but nearly every firm of patent agents has at least one trade mark attorney among its number.

Trade mark or patent attorneys should be consulted when an application for a trade mark is opposed or when a registered trade mark or design is challenged in the Trade Marks or Designs Registry or at OHIM. They can now conduct litigation in the Chancery Division and Patents County Court and advise on licences and assignments. They are trained in trade mark, design and copyright law and are well placed to advise on Registry or OHIM practice but they claim no expertise outside their specialization. As Community trade marks and designs apply throughout the EU there is no objection to instructing attorneys from other EU member states.

Solicitors

In contrast to the professions mentioned earlier, solicitors actually changed their name *from* attorneys. That term, which is still used as a professional title for lawyers in the USA and other

---

6   http://www.cipa.org.uk/members/directory/default.asp?m=f&dir=2.

7   http://www.cipa.org.uk/members/directory/default.asp?m=f&dir=1.

8   SI 1990 No. 1458 (http://www.opsi.gov.uk/si/si1990/Uksi_19901458_en_1.htm).

9   S.94 Trade Marks Act 1994.

parts of the world, used to apply to lawyers who practised in the common law courts while those practising in chancery were known as solicitors. Upon the merger of the jurisdictions in 1873 both sets of practitioners adopted the chancery name. The old titles survive in the officer of Attorney General and Solicitor General on both sides of the Atlantic. Because there are separate legal systems in the UK there are separate legal professions. Solicitors practising in England and Wales are now known as Solicitors of the Senior Courts and are now represented by the Law Society and regulated by the Solicitors Regulation Authority.[10] Scottish solicitors are regulated by the Law Society of Scotland[11] and Northern Irish solicitors by the Law Society of Northern Ireland. [12]

There are about 100,000 solicitors in England and Wales. They can best be described as legal services contractors. They offer to supply just about every conceivable type of legal service ranging from drafting wills, conveying real property and defending motorists in the magistrates' courts to preparing complex commercial agreements and managing references to the ECJ pursuant to art 234 of the Treaty of Rome. They manage their clients' business, conducting correspondence, filing documents, paying fees and buying in specialist services such as advice from barristers. Solicitors' firms vary in size from one person offices to multinational practices. Some offer a wide range of legal services while others specialize in particular areas.

There is a database of solicitors on the Law Society's website which can be searched by specialization. The results of such searches have to be treated with some caution as the information entered into the database is supplied by the practitioners themselves and does not indicate any accreditation or recommendation. It will already have become clear that IP is a dynamic discipline that is constantly changing and it is very difficult to do IP work well unless it is done full time. Claims to expertise in the subject by suburban or country practices may denote nothing more than a fee earner's interest in the topic or perhaps one big case that worked out well. Claims by the same solicitor to expertise in IP and another difficult specialization, such as planning or building work should be regarded with particular scepticism. Firms that belong to the *Intellectual Property Lawyers Association*[13] can be relied upon since membership of the association is conditional upon having a significant IP practice and commitment to the reform of IP law. Firms that are not members of that Association should be approached only if they are recommended by someone in a position to evaluate their competence such as a substantial user of specialist law firms' services or perhaps a supplier of specialist services such as patent counsel. Absent IPLA membership and an informed and impartial recommendation, enquirers should ask about the training and expertise of the relevant fee earner, recent cases or other work that he or she has done, books and articles that he or she has published, the size and extent of the IP library especially whether it includes specialist reports such as the *Reports of Patent Cases* and *Fleet Streets*. Flash powered websites and glossy brochures do not necessarily betoken excellence.

Solicitors come into their own when a lot of resources need to be managed efficiently. Such a need arises in litigation and arbitration where complaints have to be investigated, statements taken, documents gathered and witnesses interviewed, claims issued, counsel or advocates instructed, statements of case served, lists of documents prepared and exchanged, copies made and inspected, judges or masters attended, bundles prepared, counsel briefed, trial attended, judgment executed and many other things done quickly and thoroughly. All of this

---

10   http://www.sra.org.uk/home.page.
11   http://www.lawscot.org.uk.
12   http://www.lawsoc-ni.org.
13   http://www.ipla.org.uk.

requires organization and attention to detail that is way beyond most non-lawyers' capability. There are other professionals who are authorized to conduct litigation such as patent and trade mark attorneys who have experience of conducting proceedings in the UK-IPO or EPO. While it is true that those professionals are developing expertise in litigation, it must be stressed that experience derived from conducting cases in the IPO is very different from that gained in specialist litigation. Another instance where a lot of resources have to be managed is in a complex commercial transaction such as the sale or purchase of a business where banking, contractual, corporate governance, employment, tax, trust and possibly insolvency issues are likely to arise as well as intellectual property.

Although it is occasionally calamitous to instruct a solicitor on a learning curve in this field (such as when he or she fires off a letter of claim that gives rise to a threats action as in *Kooltrade Ltd. v XTS Ltd*)[14] the most likely adverse consequence is waste. A low hourly rate can be tempting but an inexperienced practitioner is likely to take far longer to accomplish things, and be less accurate than a specialist. Even if there are savings in solicitors' costs they are often more than offset by counsels' fees because many inexperienced solicitors are forever 'picking counsels' brains' as they call their pestering. After a time, counsels' clerks tire of all that and send a fee note.

Barristers

Counsel – known as *barristers* in England, Wales and Northern Ireland and as *advocates* in Scotland – are specialist advocates and legal consultants. When law firms were limited to 20 members and most solicitors were non-graduates, counsel were the aristocrats of the law – in some cases quite literally. They enjoyed exclusive rights of audience in the Senior Courts. They supplied the higher court judiciary. They contributed most of the legal scholarship. Their opinions on the law were regarded as only slightly less authoritative than judgments. They could be consulted only through solicitors or other professional intermediaries. If a client wished to consult a barrister, he or she had to visit the barrister and not the other way round. Business with counsel had to be transacted through commission agents known as clerks who were paid a percentage of counsels' fees, which they had an interest in inflating. Over the last 20 years or so the prestige of the bar has diminished as that of solicitors has increased. The bar's monopolies of higher court advocacy and judicial appointments have been abolished. Procedural reforms have reduced the scope for oral advocacy. Unrestricted recruitment at a time of diminishing demand for the bar's services has diminished its market power. Rules preventing barristers from practising in partnership or corporations have discouraged investment in marketing and technology. The preservation of a court dress and working practices that lend themselves to caricature or even ridicule have led many to dismiss the bar as at best anachronistic and at worst absurd. Yet barristers still have their uses even in specialist areas like IP.

First, they are in a better position than almost anyone else to anticipate how the law will develop. That is because they have been brought up with the judges who make the law and understand how those judges think. What a client often needs to know is how the law will apply to a new technology or affect a contemplated transaction. Book learning can assist only up to a point. Relevant statutes and cases can be identified but these are rarely conclusive. Counsel's advantage is that he or she is likely to have appeared before the judge or even

---

14   [2001] FSR 344.

against him or her when the judge was at the bar. The barrister is likely to have met the judge socially. He or she will have exchanged news and gossip about the judge with other barristers. Through contacts of this kind, counsel will usually have a pretty good idea of how the judge will decide a new issue.

Counsels' second advantage is that their knowledge and understanding of the black letter law is rivalled only by that of the most highly specialized and hence expensive solicitors. Accordingly, instructing a specialist barrister can go a long way towards levelling the imbalance between a magic circle law firm and a small provincial one. There are at least two reasons why barristers acquire such expertise. One is that they have the leisure to read and digest the law because they are spared much of the administrative work that solicitors have to do. Secondly, the formulation of an argument with the need to construe sections of statutes and apply case law helps to develop an intimate understanding of the topic.

Thirdly, as their overheads are very much lower than solicitors', barristers' services are often correspondingly cheaper. It is now possible to consult counsel without the intervention of a solicitor or other professional intermediary. Saving money is not the only advantage of public access. Another is that the barrister can help assemble the rest of a legal team. As they have dealings with lots of law firms, barristers are in an excellent position to judge which solicitors really know what they are doing as opposed to those who just know the buzz words. Yet another advantage is that the client gets the barrister of his choice. The public access contract promises that the barrister will do the work personally. He or she cannot delegate it to a partner or assistant as a solicitor can.

There are just over 12,000 barristers in independent self-employed practice in England and Wales[15] and another 580 in Northern Ireland.[16] The Scottish Bar does not publish its numbers on its website but there are thought to be well over 1,000 practising advocates. Most barristers in England still practise from the ancient splendour of Inns of Court, often in slightly squalid, if genteel, working conditions. They do so as sole practitioners and never as firms or corporations. In England and Wales barristers form loose associations known as 'chambers'[17] to share office accommodation, staff and other resources. While barristers can seek employment in solicitors' firms, industry or the public sector, they cannot then go to court much. Consequently their status is less than that of barristers in independent private practice. Most counsel offer a very broad range of work, particularly in Scotland and Northern Ireland where there is less opportunity for specialization. Many will accept anything that is offered to them, arguing that they can always look up points of law and that a skilled advocate should be able to turn his or her hand to anything. There is a grain of truth in the assertion. Sometimes a non-specialist coming to an area of law with a completely fresh mind can spot a point that specialists have missed. More often than not, however, a generalist is at a disadvantage when briefed against a specialist who knows the pitfalls of his or her area of the law, the practice of the court and the predilections and prejudices of the judge. It is important not to exaggerate the importance of advocacy. A well constructed argument or skilful cross-examination can occasionally make a difference but brilliant advocacy is no substitute for careful preparation. In that regard it is important to understand that different

---

15   Source: The General Council of the Bar – Records Office, Dec 2006.

16   Source: The Bar Library website (see http://www.barlibrary.com/about-us/the-legal-profession-in-ni).

17   In Northern Ireland as in the Republic barristers practise from bar libraries attached to the courts or from home though some hire office space in premises near the higher courts. In Scotland a hybrid exists where counsel also practise from their bar association library or from home but are organized for marketing and certain administrative purposes in 'stables' which employ clerks who perform some of the functions of clerks in England and Wales but not the all important one of fee collection which is entrusted to a private company that collects fees on behalf of all practising advocates.

styles of advocacy are appropriate for different tribunals. What goes down well before a jury in the Old Bailey will not necessarily impress a chancery interim applications judge with a long list. Notwithstanding that an IP specialist will usually do better than a non-specialist in a specialist court, it is unwise to suppose that London counsel will always outclass locals on their home turf. There are some subtle differences between practice in the Royal Courts of Justice and practice in the North which local practitioners are likely to know and outsiders may not. Attempts by London specialists to teach a local judge his or her job are rarely appreciated.

All the caveats on solicitors' claims to expertise in IP apply at least as much to counsel. There are only a handful of chambers that do IP and technology work exclusively. All but one of those chambers are in London. There are also a few recognized specialists in general chancery or commercial chambers. Most IP specialists are members of the *IP Bar Association*. Anyone claiming expertise in IP who is not a member of that Association should be asked the same questions on education, training, experience, publication and library resources that have been recommended earlier for solicitors.

PROFESSIONALS ABROAD

If you need patent, design or trade mark protection outside Europe you will probably need to consult a patent attorney or agent who practises before the IP office that grants such protection. If you have an IP dispute abroad you will need to consult a lawyer who practises In the country where the dispute arises. Patent attorneys and lawyers in the UK can introduce you to a suitably qualified colleague but they can only act for you if you have an office and qualified staff in the country concerned. There are a few transnational law practices but they tend to serve transnational companies that can afford substantial fees. Instructing such a practice is not usually open to start-ups or other SME. It is therefore essential for them to understand how IP services are delivered outside the UK.

LAWYERS IN COMMON LAW COUNTRIES

The adversarial system in common law countries by which rights are determined after a hearing before a court or tribunal creates a need for oral advocacy and case management. In some countries, such as Australia, Hong Kong, Ireland, New Zealand and South Africa, these are delivered by separate professions as in England. Such professions may be known by different names. Advocates are not called 'barristers' everywhere and litigators are called 'attorneys' in some countries. Members of those professions may specialize to a lesser degree. But the basic distinctions between different professional service providers are the same as in England. In other common law countries, such as Canada, India, Singapore and the USA, some or all of those functions can be performed by the same professional and certainly by the same firm. The size and sophistication of local law firms reflects the needs of local business. Some of the law firms serving major commercial centres such as New York and to a lesser extent Toronto, Sydney and Singapore are very large and very sophisticated indeed. The legal services market in those countries resembles that of the City of London. Indeed many American, Canadian and Australian firms are in London just as many London firms are also in New York and some or all of the other major financial centres. Firms in less developed countries tend to be smaller and less specialized. However, these are generalizations. Like all generalizations there are notable exceptions and it should never be forgotten that times are changing rapidly.

LAWYERS IN CIVIL LAW COUNTRIES

The civil law makes different use of oral advocacy and that produces a different split. Some legal services such as litigation are provided by *'lawyers'*.[18] Others such as the formation of companies, transfer of land and other non-contentious work are provided by *'notaries'*. Although *notaries* exist also in common law countries their status and functions are quite different. In common law countries they perform the administrative tasks of recording certain transactions and authenticating certain instruments. Many of them are also solicitors. In civil law countries they provide a range of non-contentious services from forming companies to transferring land. Their role is sometimes interpreted to English lawyers as combining some of the roles of a solicitor, chancery barrister and public registry and their status is very high indeed. In most civil law countries there are also professionals who practise before IP offices but they do not usually regard themselves as lawyers.

Fees

SOLICITORS

Most professionals charge for their time and disbursements. 'Disbursements' are the costs that professionals incur in delivering their services. They include fees charged by public bodies such as courts and tribunals and fees charged by other professionals, such as counsel and expert witnesses. Most professionals charge an hourly rate which can usually be negotiated depending on local supply, the experience and function of the fee earner and the local cost to the professional of providing the services. Because of the negotiability of hourly rates it is impossible to generalize. As a general rule service providers in London charge considerably more than those in other UK metropolitan centres and experienced practitioners more than juniors. An experienced specialist practising in a major law firm can command anything up to £1,000 per hour while an assistant solicitor in a small general practice outside London only £100 or so. On average patent attorneys can charge more than most solicitors but less than partners of major City practices.

COUNSEL

Counsel charge for their services rather differently. For a start, they are not allowed to hold clients' funds so they charge only for their services, sometimes for reimbursement of their expenses, but never for disbursements. They negotiate fees for specified services such as advising in conference or appearing in court. Traditionally, counsels' fees were negotiated by clerks who tended to charge whatever the market would bear, but nowadays fees bear at least some relationship to time spent on the task in hand. The fee for the first day of an oral hearing is called a *'brief fee'* or *'brief'* and the fee for each subsequent day is called a *'refresher'*. The brief is usually based on the hours likely to be spent in court plus those required for preparation. Where there is a trial with a large number of witnesses of fact and expert evidence the advocate may need to spend a week or longer on such preparation. A typical fee for an established practitioner would be £12,000 on the brief and £1,250 refresher. The brief for the same counsel to move or resist an application for an interim injunction would be about £1,700 since that

---

18   Known as *'avocats'* in French, *'abodado'* in Spanish, *'avvocato'* in Italian, *'Rechtsanwalt'* (literally *'law agent'*) in German and *'bengoshi'* in Japanese.

would require about 5 hours preparation and 2 in court. The same counsel would probably charge £750 to advise in writing on a difficult point of law and between £500 to £750 to 'settle' or draft a statement of case.

CONTINGENCY FEES

Some law firms are prepared to charge for their services on the promise of a share of any benefits that their clients recover. Such fees are known as 'contingency fees' because payment is *contingent* or conditional upon the service leading to recovering a sum of money to be shared by the solicitor or client. In the USA it is possible to enter an agreement with a lawyer to share any damages that may be awarded. Such retainers are used frequently to fund product liability and other damages claims in the USA. Those arrangements work successfully in the USA because claimants do not risk an award of costs if they are unsuccessful and damages tend to be higher than elsewhere. Lawyers in England and Wales are allowed to enter contingency fee agreements only for non-contentious work such as drafting legal instruments for a revenue generating venture. They are not allowed to litigate on a contingency retainer.

CONDITIONAL FEE AGREEMENTS

However, English lawyers can enter *conditional fee agreements* (CFA) with litigants whereby the lawyer will be paid his or her usual fees plus a supplement known as *a 'success fee'* if the client is successful but nothing if the client is unsuccessful.[19] A typical CFA together with notes and conditions can be downloaded from the website of the *Chancery Bar Association*.[20] It is very important for clients to understand that entering a CFA does not relieve them from the risk of paying the other side's costs if the claim fails. Consequently they must make provision for those costs by insurance or otherwise. CFAs work very well for road traffic and accident claims against employers where the defendants are insured, the risks of failure are low and costs are predictable. They do not work well for more complex areas of litigation such as IP where costs are much higher, delays much longer and uncertainties much greater. The prospect of a success fee in several years time rarely justifies the investment necessary to launch and maintain the claim from the solicitors' point of view. Further premium for insuring against the other side's costs is usually prohibitive. Consequently very few IP infringement claims are launched on CFAs.

Alternative business structures

These are proposed in the new Legal Services Act 2007 which received royal assent on 30 October 2007. The Act will establish a new framework for the regulation of legal services in England and Wales. In his foreword to the white paper setting out proposals for reforming

---

19   The statutory basis for CFAs is S.58 of the Courts and Legal Service Act 1990 which defines a conditional fee agreement as 'an agreement in writing between a person providing advocacy or litigation services and his client which:
    (a) does not relate to proceedings of a kind mentioned in subsection (10);
    (b) provides for that person's fees and expenses, or any part of them, to be payable only in specified circumstances;
    (c) complies with such requirements (if any) as may be prescribed by the Lord Chancellor; and
    (d) is not a contentious business agreement (as defined by section 59 of the [1974 c. 47.] Solicitors Act 1974).'
See http://www.opsi.gov.uk/acts/acts1990/Ukpga_19900041_en_3.htm#mdiv58.
20   http://www.chba.org.uk/default.asp?l=1&m=Conditional+Fee+Agreement&i=5&r=22416.

the regulation and delivery of legal services[21] the Lord Chancellor envisioned a legal services market where excellence would be delivered but which would also be responsive, flexible, and put the consumer first. [22] One of the ways in which the government hopes to deliver such a market is by promoting the development of alternative business structures (ABS). These would enable legal and certain other services to be provided to high standards and in ways that suit different consumers thereby ensuring competition and innovation.

An ABS could be any structure that could deliver legal services service, other than the structures currently used to do so in private practice including partnerships, limited liability partnerships, public and private limited companies and mutual societies. [23] The hope is that such ABS would offer high quality legal services from all legal practitioners, delivered to suit consumers, not providers. Their business models and practices should support that objective and foster innovation and diversity. The proposed legislation would remove barriers to make it easier for new providers to enter the market and thereby benefit both consumers[24] and service providers.[25]

Doing it yourself

Acting in person before the UK or other IP office or in court is not to be recommended if it can possibly be avoided, but the cost of professional services is such that sometimes there is no alternative. There are now a number of resources offering pretty good free advice and other services locally or over the internet. Here are just a few.

---

21   'The Future of Legal Services: Putting Consumers First' Cm 6679 Oct 2005 (http://www.dca.gov.uk/legalsys/folwp.pdf).
22   Page 7 Ibid.
23   Footnote 20 on page 39.
24   The white paper argued that the potential benefits for consumers would include:
- more choice: consumers will have greater flexibility in deciding from where to obtain legal and some non-legal services.
- reduced prices: consumers should be able to purchase some legal services more cheaply. This should arise where ABS firms realise savings through economies of scale and reduce transaction costs where different types of legal professionals are part of the same firm.
- better access to justice: ABS firms might find it easier to provide services in rural areas or to less mobile consumers.
- improved consumer service: consumers may benefit from a better service where ABS firms are able to access external finance and specialist non-legal expertise.
- greater convenience: ABS firms can provide one-stop-shopping for related services, for example car insurance and legal services for accident claims.
- increased consumer confidence: higher consumer protection levels and an increase in the quality of legal services could flow from ABS firms which have a good reputation in providing non-legal services. These firms will have a strong incentive to keep that reputation when providing legal services.

Page 40.
25   Expected benefits for service providers would include:
- increased access to finance: at present, providers can face constraints on the amount of equity, mainly debt equity, they can raise. Allowing alternative business structures will facilitate expansion by firms (including into international markets) and investment in large-scale capital projects that increase efficiency.
- better spread of risk: a firm could spread its risk more effectively among shareholders. This will lower the required rate of return on any investment, facilitate investment and could deliver lower prices.
- increased flexibility: non-legal firms such as insurance companies, banks and estate agents will have the freedom to realise synergies with legal firms by forming ABS firms and offering integrated legal and associated services.
- easier to hire and retain high-quality non-legal staff: ABS firms will be able to reward non-legal staff in the same way as lawyers.
- more choice for new legal professionals: ABS firms could contribute to greater diversity by offering those who are currently under-represented more opportunities to enter and remain within the profession.

Page 41.

IP CLINICS

IP clinics are free consultations with a patent or trade mark attorney or other IP professional. Several are organized around the UK by the CIPA in conjunction with some of the British PATLIB[26] libraries.[27] Except for the Birmingham clinics, all are attended by registered patent agents. Consultations are usually by appointment and the dates and times of clinics and booking information appear on the CIPA website. [28] To encourage attendance or reasonable notice of cancellation a small deposit is sometimes requested. Trade mark and design clinics are also provided by ITMA at the London branch of the UK-IPO[29] on the first Thursday of every month (except January when it is the second Thursday) between 17:00 and 18:30. Full particulars and booking forms are available from the ITMA website.[30] IP clinics are also organized by nipc® at the Elsie Whiteley Innovation Centre in Halifax on the first Wednesday of the month, the Barnsley campus of the University of Huddersfield in the morning on the second Tuesday, the Poplars Business park at Catcliffe in Rotherham in the afternoon of the second Tuesday, the Northern Technology Institute in Leeds on the third Wednesday, Gumption Centres Bradford[31] on the third Thursday; and Huddersfield Media Centre on the last Friday.[32] Flourishing inventors' clubs are attached to the Leeds[33], Liverpool[34], Manchester[35] and Sheffield[36] clinics in the North and there are others elsewhere in the UK.

UK-IPO

The Central Enquiry Office of the UK-IPO offers basic information on all areas of IP and publishes a wide range of brochures and guides, many of which can be downloaded from the IPO's website. Also available from the website are unofficial but very useful consolidations of the Patents Act 1977,[37] Registered Designs Act 1949,[38] Copyright Designs and Patents Act 1988[39] and Trade Marks Act 1994[40] together with similar consolidations of the Rules, manuals, transcripts and digests of hearing officers' decisions, tribunal practice notices and many other materials. Although the Central Enquiry Office will not offer specific legal advise it will provide much practical guidance on filings, oppositions, invalidity and many related matters. IPO staff attend many exhibitions and events across the UK and organize local IP awareness and other workshops. The telephone number for the Central Enquiry Office is 0845 9 500 505.

---

26   PATLIB is a European network of IP information centres consisting of the EPO, national IP offices and local public libraries with patent collections. The UK members of the network can be found on the PATLIB UK page ('Patent information centres in the United Kingdom') of the EOP website at http://www.epo.org/patents/patent-information/patlib/directory/unitedkingdom.html.
27   Currently at Aberdeen, Belfast, Birmingham, Bristol, Glasgow, Leeds, Liverpool, London, Manchester, Newcastle-upon-Tyne, Newport, Plymouth, Portsmouth, Sheffield and Swansea.
28   http://www.cipa.org.uk/pages/advice-clinics.
29   Harmsworth House, 13-15 Bouverie Street.
30   http://www.itma.org.uk/pdf_downloads/events/advice_clinics_07.pdf.
31   Glydegate, Bradford, BD5 0BQ Tel 08450 344 133 at http://www.gumptioncentres.co.uk/contact.html.
32   7 Northumberland Street, Huddersfield, HD1 1RL.
33   http://www.businessandpatents.org.
34   http://www.liverpoolinventors.org.uk.
35   http://www.manchesterinventors.com.
36   http://www.sheffieldinventors.org.uk.
37   http://www.ipo.gov.uk/patentsact1977.pdf.
38   http://www.ipo.gov.uk/regdesignactchanges.pdf.
39   http://www.ipo.gov.uk/cdpact1988.pdf.
40   http://www.ipo.gov.uk/tmact94.pdf.

OTHER IP OFFICES

Similar information is available in English from most other IP offices including the EPO, OHIM and WIPO. A good starting point for European patents is The 'Guide for applicants' which outlines the procedure for granting European patents and offers practical advice. Part 1[41] describes and explains how to obtain a European patent and Part II deals with PCT applications. Also available on the EPO site[42] are the EPC, Implementing Regulations and other rules[43] relating to European patents, the Official Journal, full transcripts of decisions of the Boards of Appeal and many similar details. OHIM[44] publishes on its website basic guidance on Community trade mark[45] and design law[46] as well as the CTM and CD Regulations and other EC legislation, transcripts of the leading ECJ and other cases and brochures on filings, opposition and cancellation. The WIPO website has the Paris, Bern and other IP treaties, [47] summaries of national IP laws,[48] basic information on IP[49] and many other useful materials and resources in English and several other major languages.

CITIZENS ADVICE

Basic advice on the general law and practical information on its application to particular circumstances is offered by the *Citizens Advice* website[50] and its 20,000 volunteers. There are branches known as 'Citizens Advice Bureaux' in most towns and cities in England and Wales, many attached to or located not far from courts. The address and telephone number of the nearest bureau can be obtained from the website.[51] The service handles nearly 5.5 million enquiries every year. There are similar services for Scotland[52] and Northern Ireland. [53]

PRO BONO ADVICE

'*Pro bono*' is short for '*pro bono publico*' or 'for the public good'. It is an American term that has been imported into the UK to refer to many free legal advice and representation schemes that many barristers, solicitors and other professionals offer throughout the UK. One of the best schemes is the *Bar Pro Bono Unit*[54] which offers advice, representation and help in all legal areas of the law, including IP, to those who cannot afford to pay and do not qualify for legal aid. Examples of cases where the Unit has been able to help appear on its website.[55] The Unit is supported by the Bar Council, the Inns of Court and several large London chambers.

---

41   http://www.european-patent-office.org/legal/guiapp1/e/index.htm.
42   http://www.epo.org.
43   http://www.european-patent-office.org/legal/epc/e/contents.html.
44   http://oami.europa.eu.
45   http://oami.europa.eu/en/mark/role/brochure/br1en.htm.
46   http://oami.europa.eu/en/design/default.htm.
47   http://www.wipo.int/treaties/en.
48   http://www.wipo.int/members/en.
49   http://www.wipo.int/about-ip/en.
50   http://www.citizensadvice.org.uk/index.htm.
51   http://www.citizensadvice.org.uk/index.htm.
52   http://www.cas.org.uk.
53   http://www.citizensadvice.co.uk.
54   http://www.barprobono.org.uk.
55   http://www.barprobono.org.uk/?cID=case_examples.

OTHER USEFUL WEBSITES

Statutes since 1988, statutory instruments since 1987 and all the legislation of the Scottish, Welsh and Northern Ireland representative assemblies and their respective governments appear on the website of the Office of Public Sector Information (OPSI).[56] The Civil Procedure Rules which govern civil litigation in the Senior and County Courts appear on the Ministry of Justice website.[57] That site is linked to HM Courts Service[58] website which contains forms used in litigation, guides to the practice of the Chancery, Patents and other courts, a database of court addresses and contact details and other information. As for case law, transcripts of the speeches of the law lords in the House of Lords and their judgments in the Privy Council together with judgments of the Senior Courts of England and Wales, the Court of Session, Court of Judicature of Northern Ireland, Irish Supreme Court, the ECJ and many other courts and tribunals are to be found at BAILII (*British and Irish Legal Information Institute*). [59] BAILII is linked to similar Legal Information Institutes for the laws of Australia, Canada, France, Hong Kong, New Zealand, USA and many other countries. European legislation and other materials are accessible through the *Europa* website,[60] the portal for the EU institutions. Particularly useful are the Industrial Property,[61] copyright and related rights[62] and antitrust[63] pages.

---

56   http://www.opsi.gov.uk.
57   http://www.justice.gov.uk/civil/procrules_fin/index.htm.
58   http://www.hmcourts-service.gov.uk/index.htm.
59   http://www.bailii.org.
60   http://www.europa.eu.
61   http://ec.europa.eu/internal_market/indprop/index_en.htm.
62   http://ec.europa.eu/internal_market/copyright/index_en.htm.
63   http://ec.europa.eu/comm/competition/antitrust/overview_en.html.

11 *Threats Actions*

Readers will remember Mr. Pepys's discomfort upon learning about threats actions; how he had to make a phone call. He was not the first solicitor for whom they were an unwelcome discovery and he will not be the last. But at least he did not learn about them the hard way, that is to say in a letter of claim or even a *claim form*. Since non-specialist solicitors are more likely to land themselves in lumber than anyone else this chapter is written in slightly different language from the rest of this effort. I have adopted the sort of simplified legal speak that those chaps like – the sort of language that they got used to from the 'Nutshell' guides when they were cramming for their vocational exams and had much, much better things to do than read statutes or case law.

What is a 'threats action'?

A threats action is a right of action for persons who are aggrieved by threats to sue for infringement of a patent, registered design, unregistered design right or registered Community design or a registered or Community trade mark that turn out to be groundless. Proceedings may be brought not only against those who make those threats but also against those who convey them such as solicitors. The right of action does not cover all threats. Saying 'I'll sue you' to an alleged manufacturer or importer of something that infringes your client's right is usually alright. So, too, is sending a copy of your client's patent specification or certificate of registration to the horrible little man who is giving your client grief. But anything else – well tricky, better read on.

Legislative policy

The policy behind these statutes was explained by Mr Justice Lightman in *L'Oréal (UK) Ltd. v Johnson & Johnson* as:

> clearly to stop patentees who were (in Pope's words about Addison) 'willing to wound but afraid to strike' from holding the sword of Damocles above another's head.[1]

The legislative intention is obvious from the order in which the threats action provision appears in the Patents Act 1977. The section number is 70, which is immediately before S.71 conferring jurisdiction upon the court to make declarations of non-infringement and S.72, setting out grounds for the revocation of patents. Patents are monopolies that can operate against the public interest. All these provisions are there to try to prevent their abuse though in different ways. Basically the harm that the legislation is trying to prevent is what we nowadays might call 'viral anti-marketing'. Putting it about among retailers that you can get into a whole heap of trouble if you stock or sell beautifully made and less expensive imported product B instead of

---

1   [2000] EWHC Ch 129 (7th March, 2000) at http://www.bailii.org/ew/cases/EWHC/Ch/2000/129.html, also at [2000] FSR 686, 693.

clunky old locally made product A which just happens to be supplied by the person spouting the threats. A perfect example comes from *Kooltrade Ltd. v XTS Ltd.*[2] where the defendant's solicitors wrote to the internet and mail order sales arm of a major retailer alleging that a baby carriage that they had bought from the claimant infringed their non-existent patent and design rights. The retailer immediately dropped the product line and did not buy anything else from the injured supplier. Actions of this kind can be devastating because who needs to buy into a lawsuit, particularly in England where costs for patent litigation are notorious?[3]

The legislation

This cause of action was created by S.32 of the Patents, Designs and Trade Marks Act 1882. A similar provision has appeared in every subsequent patent statute. The present provision is S.70 of the Patents Act 1977 which is set out in full because it has been amended substantially by the Patents Act 2004:

(1) *Where a person (whether or not the proprietor of, or entitled to any right in, a patent) by circulars, advertisements or otherwise threatens another person with proceedings for any infringement of a patent, a person aggrieved by the threats (whether or not he is the person to whom the threats are made) may, subject to subsection (4) below, bring proceedings in the court against the person making the threats, claiming any relief mentioned in subsection (3) below.*

(2) *In any such proceedings the claimant or pursuer shall, subject to subsection (2A) below, be entitled to the relief claimed if he proves that the threats were so made and satisfies the court that he is a person aggrieved by them.*

(2A) *If the defendant or defender proves that the acts in respect of which proceedings were threatened constitute or, if done, would constitute an infringement of a patent –*
    (a) *the claimant or pursuer shall be entitled to the relief claimed only if he shows that the patent alleged to be infringed is invalid in a relevant respect;*
    (b) *even if the claimant or pursuer does show that the patent is invalid in a relevant respect, he shall not be entitled to the relief claimed if the defendant or defender proves that at the time of making the threats he did not know, and had no reason to suspect, that the patent was invalid in that respect.*

(3) *The said relief is –*
    (a) *a declaration or declarator to the effect that the threats are unjustifiable;*
    (b) *an injunction or interdict against the continuance of the threats; and*
    (c) *damages in respect of any loss which the claimant or pursuer has sustained by the threats.*

(4) *Proceedings may not be brought under this section for –*
    (a) *a threat to bring proceedings for an infringement alleged to consist of making or importing a product for disposal or of using a process, or*

---

2   [2001] FSR 158.
3   Lord Esher MR's famous dicta in *Ungar v Sugg* (1892) 9 RPC 113 'that a man had better have his patent infringed, or have anything happen to him in this world, short of losing all his family by influenza, than have a dispute about a patent' which appears or is referred to more than once in this screed was made in the context of a threat of litigation.

(b)   a threat, made to a person who has made or imported a product for disposal or used a process, to bring proceedings for an infringement alleged to consist of doing anything else in relation to that product or process.

(5)   For the purposes of this section a person does not threaten another person with proceedings for infringement of a patent if he merely –

(a)   provides factual information about the patent,

(b)   makes enquiries of the other person for the sole purpose of discovering whether, or by whom, the patent has been infringed as mentioned in subsection (4) (a) above, or

(c)   makes an assertion about the patent for the purpose of any enquiries so made.

(6)   In proceedings under this section for threats made by one person (A) to another (B) in respect of an alleged infringement of a patent for an invention, it shall be a defence for A to prove that he used his best endeavours, without success, to discover –

(a)   where the invention is a product, the identity of the person (if any) who made or (in the case of an imported product) imported it for disposal;

(b)   where the invention is a process and the alleged infringement consists of offering it for use, the identity of a person who used the process;

(c)   where the invention is a process and the alleged infringement is an act falling within section 60 (1) (c) above, the identity of the person who used the process to produce the product in question;

and that he notified B accordingly, before or at the time of making the threats, identifying the endeavours used.

Equivalent provisions appear in the Registered Designs Act 1949,[4] Copyright, Designs and Patents Act 1988,[5] the Trade Marks Act 1994[6] and the statutory instruments implementing the

---

4   S.26 provides:

(1)   Where any person (whether entitled to or interested in a registered design or an application for a registered design or not) by circulars, advertisements or otherwise threatens any other person with proceedings for infringement of [the right in a registered design], any person aggrieved thereby may bring an action against him for any such relief as is mentioned in the next following subsection.

(2)   Unless in any action brought by virtue of this section proves that the acts in respect of which proceedings were threatened constitute or, if done, would constitute, an infringement of [the right in a registered design] the registration of which is not shown by the [claimant] to be invalid, the [claimant] shall be entitled to the following relief, that is to say —

(a)   a declaration to the effect that the threats are unjustifiable;

(b)   an injunction against the continuance of the threats; and

(c)   such damages, if any, as he has sustained thereby.

(2A)   Proceedings may not be brought under this section in respect of a threat to bring proceedings for an infringement alleged to consist of the making or importing of anything.

(3)   For the avoidance of doubt it is hereby declared that mere notification that a design is registered does not constitute a threat of proceedings within the meaning of this section.

5   S.253 provides:

(1)   Where a person threatens another person with proceedings for infringement of [national unregistered] design right, a person aggrieved by the threats may bring an action against him claiming -

(a)   a declaration to the effect that the threats are unjustifiable;

(b)   an injunction against the continuance of the threats; and

(c)   damages in respect of any loss which he has sustained by the threats.

(2)   If the [claimant] proves that any threats were made and that he is a person aggrieved by them, he is entitled to the relief unless the defendant shows that the acts in respect of which proceedings were threatened did constitute, or if done would have constituted an infringement of the design right concerned.

(3)   Proceedings may not be brought under this section in respect of a threat to bring proceedings for an infringement alleged to consist of the making or importing of anything.

(4)   Mere notification that a design is protected by design right does not constitute a threat of proceedings within the meaning of this section.

6   S.21 provides:

(1)   Where a person threatens another with proceedings for infringement of a registered trade mark other than:

Community trade mark, Madrid Protocol and Community design regulations into the UK. There is also similar in legislation in countries whose laws are modelled on ours. Some, such as India and Australia, even extend threats actions to copyright[7] which we have never done here.

What is an Actionable Threat?

In *L'Oréal (UK) Ltd. v Johnson & Johnson*[8] Mr Justice Lightman adopted the following definition:

> *In summary, the term 'threat' covers any intimation that would convey to a reasonable man that some person has [trade mark] rights and intends to enforce them against another. It matters not that the threat may be veiled or covert, conditional or future.*[9]

A general warning to the public or trade that a patentee has patent rights and means to enforce them will not suffice[10] but an advertisement warning traders not to deal in 'rubbishy imitations' by a similar name was actionable when the only product competing with the defendant's *'vanguard'* was the claimant's *'vizard.'* The test is subjective: how would the communication be understood by the recipient in the position of the claimant?[11] As Mr Justice Aldous put it in *Bowden Controls*:

> *I have to take into account the commercial background and knowledge of a recipient of the type to whom these letters sent ... Even if he thought that suppliers did not consider it practical to sue manufacturers, I believe that the recipient would consider what was the purpose of the letter. He would conclude that the purpose of the letter was to give him information and a warning. That requires the answer: a warning as to what?*

A communication that conveys that message is actionable even if expressed informally and without mentioning patent proceedings. An informal conversation between courteous

---

(a)   the application of the mark to goods or their packaging;
(b)   the importation of goods to which, or to the packaging of which, the mark has been applied, or
(c)   the supply of services under the mark,
any person aggrieved may bring proceedings for relief under this section.
(2)   The relief which may be applied for is any of the following –
(a)   a declaration to the effect that the threats are unjustifiable;
(b)   an injunction against the continuance of the threats; and
(c)   damages in respect of any loss he has sustained by the threats;
and the [claimant] is entitled to such relief unless the defendant shows that the acts in respect of which proceedings were registered constitute (or if done would constitute) an infringement of the registered trade mark concerned.
(3)   If that is shown by the defendant, the [claimant] is nevertheless entitled to relief if he shows that the registration of the mark is invalid or liable to be revoked in a relevant respect.
(4)   The mere notification that a trade mark is registered, or that an application for registration has been made, does not constitute a threat of proceedings for the purposes of this section.
7   See S.202 of the Australian Copyright Act 1968 at http://www.austlii.edu.au/au/legis/cth/consol_act/ca1968133/s202.html and S.60 and S.60 of the Indian Copyright Act 1957 at http://www.commonlii.org/in/legis/num_act/ca1957133.
8   [2000] FSR 686, 693.
9   Adopted from paras 10-402 and 403 of the *Encyclopaedia of UK and European Patent Law.*
10   As in *Crowther v United Flexible Metallic Tubing Co. Ltd.* (1905) 22 RPC 549.
11   Per Aldous J in *Bowden Controls Ltd. v Acco Cable Controls Ltd. and another* [1990] RPC 427, 432 and Lightman J in *L Oréal (UK) Ltd. v Johnson & Johnson* [2000] FSR 686, 693).

businessmen in which neither party says anything about solicitors or claim forms may convey such a message:

> *I think that an interview of this kind, a serious interview between businessmen, although nobody speaks of solicitors and writs, has no real meaning except to convey to the person whom I regard as having been threatened, that the threatener has legal rights and means to enforce them.*[12]

So, too, can a threat that is made in response to an enquiry[13] though that danger is now mitigated considerably in the case of patents by the new paragraphs (b) and (c) of S.70 (5) of the Patents Act 1977 which were inserted by the 2004 Act. A threat made ostensibly in relation to another cause of action can be actionable[14] as indeed can the mention of a UK trade mark in a cease and desist letter in respect of foreign intellectual property rights.[15] A letter of claim (aka 'letter before action' and 'cease and desist') can be a threat[16] but not necessarily a letter from a solicitor warning that he intends to advise his client to institute patent infringement proceedings since clients (in some cases sensibly) do not always follow their solicitors' advice.[17] Each case turns on its own facts and it is very difficult to lay down any hard and fast rules. Also, since the 2004 Act has modified the law as to patents but not trade marks, registered or unregistered designs what is now safe in respect of patents is not necessarily safe in respect of other rights.

WHO IS A 'PERSON AGGRIEVED'?

Claims must be brought by a *'person aggrieved'* by a threat. The scope of these words is very wide indeed. They certainly include persons to whom a threat is addressed, one of the suppliers of a person who has been threatened or, indeed, the controlling shareholder of a small private company if he or she depends on that company for a livelihood. Typically the person threatened will be a wholesaler, retailer or other distributor. It is not necessary to suffer actual loss or damage in order to have a grievance[18] though unless you can demonstrate such loss or damage you are unlikely to get any damages or an inquiry as to damages.[19]

AGAINST WHOM CAN AN ACTION LIE?

It will be remembered that this is where Mr. Pepys's heart missed a beat and he had to make an urgent phone call. An action can lie against a solicitor or patent attorney who communicates a threat as well as against the client who instructs him to do so.[20] Some statutes like the Australian Copyright Act 1968 provide a limited immunity for threats made by barristers and solicitors in the course of their work.[21] I did try to argue for the insertion of a similar provision in the consultation for the new Patents Act 2004 but the great and the good of the UK patent

---

12   As in *Lunar Advertising Co. Ltd. v Burnham & Co,* (1928) 45 RPC 258, 260.
13   As in *L'Oréal (UK) Ltd. v Johnson & Johnson* [2000] FSR 686.
14   As in *C & P Development Co. (London) Ltd. v Sisabro Novelty Co. Ltd.* (1953) 70 RPC 277 and *Vandervell Products Ltd. v Usher* [1961] RPC 206.
15   As in *Prince Plc v Prince Sports Group Inc.* [1998] FSR 21.
16   *Brain v Ingledew Brown & Bennison* [1997] FSR 511).
17   *Earles Utilities v Harrison* (1934) 52 RPC 77.
18   *Brain v Ingledew Brown & Bennison* [1997] FSR 511.
19   See *Kooltrade* at [2001] FSR 158.
20   *Brain v Ingledew Brown & Bennison* [1997] FSR 511.
21   S.202 (3) provides:
      Nothing in this section renders a barrister or solicitor of the High Court, or of the Supreme Court of a State or Territory, liable to an action under this section in respect of an act done by him or her in his or her professional capacity on behalf of a client.

establishment were against me. In short, proceedings may lie against anyone who threatens proceedings whether the proprietor of the patent or other right or not. It used to be thought that there was no cause of action by the proprietor of a patent application because S.70 of the 1977 Act omitted the words 'or an application for a patent' which used to appear in S.65 of the 1949 Act but that argument was dismissed by Mr. Justice Laddie in *Brain v Ingledew Brown & Bennison*.[22]

REMEDIES

The legislation provides the following remedies:

(a) declarations that the threats are unjustifiable;
(b) injunctions against a continuance of the threats; and
(c) damages sustained by the threats.

Damages have become increasingly important as a remedy with the growth of mail order and e-commerce distribution. In one unreported case in which I was instructed, the master assessed damages for loss of sales resulting from threats causing a product to be delisted from a mail order catalogue at just under £50,000. At the time the product was withdrawn from sale by the retailer, only a handful of articles had actually been sold and the other side argued unsuccessfully that if the product was any good it would still sell. In accordance with usual Chancery procedure, damages are generally assessed upon an inquiry although the court may deal with the question at trial. A claimant must prove that he has suffered some loss as a result of the threats (as opposed to some other cause such as the actual issue of proceedings).[23] If he can show causation and some loss the court will generally grant an inquiry even if the evidence of loss is weak as in *Brain*. However, an inquiry is not automatic and was refused in *Prince Plc v Prince Sports Group Inc*.[24] where the threat was made in a domain name registration dispute.

DEFENCES

These have been extended in the case of patents (but not in the case of other rights) by the 2004 Act. Essentially, they are:

* the threats were justified;
* the threat fell within a statutory exception;
* the threat was a mere notification of the existence of the intellectual property right;
* the threat was entirely in respect of foreign litigation; and
* the threat was made in 'without prejudice' negotiations.

JUSTIFICATION

It has always been a defence to show that the acts of which the defendant complained infringed or would have infringed his patent, design or trade mark unless the claimant can show that the right is invalid.[25] That defence has now, however, been extended in the case of patents by the new sub-section (2A). If the defendant proves that the acts in respect of which

---

22   [1997] FSR 511.
23   *Carflow Products (UK) Ltd. v Linwood Securities (Birmingham) Ltd.* [1998] FSR 691.
24   [1998] FSR 21.
25   See S.70 (2) and (2A) Patents Act 1977, S.26 (2) Registered Designs Act 1949, S.253 (2) Copyright, Designs and Patents Act 1988 and S.21 (2) Trade Marks Act 1994.

proceedings were threatened constitute or, if done, would constitute an infringement of a patent the claimant shall be entitled to the relief claimed only if he or she can show that the patent alleged to be infringed is invalid in a relevant respect. Moreover, even if the claimant does show that the patent is invalid in such a respect, he or she shall not be entitled to the relief claimed if the defendant proves that at the time of making the threats he or she did not know, and had no reason to suspect, that the patent was invalid in that respect. Patent litigation is often sparked off by a threats action in which the defendant counterclaims for infringement in respect of which the claimant counterclaims to the counterclaim for revocation.

EXCEPTED ACTS

Threats in respect of the alleged making or importing of a product (or in the case of threatened patent proceedings using a process) were never actionable under S.70 of the Patents Act 1977 or indeed the equivalent provisions of the Registered Designs and Copyright, Designs and Patents Act 1988. Similarly, threats in respect of alleged application of a mark to goods or their packaging, importation of goods to which a mark has been applied, or the supply of services[26] under a mark only fall outside S.21 of the Trade Marks Act 1994. It used to be the law that a threat of proceedings for say selling as well as making or importing an infringing product was still actionable since the statutory exception was confined to the acts of making and importing[27] but the exception has now been widened. The new S.70 (4) (b) means that proceedings may no longer be brought for a threat made to a person who has made or imported a product for disposal or used a process, to bring proceedings *for an infringement alleged to consist of doing anything else in relation to that product or process*. So the previous case law, which actually arose in a case from Huddersfield where the solicitor for some reason or other instructed a barrister 200 miles away instead of his local home based expert 5 minutes away[28] whom his firm already used to instruct, has now changed.

MERE NOTIFICATION

Merely notifying a party that a patent, design or trade mark registration or national unregistered design right subsists has never been actionable provided that that is all that is said or done. The defence did not apply if anything was added to the notification, such as an indication that the patent or other intellectual property right will be enforced.[29] The only safe thing to do (and that is still the case with designs and trade marks) was to send a copy of the specification, the certificate of registration or whatever together with a compliments slip or at the most an invitation to discuss a licence. Everyone in the intellectual property community knew what such a communication meant and a shrewd patent solicitor would often respond with an innocent looking letter asking simply 'why have you sent us this?' hoping to provoke his or her opponent into making a threat. The mere notification exception has been extended in respect of patents (but not in respect of anything else) by two new sub-sections that have been inserted by the 2004 Act. S.70 (5) now makes clear that a person does not threaten another person with proceedings for infringement of a patent if he or she merely provides factual information about the patent, makes enquiries of the other person for the sole purpose of discovering whether, or by whom, the patent has been infringed or makes an assertion about

---

26   Mr. Justice Neuberger (as he then was) held in *Prince* that the supply of services under a mark does not include the use of the mark as a domain name.

27   See *Cavity Trays Ltd. v RMC Panel Products Ltd.* [1996] RPC 361.

28   *Cavity Trays Ltd. v RMC Panel Products Ltd.* [1996] RPC 361.

29   *Rosedale Associated Manufacturers Ltd. v Airfix Products Ltd.* [1956] RPC 360.

the patent for the purpose of any enquiries so made. Also, there is a new defence under S.70 (6). In proceedings for threats made by one person (A) to another (B) in respect of an alleged infringement of a patent for an invention, it is now a defence for A to prove that he used his best endeavours, without success, to discover the identity of any person who made or imported an allegedly infringing product, or the identity of a person who used an allegedly infringing process.

THREATS OF PROCEEDINGS ABROAD

A threat to bring proceedings abroad for infringement of a foreign patent is not actionable in the UK[30] but a veiled threat of proceedings in the UK can still be actionable even if the only proceedings likely to be brought are for the infringement of a foreign intellectual property right.[31] A threat to bring proceedings for the infringement of a European patent or a Community trade mark or design in England is clearly actionable.

'WITHOUT PREJUDICE' COMMUNICATIONS

The words 'without prejudice' in a letter, fax, email or other document are understood in England and the rest of the common law world to mean that the communication relates to settlement discussions and that it should not be shown to a court or arbitrator while the dispute is still going on. Similarly, nothing said in a 'without prejudice' discussion or mediation can be repeated. The privilege is very useful because it enables the parties and their legal representatives to speak off the record without their words being used against them. The privilege was never absolute and it was thought until the Court of Appeal's decision in *Unilever Plc v The Procter & Gamble Co.*[32] that a threat made in a 'without prejudice' meeting or communication was one of those exceptions. The Court of Appeal has held that the public interest in promoting settlement requires the exclusion of threats made in genuine settlement negotiations. On the other hand, the words 'without prejudice' will be ignored if made in any other circumstances such as a letter to a retailer.[33]

PRACTICAL CONSEQUENCES

The risk of threats actions limits the extent to which information and documents can be exchanged before a hearing yet there are occasions when it is necessary to give notice of the subsistence of a claim. A person who imports, possesses, deals in or distributes articles that infringe an unregistered design right can be held liable for their acts only if he or she knew or had reason to believe them to be such. Yet another good reason for seeking specialist professional advice.

---

30   *Egg Fillers and Containers (Aust) Pty Ltd. v Holed-Tite Packing Corp.* (1933) 51 RPC 9.
31   *Prince Plc v Prince Sports Group Inc.* [1998] FSR 21.
32   [2000] FSR 344.
33   *Kooltrade Ltd. v XTS Ltd.* [2001] FSR 158).

12 *A Few Last Tips*

In conference, Mr Aardvark remarked that there were a number of things that he would have done differently had he known then what he knows now. So what about you? What have you learned? If I have done my job properly, you should have picked up at least the following tips:

1. Intellectual property is not an end in itself. It is there to help give your business a competitive edge over the competition.
2. There is no point in having an intellectual property right unless you can enforce it. And that generally means being able to sue in the civil courts.
3. Consider IP insurance. There are not many viable alternatives.
4. Provide for IP enforcement in your business plan.
5. Dispute resolution must be planned and managed.
6. Monitor the competition at all times.
7. Assemble a team of good specialist advisers before you need to call on them.
8. Dispute resolution decisions must make business sense.
9. Establish a clear chain of command to cope with any dispute.
10. Seek professional advice but remember these is no such thing as a one-stop shop.
11. Learn from the experience of others.
12. Read as widely as possible.

Tip #1: Intellectual Property is not an end in itself. It is there to give you a competitive advantage

Patents, registered designs and trade marks cost money. According to the European Patent Office in 2005,[1] the cost of obtaining and maintaining a typical European patent[2] over 10 years is €37,500.[3] Very few inventions justify that kind of expenditure. As Peter Bissell and Graham Barker make clear at the beginning of their book 'The Business of Invention', most patents are never worked at all and of those that are worked, very few even cover the costs of obtaining them. Only a minuscule percentage actually make money for their owners.

A CAUTIONARY TALE

Some time ago I met a lovely couple at the first meeting of an inventors' club. The husband had invented a very ingenious device that had actually been marketed. He had consulted

---

1   Research carried out by the Roland Berger Market Research: 'A representative survey on the cost of obtaining a European patent' (http://www.european-patent-office.org/epo/new/cost_analysis_2005_en.pdf).
2   A specification of 18 pages (11 description, 3 claims, 4 drawings) with 10 claims designating France, Germany, Italy, Spain, Switzerland and the United Kingdom.
3   Ibid.

patent agents who had advised him on the law and told him that the belt and braces approach was to apply for a patent in all the countries in which he hoped to make or market his product. He followed their advice using a nest egg that he and his wife had set aside to buy, among other things, a caravan for their retirement. Having secured a very impressive portfolio of certificates from the European Patent Office, US Patent and Trademark Office, Japan Patent Office and several other countries, he hawked his invention around the industry looking for someone to take a licence from him. Eventually he did find a small company which made a test run but they found the product difficult to shift and in due course terminated the licence. The wife was devastated by the experience. Over a drink in a wine bar after the meeting she told me with tears in her eyes of their plans for their retirement. The top-of-the-range model they had in mind. All the parts of the country they wanted to visit. About the possibility of a trip to the Continent. But, instead, all they had to show for their life savings was a seemingly valueless pile of patent specifications.

THE DILEMMA

A cautionary tale if ever there was one. However, if – just if – your invention turns out to be the world beater that you think it may be when you dream it up in the bath, and you haven't protected it properly, you could end up tearing your hair out. So this is the dilemma. You could, and probably will, squander your seed corn on patent, design or trade mark protection that you are unlikely ever to need. But if you do not have that protection it is just possible that you could lose everything. Deciding what protection, if any, to take out is a bit like playing crane, scissors, paper, stone.

CRANE, SCISSORS, PAPER, STONE

This is a game[4] between two. The players shake hands three times. On the third shake they break and each player forms his or her hand into a shape such as a claw representing a *crane*, two outstretched fingers representing *scissors*, a flat palm representing *paper* or a clenched fist representing *stone*. If one chooses 'paper' and the other 'scissors' the player choosing scissors wins while the loser suffers a forfeit such as a slap on the wrists. Had the loser chosen 'stone' instead of paper, he or she would have won because stone blunts scissors. If the player who had chosen 'scissors' had chosen 'stone' instead, the player choosing 'paper' would have won because 'paper' wraps up 'stone'. 'Cranes' trump everything except 'paper' because they can pick up everything except paper. However, they are vulnerable to 'paper' because they could also be wrapped up. Inventors have to make similar snap decisions when deciding

* whether to apply for a patent at all;
* if so where to seek patent protection;
* how to enforce such protection; and so on.

A patent may keep competing products out of a market but it is no use at all without the means of enforcing it. That is like scissors cutting paper but blunted by stone. Having legal protection and the means to sue are pointless if there is no demand for the invention. That is like paper wrapping up stone. Strong demand will not last should competitors be free to come into the market. That is like returning to scissors and paper. This is an exercise that all businesses have to do from the mighty multinational to the back room start-up. Though the

---

4   A version of the game is described on the Fisher Price website: see 'Play & Learn Family Activities' at http://www.fisher-price.com/uk/playtime/learn.asp?min=1.5&max=2.

task may be easier for multinationals in that they have massive resources, years of experience and teams of well qualified lawyers and patent attorneys at their disposal, they still face uncertainties. That means that they can still get things wrong.

A SUGGESTED METHODOLOGY

As I said above, businesses invest in branding, design, technology and creative works to give them an edge over the competition. There are, of course, many other ways of obtaining a competitive advantage. One may be to market more aggressively. Another may be to reduce prices by shifting production abroad. Yet another may be to develop a new product. Each of these may be a much better investment than securing a legal monopoly for 20 years. On the other hand, there are some products that would not be developed without intellectual property protection. The reason why pharmaceutical companies apply for patents and trade marks just about everywhere is that they need the monopolies that those rights afford to amortize their product development costs. They cannot simply switch to a new product because lead times are too long. Nor can they easily transfer production to a country with low production costs.

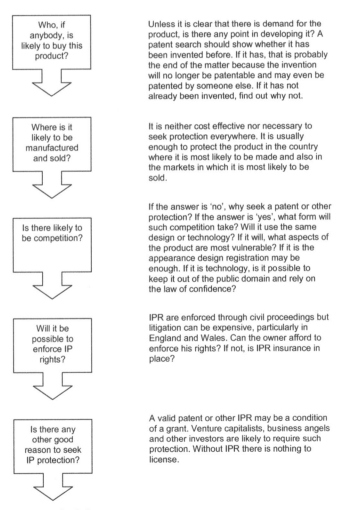

Figure 12.1   Patent decision process

Indeed, if they do so they may inadvertently nurture a potential competitor. In the course of a patent term India has developed from being a relatively backward, largely centrally planned economy with only a tiny pharmaceutical industry supplying mainly domestic demand into a major drugs manufacturer. It is prudent to compare the costs of obtaining and maintaining IP protection with the likely benefits to be gained and with all the other uses to which such money could be put.

DO YOU NEED PATENT PROTECTION AND IF SO WHERE

The couple who had spent money they had set aside for a caravan on patenting would probably have thought twice about making that investment had they asked themselves the questions shown in Figure 12.1. The high cost of patenting has already been mentioned. Not even the largest companies can justify every possible type of legal protection for every one of their products in every country of the world. They have to be selective and they base their selections on estimates of likely revenues, identification of probable threats to those revenues and evaluation of the most effective means of meeting them. Those with far fewer resources and less experience of intellectual property have to do likewise.

Tip #2: There is no point in having an Intellectual Property Right unless you can enforce it

As I have said at least once in this book, an IP right is essentially a right to bring a lawsuit. While certain infringements, such as copyright and trade mark infringements on a commercial scale,[5] are criminal offences as well as actionable wrongs in many countries of the world, primary responsibility for policing and enforcing IP rights rests with the owners of those rights. Civil litigation is not cheap anywhere but it is particularly expensive in the United Kingdom. Attempts have been made to find alternatives to litigation in the UK but the only schemes that have taken off in a big way are the domain name dispute resolution schemes for generic and country code top level domain names operated by ICANN[6] and various national domain name space authorities.[7]

Tip #3: Consider IP insurance

Since very few small businesses can stand the costs of litigation in England and Wales, the only viable option for most of them is intellectual property indemnity insurance. It is necessary to seek such cover because most general liability policies exclude or limit intellectual property claims. Premiums start at around £4,000 a year for a single patent or other IP right in the UK alone and can rise to tens of thousands of pounds for worldwide cover. It is possible that competition and greater experience of the market will bring down those rates in time but, at present, there are only a handful of brokers who specialize in this business and there is very

---

5   Art 61 of Agreement on Trade-related Aspects of Intellectual Property Rights, which is an annex to the Agreement establishing the World Trade Organization, requires contracting parties to impose criminal liability for piracy and counterfeiting. (http://www.wto.org/english/docs_e/legal_e/27-trips_05_e.htm#5.)
6   Internet Corporation for Assigned Names and Numbers (a company incorporated in California responsible for administering the international domain name system) http://icann.org.
7   Such as Nominet's Dispute Resolution Service for .uk names.

little difference in the premiums that they charge. Some brokers can arrange for premiums to be paid by instalments in certain circumstances. Discounts are available through various schemes such as those operated by IP Wales[8] and ACID[9] for their members. Because of such heavy premiums, I meet considerable resistance when I advise small businesses to consider IP insurance. One response that I often encounter from cash-strapped inventors and entrepreneurs is that they will look for a lawyer who is prepared to act on a 'no win no fee retainer' if and when they need to go to law. Another is that after-the-event insurance is always available. Both arguments are misconceived.

'NO WIN NO FEE' NOT AN OPTION IN THE UK

The first misconception is that American style contingency fee retainers are available for litigation in this country. It is not possible for lawyers in the UK to accept instructions for litigation on the promise of a share of any damages that may be awarded in the way that is done in the USA. It is possible for lawyers in England and Wales to accept instructions under a CFA ('conditional fee agreement') but those agreements are very different from 'conditional retainers' even though they are also referred to commonly as 'no win, no fee' agreements. Like a contingency retainer, a CFA provides for a lawyer to receive a fee only if the litigation is successful. Unlike a contingency retainer, the conditional fee is paid not out of the damages awarded to the successful party, but forms part of the costs that may be assessed by the court and recovered from the unsuccessful party in the usual way. The incentive for lawyers to accept instructions on this basis is that they may recover an uplift of up to 100 per cent of the amount to which they would normally be entitled known as a 'success fee.' A party who enters a CFA remains liable for the other side's costs. If that party is a limited company it may be required to deposit or otherwise guarantee the payment of tens of thousands of pounds as security for those costs. There is often considerable investigatory and other preparatory work to be done before the lawyer can decide whether to enter a CFA for which he or she could charge his normal fee. Although there are some types of litigation such as personal injuries and debt recovery where CFAs work very well, these agreements are not well suited to IP litigation. There are a number of reasons for that. First, the costs of IP litigation tend to be very much higher. Secondly, questions of liability and the amounts payable by way of damages or upon an account of profits are tried on separate occasions. Accordingly, lawyers have to factor in the reality that they have to wait much longer to be paid than they would in other litigation. Thirdly, there are usually more uncertainties. For all these reasons, CFAs are no substitute for before-the-event insurance.

NOR IS AFTER-THE-EVENT INSURANCE.

There are several reasons for that. First, insurers will take these risks only if counsel is prepared to advise that there is a 65 per cent or better chance of success. There are not many circumstances where that is possible. Secondly, premiums are very high, typically one third of the risk insured against. Thirdly, it is usually necessary to do at least as much investigatory and preparatory work for after-the-event insurance as would be done by a lawyer contemplating a CFA. Again, the lawyers doing this work would expect to be paid.

---

8   See 'IP Insurance: IP Wales has worked with HSBC Bank to develop an IP Insurance product tailored to the needs of the small & medium-sized enterprise community' at http://www.ipwales.com/ip_insurance/index.asp.

9   Anti-copying in Design: see http://www.reactinsurance.com/cust-bin/page.pl?id=acid/&p=home.

WHAT ABOUT COLLECTING SOCIETIES?

The only viable alternative to insurance that may be available is to join a *'collecting society'*. These are societies or other bodies that represent groups of IP rights owners. Several of them such as the *Performing Rights Society* and the *Mechanical Copyright Protection Society* are almost household names in the United Kingdom because their stickers are to be seen in pubs and restaurants throughout the country. Such bodies grant licences to perform, reproduce or make some other use of the works of their members (often referred to as their 'repertoire') in return for a single licence fee which is paid into a fund that is administered by the collecting society for distribution to its members after deduction of its administrative costs and other expenses. Users of a repertoire who fail to take the appropriate licence or whose use exceeds the terms of their licence are pursued through the courts in the usual way. Several collecting societies in the UK have reciprocal arrangements with collecting societies in other countries thereby enabling British IP owners to recover royalties for the use of their work abroad and foreign owners to recover royalties for use of their work here. Collecting societies exist for various copyright owners plus some musicians and other performers, but not for owners of other IP rights.

Tip #4: Provide for IP enforcement in the business plan

Since the principal assets of most if not all businesses are their brands, technology or design of their products consideration should be given to the protection and exploitation of those assets at the earliest possible stage. That is usually when a business plan is drawn up. It is nowadays quite common for businesses to include patenting or trade mark registration in their business plans if only to qualify for grants, loans or investment, but it is still far from common for them to consider IP enforcement and, more particularly, the funding of such enforcement. In view of the high cost of litigation, that can be fatal. Businesses and their professional advisors should always include intellectual property insurance or some other means of funding enforcement in their budgeting. It is also in the interests of bankers, business angels, venture capitalists and other lenders and investors to insist on such cover or other provision when contemplating loans, investment or other assistance. So, too, in many cases is such provision in the interests of licensees and distributors.

Tip #5: Dispute resolution must be planned and managed

My experience of nearly 30 years at the English Bar is that far more disputes are resolved by the laws of economics than by the laws of England. Sometimes that is because one of the parties finds that it has miscalculated the cost to itself or the resolve of the other. Sometimes it is because both parties realize that the cost of fighting will exceed the benefit of any courtroom victory. The way to avoid this difficulty is to plan ahead just like any other business project. A good example of dispute resolution planning is the *Litigation and Settlement Strategy* of HM Revenue & Customs.[10] The declared objectives of the strategy are closing the tax gap and providing taxpayers with a clear understanding of the law. [11] HMRC pursues those objectives by seeking non-confrontational solutions wherever possible, focusing on issues that best serve

---

10   See http://www.hmrc.gov.uk/practitioners/lss.pdf.
11   See http://www.hmrc.gov.uk/practitioners/lss-intro.htm.

those objectives, choosing cases for their wider impact as well as for their own value, pressing for full value settlement where there is a strong case and not pursuing weak arguments. Though objectives and resources will vary from litigant to litigant, the methodology will be the same.

DISPUTE RESOLUTION STRATEGY FOR IPR OWNERS

The best time to start planning for dispute resolution is before any dispute arises. Ideally, provision for IPR enforcement should be in the business plan. The first and probably most important step is to make sure that appropriate legal protection of the brand, product, process, work of art or other intellectual asset is in place. Such protection may require a patent, trade mark or design registration, licence, confidentiality agreement or other legally enforceable right as well as sufficient funds for enforcement. Unless the IPR owner belongs to a collecting society or can raise large sums of money at short notice, he or she is likely to rely on IP insurance for such funding. The second step is to monitor the competition, particularly any patent, design or trade mark applications that a competitor may make. The third is to assemble a team of lawyers and patent attorneys with the right skill mix who understand their client's business and are ready to act at very short notice. The fourth is to establish a clear chain of command. Someone should be put in charge of dispute resolution and given an adequate budget and all necessary decision making powers. One of that manager's tasks will be to decide which matter to contest and which to ignore or compromise on. Whenever an issue is contested, he or she should determine the objectives, allot a budget and either take charge of the project or delegate it to someone who can be relied upon.

Tip #6: Monitor the competition

There are several ways of monitoring the activities of competitions. One way is to keep an eye on UK-IPO and other patent office websites and journals for applications that could threaten your business. Most patent and trade mark attorneys offer that service. So, too, do some public libraries. For instance, the *'Currentscan'* patent watch service offered by the British Library[12] offers:

- competitor watches: regular reports on the latest patent applications filed by companies or individuals;
- sector watches: regular reports on the latest patent applications in specific technical fields; and
- status watches: regular reports on the progress of patent applications in a number of countries.

A similar service is offered by the Business and Patents section of Leeds Central Library.[13] If a competitor is likely to conceal its activities a specialist private investigator like *Amsel & Co.*[14] should be considered. Investigators carry out studies using desk and market research, place trap orders, carry out market samples and even initiate and conduct confidential negotiations on an IPR owner's behalf. It is also sensible to visit competitors' stands at trade shows, bookmark their websites, scour the trade press for news and articles and talk to distributors, end-users and others in the market.

---

12   http://www.bl.uk/services/current/patents.html.
13   http://www.businessandpatents.org.
14   http://www.amsel.co.uk.

Tip #7: Assemble a team of specialist professional advisors before you need them

Although a good lawyer can only do so much with a weak case, a bad lawyer can undoubtedly lose a strong one. Looking for good legal representation is not something that can be put to one side until after a dispute has occurred. There is rarely enough time for that since instructions have to be given, advice sought and action taken very quickly once a dispute erupts. A good specialist knowledge and understanding of IP law is always necessary but it is never sufficient of itself. The lawyer must also know the client and understand its business intimately. One way to procure that combination of specialist skill and intimate knowledge and understanding of the business is to employ an in-house lawyer or patent attorney. If employing an in-house lawyer is unaffordable or otherwise impractical, look out for lawyers who act for similar businesses or who have acted for similar ones in the past. Their interest in and knowledge of an industry can be gauged from their publications and seminars. If you know their clients, ask what sort of service they received. Lawyers with a genuine interest in IP will produce a fair volume of high quality material. The rest will rely simply on their brochures. When you find a good lawyer or other professional advisor, open a dossier on him or her. File or bookmark his or her articles, handouts, cases and other information. Finally, remember that it is no longer necessary to instruct a solicitor or other intermediary in order to consult counsel. Many specialist barristers will advise and draft legal instruments under the Bar Council's public access scheme.

Tip #8: Dispute resolution decisions must make business sense

This has already been covered extensively but it needs to be stressed. As with all business decisions, the expected benefit of initiating a dispute must justify the probable risks and costs. When deciding whether or not to pursue a damages claim, for example, relevant considerations will be the likely award, the defendant's ability to satisfy judgment, the expected costs and the prospects of success. If the preferred remedy is an injunction, the nature and extent of the threat to the claimant's business will be relevant.

Tip #9: Establish a clear chain of command

Disputes tend to take on a life of their own unless they are managed properly. Objectives and policy should be set by the board, partners or proprietor and a realistic budget allocated to meet those objectives. One of the directors or partners or some other senior manager should be put in charge of dispute resolution. He or she will draw up guidelines as to when and how a challenge will be contested. Typically these will provide for the resolution of disputes as quickly and cost-effectively as possible. They will establish procedures for handling and storing documents, recording conversations and registering events. They will indicate when professional advice should be sought and from where it should be obtained. They will provide guidance on initiating complaints, avoiding liability for groundless threats, the form and contents of letters of claim and response, the best method of resolving particular types of disputes, timescales and deadlines. Expenditure on dispute resolution should be planned and reviewed periodically. If and when a dispute arises, the person with overall charge of dispute resolution should decide how to respond to it promptly. If he or she decides to sue, arbitrate or use some alternative means of dispute resolution, he or she will prepare a dispute resolution strategy, instruct in-house and outside professional advisors to carry it out, monitor performance and generally oversee the conduct of the dispute. In a very large enterprise it may be necessary to delegate case management to others.

Tip #10: Seek professional advice but remember that there is no 'one-stop shop'

Every inventor or entrepreneur is likely to require a number of different professionals at various times. These will include an accountant to supervise the bookkeeping, prepare accounts and tax returns and advise on general matters, a patent or trade mark agent to apply for a patent, trade mark or design registration, a solicitor for general legal business, a barrister for representation before courts or tribunals, drafting complex legal instruments and advice on difficult points of law, to mention just a few. All of these professionals offer services that are useful and sometimes indispensable.

However, it has to be understood that these professionals will advise only on their areas of expertise and not outside them. A patent agent, for instance, will advise on how to obtain optimum protection for his or her client's invention. It is not his or her job to consider whether such optimum protection is necessary or even desirable for the invention in hand. That is how the couple I mentioned at the beginning of this chapter spent their nest egg on patents in Europe, the USA and Japan for an invention that is unlikely ever to be made or marketed. Other professionals such as accountants or business advisors might have considered such matters but they were only consulted on say drawing up a business plan.

Consequently, it has to be stressed that while there is some overlap between the services offered by some of those professionals there is not yet any such thing as a 'one-stop shop' or single source for all professional services. That may change shortly as Part V of the Legal Services Act provides for alternative business structures which could included multidisciplinary practices but for the moment professional men and women practise in specialist firms or as sole practitioners. Members of one profession will often refer their clients to members of another – accountants to lawyers, for instance, and *vice versa*. Several firms of patent agents practise with law firms in the same building, in one or two cases under the same name. Solicitors and patent agents have traditionally consulted barristers on behalf of their clients.

Possible the nearest things to one-stop shops for the time being are the 'clinics' and 'workshops' hosted by patent libraries and inventors' clubs around the country. At these events a patent agent, lawyer, business advisor, patent librarian and other professionals may be consulted free of charge. I organize clinics at Barnsley, Bradford, Halifax, Huddersfield, Leeds and Rotherham. Others in the North of England are arranged by the central libraries in Leeds, Liverpool, Manchester and Sheffield. Particulars of some of these clinics are posted from time to time on the website of the Chartered Institute of Patent Agents.

Tip #11: Benefit from the experience of others

Patent clinics and workshops are just some of the services offered by inventors' clubs. Others arrange for talks by professionals, business angels and other speakers. Most have websites and many publish newsletters and journals. Most importantly, they provide a forum for inventors and their advisors to meet and share experiences. Often some of the best advice that I can give to a client is to enquire whether there is an inventors' club in their area, to join it if there is such a club, or to start one of their own if there is not. Had Mr Aardvark joined such a club he may well have found out about design registration and IP insurance at a time when he could have made use of that information. Were he to join such a club now, he could still pass on what he has learned from experience to someone who might otherwise have learned those lessons the hard way.

Tip #12: Read as widely as possible

Finally, read, read and read again. There is a lot of good information on the internet. Good places to start are the websites of the UK-IP Office,[15] the British Library,[16] the World Intellectual Property Organization,[17] the European Patent Office,[18] OHIM (the EC trade marks and design registry)[19] and indeed my chamber's IP information site.[20] Several of those sites offer very good booklets, forms and model agreements which can be downloaded. For instance, one of the best is 'Confidentiality and Confidential Disclosure Agreements' which contains a model confidentiality agreement that has been prepared by two friends and neighbours, Peter Bissell and Graham Barker. Peter and Graham have written *The Business of Invention: the Essentials of Success for Inventors and Innovators* which is highly recommended for individual inventors and small businesses. It is available only from their website.[21] Many patent agents and business advisors distribute it to their clients. This effort has been inspired by their work and is intended to supplement it.

Epilogue

Well this is just about it. I have actually finished this penance. My family never thought they would live to see this day. Neither did my publisher. Neither did I. I hope none of you actually need to use this book but if you do I should be interested to learn which of my suggestions worked, which did not. I wish all my readers the very best of luck with their respective businesses.

---

15   www.patent.gov.uk.
16   http://www.bl.uk/collections/patents.html.
17   http://www.wipo.int/portal/index.html.en.
18   http://www.european-patent-office.org/index.en.php.
19   http://oami.europa.eu/en/default.htm.
20   www.ipit-update.com.
21   http://www.abettermousetrap.co.uk.

Appendix

Letter of Claim

1. OUR CLIENT

We act for ABC Computer Systems Ltd ('ABCS'), a private company incorporated in England and Wales under the Companies Act 1985 under company number .... which carries on business from 128 The Arches, Manchester M99 9ZZ.

2. THE CLAIM

Our client complains that you have infringed its copyright in the suite of applications programs that it wrote for you in 2002 which are listed on pages ...... to .... ('the Software') of the enclosed paginated bundle of documents ('the Bundle') by making and marketing the programs that are listed on pages ...... to .... ('the Infringing Package') of the Bundle in 2005 without its consent. Our client has instructed us to issue proceedings against you for infringement of copyright without further notice unless you respond punctually and constructively to this letter of claim.

3. THE COPYRIGHT WORKS

The Software was written by our client's employees between 1990 and 2002 in the course of their employment. As we have already stated, our client is and was then incorporated in England and Wales and each and every member of its staff was a British subject and citizen residing and domiciled in England and Wales. The Software and the components comprising the same are the product of considerable skill and labour. It follows that they are original literary works in which copyright subsists and that our client is the owner of that copyright by virtue of S.11 (2) of that Copyright, Designs and Patents Act 1988.

4. THE CODE AND PRACTICE DIRECTION

In writing this letter of claim we have followed the Practice Direction-Protocols ('the PD-Protocols') and Code of Practice for pre-action conduct in intellectual property disputes ('the Code') and we expect you to do the same. Copies of the PD-Protocols and Code appear on pages 1 to ...... and ...... to .... of the Bundle respectively. We respectfully remind you that the Court has power under the Civil Procedure Rules to penalize non-compliance with PD-Protocols.

5. INFRINGEMENT

In making the Infringing Package you have reproduced a substantial part of the Software without our client's licence thereby infringing the copyrights subsisting in that work. We give just 3 examples:

[Insert a full description of the similarities relied upon]

6. REMEDIES SOUGHT

Our client requires your promise never to infringe its copyright or other intellectual property right ever again. All copies of the Infringing Package and anything else that infringes our client's copyrights or other intellectual property must be delivered up to us. A director or other officer of your company must verify by statutory declaration that that has been done. He or she must also state how many copies of the Infringing Package were supplied, identify the persons to whom they were supplied and indicate the moneys that you have received from each customer. Our client will then let you know whether it wishes you to compensate it for its loss and damage or to account to it for your profits. If it elects compensation you should be aware that it will seek additional statutory damages of £100,000 or such other sum as the justice of the case may require having regard to the flagrancy of the infringement and the benefits you have derived pursuant to S.97 (2) of the 1988 Act.

7. FUNDING

At present, our clients are paying their own costs. If they have to sue you they reserve the right to negotiate funding under a conditional fee agreement which would entitle them to a success fee in addition to the compensation and costs mentioned above.

8. WHAT YOU MUST DO NOW

As we shall allow you a reasonable opportunity to take legal advice, we expect you to acknowledge this letter on or before 17:00 on [Tuesday, 2 January 2007] and respond fully by 17:00 on [Tuesday, 16 January 2007]. Should you admit our clients' claim, you can resolve this dispute without resort to litigation by giving our client the remedies sought above by 17:00 on [Tuesday, 16 January 2007]. Should you dispute the claim, your response should comply with paragraph 4.6 of the PD-Protocols as modified by the Code. Should you dispute any issue of fact or law raised in this letter, our clients are willing to refer such issue either to arbitration before an arbitrator agreed by us or in default of agreement within 14 days appointed by the WIPO Arbitration and Mediation Centre or other form of alternative dispute resolution. If you or your legal advisors require more time or more information to answer this letter, you must advise us in good time so that we can consider such request.

Letter of Response

Although you have not given us the time to which we are entitled under paragraph 4.4 of the *Practice Direction: Protocols* and paragraph 4 of the *Code of Practice for pre-action conduct in intellectual property disputes* (copies of which we enclose since you do not appear to have heard of them) much less than the time that we require to complete our enquiries, we believe that we already have enough information to answer your letters of 27 September 2007.

1. TRADE MARK INFRINGEMENT

In response to paragraph 2 of your letter of claim we deny our client has infringed your client's trade mark. The latter part of our client's corporate name is entirely descriptive and it is in any case distinguished by the name and silhouette of the founder of the company. By contrast your client's trade mark is an abbreviation of its corporate name set against a black oval background. While our clients trade in the same industry there are substantial differences between the services supplied by your client and those supplied by ours and also in the markets that they each serve. Comparing our client's sign and the services that it supplies with the registered trade mark and its specified goods and services there seems to be no likelihood of confusion, much less any likelihood of association with the registered mark. Even if there were such likelihood, our client would be entitled to rely on S.11 (3) of the Trade Marks Act 1994 as it has traded continuously under its corporate name in the former mill towns of Lancashire for well over 70 years.

2. INVALIDITY OF THE REGISTERED MARK

We are still taking statements and gathering documents but it seems that our client's founder, Fred Bloggs, first traded under its current name in Wigan in 1937. He opened his second branch in Blackburn in 1952 expanding the original premises by 13,000 square feet in 1952. Shortly afterwards, he opened another branch in Burnley followed by others in Bolton, Rochdale and Rawtenstall. You will see from the trading and profit and loss account for the year ended 31 December 1998 on page 1 of the annexed bundle that our client's turnover was not far short of £10 million for the year immediately before your client applied for its mark. We also enclose copies of newspaper advertisements, brochures and business stationery from that time on pages 2 to 13 of the bundle. It follows that our client had an earlier right within meaning of S.5 (4) of the Trade Marks Act 1994 in that it could have brought an action for passing off against your client and it is also entitled to counterclaim for a declaration of invalidity in respect of your client's trade mark registration in the proceedings that you threaten to launch against it.

3. CONCLUSION

In the circumstances, we regret that we cannot advise our client to give any of the undertakings that you seek in your letter. We are instructed to accept service of your issue proceedings and, of course, resist them strenuously. We shall also counterclaim for the relief indicated.

Particulars of Claim

Claim No:_____

In The High Court Of Justice

Chancery Division, Intellectual Property

Manchester District Registry

Between

ABC COMPUTER SYSTEMS LIMITED

Claimant

-and-

(1)	**DEF HOLDINGS Plc**
(2)	**DEF MOTORS LTD.**
(3)	**DEF COMPUTER SERVICES LTD.**

Defendants

PARTICULARS OF CLAIM

THE PARTIES

1. The claimant is and at all material times has been a private company incorporated with limited liability under the provisions of the Companies Act 1985 having its registered office and principal place of business at 128, The Arches, Chapel Street, Manchester M99 9ZZ. It carries on business as a software house specializing in the design and development of applications software for the motor trade.
2. The first defendant is the holding company of a group of companies which carry on business in a number of industries including the motor trade. The second defendant owns and operates a chain of garages in Northern England and North Wales. The third defendant provides computer services to the first defendant and its subsidiaries.

THE AGREEMENT

3. By a written agreement dated 27 October 2001 the first defendant commissioned the claimant to write a suite of applications programs for use by the second defendant in its business (a copy of which appears on pages 1 to 26 of the bundle of documents annexed hereto ('the Bundle') and deliver the same on 2 sets in machine code of optical media to the first defendant.

4. Clause 7.1 of such agreement provided that the claimant should retain copyright and any other intellectual property right in such programs. Clause 7.2 permitted the first defendant to grant licences to loan and run and make a reasonable number of spare copies of such software in the course of and for the purposes of their agreement.
5. Clause 19 required the claimant to deposit the source code of such software with the BV International Escrow Center of Curacao with provisions for such source code to be released to the first defendant in a number of specified circumstances one of which was 'imminent insolvency or serious financial difficulty.'
6. Clause 8 required the fee for the claimant's services to be paid in 3 equal instalments, the first upon entering the above-mentioned agreement, the second upon delivery of the above mentioned media and the third within 90 days of such delivery.

THE COPYRIGHT WORKS

7. Pursuant to such agreement, the claimant wrote, delivered and installed the programs listed on pages 27 to 29 of 'the Bundle'.
8. Each and every one of those programs was written by the claimant's staff in the course of their employment all of whom were British subjects and citizens resident and domiciled in England and Wales at all material times. Each and every program required substantial skill and labour.
9. In the premises, the suite of programs and its components were original literary works in which copyright subsists and the claimant is the first owner of such copyrights by reason of s.11 (2) of the Copyright Designs and Patents Act 1988.

THE RELEASE OF THE SOURCE CODE

10. The first defendant punctually paid the first instalment of the claimant's fee but not the second or third.
11. By a letter to the first defendant's finance director dated 19 September 2003, the claimant's managing director requested payment of its fees (page 30 of the Bundle) observing that the late payment had already caused the claimant acute financial difficulty and threatened the future of the claimant company.
12, By a letter dated 21 September 2003 (pages 31 and 32) the group solicitor of the defendant companies asked the above-mentioned escrow agent to release the source code to the above-mentioned software from escrow on the ground that the claimant was in such deep financial difficulty that it would be unlikely to maintain the above-mentioned software and enclosed the claimant's request for payment as evidence of such difficulty.
13. On 30 September 2007 the same escrow agent released such source code to one or more of the defendants.

THE INFRINGEMENT

14. On a date or time unknown to the claimant the second defendant reproduced substantial parts of such source code without the claimant's knowledge or consent to make a competing software product known as 'Top Ghia' which the third defendant markets to the motor trade in competition with the claimant's products.

Particulars of Similarity

[Illustrate the similarities between the claimant's source code and 'Top Ghia' and display samples of such similar code in the Bundle]

15. By reason of such copying and marketing the defendants and each of them have infringed the claimant's copyrights.
16. Because of such infringement, the claimant has suffered loss and damage the precise nature and full extent of which can only be quantified upon an inquiry.

RIGHT TO ADDITIONAL DAMAGES

17. By a letter dated 17 December 2006 (pages 42 to 44 of the Bundle) the claimant's solicitors asked the defendants to cease and desist from their infringement and to provide such information and documentation as might be required to assess the claimant's loss.
18. The defendants did not reply in writing, but one of the first defendant's sales managers told one of the claimant's customers that little firms like ABC should know better than to threaten big companies like his because they could snap their fingers at the law as judges and politicians were '10 a penny' in England. He added that 'the claimants could whistle for their fee. His company would have the software at its price whatever the contract said.'
19. In the premises, the flagrancy of the defendants' conduct is such that the justice of the case requires additional damages in the sum of £100,000 or such other sum as the court thinks fit.
20. The claimant is entitled to interest upon all sums due to it from the defendants whether by way of damages or upon an account of profits computed on a day to day basis at the annual rate of 8 per cent pursuant to S.35A of the Senior Courts Act 1981.

AND THE CLAIMANT CLAIMS

1. Perpetual injunctions to restrain the defendants, their employees or agents from infringing the claimant's aforementioned copyrights.
2. Delivery up of all copies of Top Ghia and any and all other infringing copies of the claimant's copyright works.
3. An inquiry as to damages (including additional damages under S.97 (2)) or at the claimant's option an account of the defendants' profits.
4. Accrued interest upon all sums due to the claimant under S.35A of the Senior Courts Act 1981.
5. Further or other relief.
6. Costs.

EKUNDAYO BURREH-HAMILTON

SERVED this 9th day of May 2007 by Dewey, Screwem & Howe (ref SP/mt) of 321 Deansgate, Manchester, M3 2RJ, solicitors for the claimant.

Defence

In The High Court Of Justice

Chancery Division, Intellectual Property

Liverpool District Registry

Between

HARRY PORTER

Claimant

-and-

FANNY'S FASHIONS LIMITED

Defendant

DEFENCE

1. As to paragraph 1 of the particulars of claim, the defendant admits that the claimant is a well known fashion designer but is unable to admit or deny and requires the claimant to prove that he is a British citizen and subject resident and domiciled in England and Wales.

2. The defendant can neither admit nor deny, and requires the claimant to prove, that the claimant is the creator of the handbag designs referred to in paragraph w of the particulars of claim.

3. Paragraph 2 is denied: the design referred to therein was not original within the meaning of S.213 (1) of the Copyright Designs and Patents Act 1988 because it was commonplace in the design field at the time of its creation.

PARTICULARS

[Insert particulars relied upon]

4. Further, design right cannot and does not subsist in:
    *   the carrying strap as that enables the handbag to be placed around the neck or shoulder of the wearer so that that article bag may perform one of its functions,
    *   the ornamentation of that strap since it is dependent upon the appearance of the wearer's shoes with which the article is intended to be worn; and
    *   the decoration of the leather since that is surface decoration.

5. Paragraph 5 is denied: the design of the bag was commissioned by the defendant as special purchase merchandise wherefore design right belongs to the defendant pursuant to S.215 (2) of the Copyright Designs and Patents Act 1988.

6. Paragraphs 6 to 9 inclusive are admitted.

7. If, which is not admitted, the claimant's design right has been infringed the defendant is entitled to elect for a licence of right on such terms as the parties can agree or in default of agreement as the comptroller may determine.

8. If, which is denied, the claimant has suffered loss or damage it is not through any wrongdoing by the defendant.

9. Save as is herein before expressly admitted or not admitted, each and every allegation in the particulars of claim are denied as though the same were set out seriatim and separately traversed.

ZAINAB BANGURA

SERVED this 12th day of November 2007 by Prince, Conteh & Partners, Bonthe House, Lumley Street, Hastings, Sussex, solicitors for the Defendant

Index

Figures are indicated by bold page numbers, tables by italics.

*For Product Safety Concerns and Information please contact
our EU representative GPSR@taylorandfrancis.com Taylor & Francis
Verlag GmbH, Kaufingerstraße 24, 80331 München, Germany*

T - #0039 - 100325 - C0 - 246/174/11 - PB - 9781032837833 - Gloss Lamination